Lincoln County
Tennessee

𝕸𝖆𝖗𝖗𝖎𝖆𝖌𝖊𝖘

1838–1860

Historical Records Project

Heritage Books
2024

HERITAGE BOOKS

AN IMPRINT OF HERITAGE BOOKS, INC.

Books, CDs, and more—Worldwide

For our listing of thousands of titles see our website
at
www.HeritageBooks.com

A Facsimile Reprint
Published 2024 by
HERITAGE BOOKS, INC.
Publishing Division
5810 Ruatan Street
Berwyn Heights, MD 20740

Originally published 1938

International Standard Book Number
Paperbound: 978-0-7884-8911-2

LINCOLN COUNTY

MARRIAGES
1838-1860

NEW INDEX

Note: Page numbers in this index refer to those of the original volume from which this copy was made. These numbers are inserted within parentheses throughout the text, as (p 124)

Allen, Sarah E. 274
Allen, William, 158
Allesson, Bettie, 344
Alley, Augustus N. B. 106
Alley, Catherine, 270
Alley, Sarah A. 144
Allisen, William B. 147
Allison, Catherine, 342
Allison, Elizabeth J. 176
Allison, G. B. 4
Allison, George W. 383
Allison, Jacob B. 283
Allison, Joseph P. 9,178
Allison, Nancy A. 145
Allison, Wm. L. 284
Allsup, B.M.G. 68,154,161,164,203
    240,251,257,268,273,303,309,346
    350,357
Allsup, Dorsas, 11
Allsup, J. V. 322
Allsup, Prissilla A. 295
Allsup, Rachel J. 328
Allsup, Sarah J. 280
Alstead, Manual, 4
Alsup, Margaret M. 208
Alsup, Mary, 69
Ambrox, Marica, 352
Ancher, Lodourick, 11
Anderson, A.M. 286
Anderson, Allen L. 24
Anderson, Cinith J. 124
Anderson, D. A. 354
Anderson, Margret R. 248
Anderson, Mary C. 61,119,159,300
Anderson, Nancy, 220
Anderson, Richard, 98,107,118
Anderson, Sarah, 140,294
Anderson, Wm. 5,8,14,21,55,56,58,324
Anderton, Peter J. 304
Andrews, Frances H. 305
Andrews, George A. 379
Andrews, James, 88
Andrews, Morgan, 254
Andrews, Samyva, 223
Andrews, William C. 52
Anthony, Amgi, 67
Anthony, Caroline, 166
Anthony, Pamila, 121
Anthony, Wm. W. 364
Aoney, Lewis F. 88
Archer, Lodowick, 11
Arondale, Jas. 149
Armstrong, Andrew B. 151
Armstrong, D.M. 380
Armstrong, Elizabeth, 273
Armstrong, James B. 165,356
Armstrong, James H. 258

Armstrong, Jane Caroline, 372
Armstrong, John, 86,207
Armstrong, John F. 233
Armstrong, John M. 280
Armstrong, Josiah, 231
Armstrong, Martha Ann, 304
Armstrong, Mary Ann, 171
Armstrong, Mary R. 222
Armstrong, Sarah Jane, 188,298
Armstrong, Thomas H. 27
Armstrong, W. T. 351
Arnal, W.W. 342
Asa, Elizabeth, 345
Ashby, Frances S. 140
Ashby, Hannah G. 227
Ashby, John, 104
Ashby, John L. 54,269,285,287,295
    297,299,302,325,334,336,338,354
    355,357,366,374
Ashby, John S. 306
Ashby, Lewis, 117
Ashby, Lurina, 211
Ashby, Martha A. 258
Ashby, Mary J. 342
Ashby, Nancy, 40,354
Ashby, Nancy Ann, 252
Ashby, Peter, 89
Ashby, Rachel, 151
Ashby, Rebecca E. 363
Ashby, Rebecca M. 238
Ashby, Salina F. 281
Ashby, Travis, 107,126,145,235,236
    257
Ashby, William H. 242
Ashby, Wilson, 345
Ashby, Wm. 40,378,380
Ashley, John L. 276
Ashley, Mary D. 291
Ashworth, William, 153,294
Askins, Susan H. 364
Askins, William, 258
Atwood, Thomas, 16
Aurin, Samuel G. 220
Austin, Henry, 221
Austin, Jesse, 185
Austin, John R. 361
Austin, William, 140
Ayers, B.W. 66
Ayers, Matilda, 35
Ayres, Elvira Jane, 226

B

Bachman, Wm. J. 361
Backman, W.B. 287
Baggett, John S. 30
Bagley, Elisha, 17

Beard, Iva W. 226
Beard, Jacob C. 122
Beard, Margaret, 124
Beard, Martha. 37
Beard, Samuel C. 225
Beard, W. W. 225
Bearden, Benjamin E. 55
Bearden, Daniel H. 183
Bearden. Elephaz, 229
Bearden, F. M. 90
Bearden, John, 1
Bearden, L. C.C. 282
Bearden, L. L. E. 284
Bearden, M. E. V. 349
Bearden, Nancy B. 251
Bearden, Pleasant, 46,58
Bearden, W. M. 21
Bearden, William, 169
Beardin, Josephine, 215
Beasley, Emeline, 107
Beasley, George W. 55
Beasley, Henry, 157
Beasley, Letetia, 94
Beasley, Martha A. 87
Beasley, Mary, 29
Beatie, Madison, 83
Beaty, Caroline J. 50
Beaty, Cathrine V. 214
Beaty, David M. 91
Beaty, John M. 97
Beaty, Martha A. 112
Beaver, A.J. 175
Beaver, Pleasant A. 302
Beavers, Asena, 23
Beavers, Betsey, 22
Beavers, Elizabeth, 340
Beavers, Mary, 284
Beavers, Priscella, 115
Beavers, Samuel, 193
Beavers, Sarah, 142
Beavers, Sarah Frances, 16
Beavers, Sarah P. 314
Beavers, William, 152
Beck, Calvin, 12
Beck, David W. 139
Beck, George L. 319
Beck, Henry, 124
Beck, James C. 303
Beck, Lillie Wilson, 371
Beck, Louisa, 223
Beck, Wilburn, 11
Beck, William P. 182
Becket, William M. 295
Beckett, William, 295
Beddenfield, Elizabeth, 130
Beddingfield, Alice M. 261
Beddingfield, M. T. 373

Bedford, Alexander M. 176
Bedford, Ann, 94
Bedford, Benjamin, 292
Bedford, I. L. 9
Bedford, W. M. 9
Bedwell, John B. 108
Bedwell, Louisa Jane, 220
Bedwell, M. M. 49
Bedwell, Major M. 48,51,84
Bedwell, Rebecca, 81
Bedwell, T. R. 362
Bedwell, William L. 247
Beeler, James C. 133
Beggerly, Mary E. 141
Beggorly, Mary, 26
Bell, A. A. 204,214,301,326
Bell, A. H. 295
Bell, Annia M. 95
Bell, Barthena, 110
Bell, Eliza, 340
Bell, Francis H. 287
Bell, James M. 22
Bell, John, 6,20,23,34,38
Bell, Louisa M. 62
Bell, Margaret M. 45
Bell, Martha A. 202
Bell, Mary Catherine, 379
Bell, Sarah, 121
Bell, Sarah M. 48
Bell, T. M. 335
Bell, Thomas W. 27
Bends, Martha J. 174
Benedict, Horace L. 200
Bennet, Albert, 146
Bennet, John L. 327
Benningfield, Mary M. 309
Benson, Benjamin C. 23
Benson, Currin D. 118
Benson, D. A. 353
Benson, Levin, 155
Benson, Mary E. 328
Benson, Nepolin, 213
Berrien, Hester Ann, 306
Berry, A. H. 291,357,358,345,362
Berry, Andrew J. 57
Berry, Benjamin H. 66
Berry, E. F. 204
Berry, Jackson, 12
Berry, James W. 310
Berry, Jane, 1
Berry, M. A. 306
Berry, Mary E. 212
Berry, R. H. 325
Berve, Benjamin, 197
Best, Angeline, 71
Bethany, Charles, 86
Bethany, Charles H. 70

Bramblet John, 265
Bramlon, Jackson, 13
Brandon, A. G. H. 272
Brandon, Benjamin B. 75
Brandon, Catharine, 53
Brandon, L. 90,110,152,173,210,235
    248,252,256,268,276,298,299,345
Branham, Susan E. 327
Brannen, Benjamin, 131
Brannon, Margaret, 13
Branson, Franklin D. 258
Branson, Sarah Jane, 220
Brass, Mariah A. 290
Bray, E. A. 381
Bray, Elijah A. 248
Bray, G. H. R. 266
Bray, James E. 301
Bray, James H. 92
Bray, N. R. 210
Bray, W. C. 302
Brazelton, Daniel, 136
Brazier, Mary, 152
Brazier, Polly, 333
Bremo, Emeline, 130
Brents, F. W. 274
Brents, James, 277
Brents, Thomas W. 55
Breston, Wesley, 185
Brewer, E. H. 355
Brewer, Elisha M. 71
Brewer, George, 263,264
Brewer, James R. 347
Brewer, Joel S. 287
Brewer, John H. 380
Brewer, Mary, 13
Bridges, Elizabeth, 143
Bridges, Mary M. 72
Bridges, Narcissa J. 113
Bridges, W. 95
Bridges, Willis, 110
Bright, Charles, 109
Bright, James M. 341
Bright, Mana E. 63
Bright, Martha R. 9
Bright, Mary, 35
Bright, Mary A. 320
Brim, Mary Jane, 169
Brimage, Sarah, 165
Brin, Jas. W. 219
Brin, Mahala, 185
Brin, Rebecca, 176
Brine, Arnold, 3
Briner, Martha, 186
Brinn, Nancy, 222
Bristen, William, 146
Bristow, J. B. 19
Britten, George H. 375
Broadway, Agnes, 16

Broadway, Francis A. 16
Broadway, George, 81
Broadway, James W. 112,252
Broadway, Mary, 134
Broadway, Ruth, 33
Broadway, Sarah, 143
Broadway, William, 164
Brooks, Joseph, 307
Brothertin, Sarah E. 380
Brotherton, Lyda C. 318
Brow, 15
Brown, A. M. 286,288
Brown, Amy M. 129
Brown, Anna, 276
Brown, Artismey J. 227
Brown, Catharine E. 157
Brown, Clarasa, 249
Brown, David F. 274
Brown, Dilila, 107
Brown, Edward A. 97
Brown, Elizabeth, 64,66,80,247,286
Brown, Emariah, 183
Brown, Emeline E. 102
Brown, George W. 107,185
Brown, H. V. 348
Brown, Harriet Ann, 364
Brown, Henry, 112
Brown, Hezekiah, 51
Brown, J. C. 350
Brown, J. D. 142
Brown, J. J. 153
Brown, J. M. 362,382
Brown, James, 374
Brown, James E. 107,329
Brown, James M. 309
Brown, James P. 4,81
Brown, James S. 235
Brown, James W. 103
Brown, Jane, 326
Brown, John, 86,177
Brown, John L. 90
Brown, John M. 320
Brown, John N. 167
Brown, Joshua D. 140
Brown, Marth, 258
Brown, Martha J. 73,293
Brown, Mary, 40,102,172
Brown, Mary Ann, 4,136,141,255,277
    329
Brown, Mary Frances, 7
Brown, Mary S. 239
Brown, Nancy, 288,320
Brown, Nancy H. 179
Brown, Nancy M. 187,220
Brown, R. M. 349
Brown, R. S. 90,147
Brown, Raney, 301
Brown, Relda J. 130

Chapman, B. 298,308
Chapman, Elizabeth, 178
Chapman, Harriet, 72
Chapman, John, 110,210
Chapman, Martha, 333
Chapman, Mary Ann, 92
Chapman, Nancy, 139
Chapman, Sarah, 248
Chapman, William, 308
Chasteen, Thomas, 165
Chastine, John, 80
Cheaser, Mary Ann, 213
Cheatam, Albert, 190
Cheatam, Elizabeth F. 104
Cheek, Samuel, 329
Cheeser, Nancy E. 338
Chellan, John G. 225
Chesser, W. Y. 210
Chesor, C. T. 338
Chewing, Virginia A. 45
Chick, Angeline, 371
Chick, William D. 246
Chilcoat, James R. 65,67,312,372
Chilcoat, Parthenia, 320
Childress, A. J. 194,219,222,224
    281,283
Childress, Delina, 97
Childress, James, 32
Childs, Fennett W. 298
Childs, Martha A. E. 128
Childs, Thomas, 1,2,9,16,30,33,36
    37,40,41,52,67,103,105,107,108
    111,119,126,135,152,183,189,196
    216,223,240,245,255,286,349
Childs, Wm. W. 287
Chiles, W. P. 328
Chiles, Alpha N. 370
Chimault, Stephens, 178
Chitwood, Ann M. 77
Chitwood, Dillia E. 379
Chitwood, James F. 78
Chitwood, Lucinda E. 293
Chitwood, Folly, 200
Chitwood, Sarah Jane, 216
Christian, B. 270,271,272,275,278
    284,285
Christian, Eliza, 4
Christie, Ephraim F. 53
Church, George, 280
Church, Ruthy, 190
Cimmons, William H. 96
Claborn, Martha, 187
Claiborn, Eliza M. 2
Clantin, John, 171
Clanton, Amanda, 29
Clanton, Mary E. 29
Clark, A. J. 4

Clark, Albert, 53
Clark, Benjamin F. 376
Clark, Benj. 3,7,10,11,28,34,35,38
    40,41,48,54,58,97,98,100,106
    114,118,122,135,142,145,149,155
    182,187,198,226,229,245,283,322
    323,334,338,371,375,389
Clark, Bolin, 27
Clark, Elainer B. 182
Clark, Eliza A. 83
Clark, Elizabeth, 378
Clark, Elizabeth B. 182
Clark, James, 28,362
Clark, James A. 368
Clark, James C. 344
Clark, James L. 308
Clark, James T. 195
Clark, John, 194,332
Clark, John L. 371
Clark, John M. 57
Clark, Joseph, 11, 102
Clark, Joseph S. 252
Clark, L. L. 356,368
Clark, Louisa, 235
Clark, Lucy C. A. 281
Clark, Martin V. 368
Clark, Matilda, 123
Clark, Mary, 98
Clark, Mary A. 83
Clark, Mary Ann, 93
Clark, Mary Jane, 271
Clark, Mary W. 132
Clark, Micajah, 1
Clark, Nancy, 10
Clark, Obadiah, 208
Clark, Phebe Elizabeth, 362
Clark, Rosannah, 33
Clark, Seneca, 220
Clark, Thomas, 150
Clark, Thomas A. 255
Clark, Thomas W. 139
Clark, Thos. J. 307
Clark, William, 8
Clarke Caroline, 147
Clarke, Eliza J. 210
Clarke, John (Jr), 149
Clarke, John W. 204
Clarke, Lucinda, 167
Clarke, Margarit R. 84
Clarke, Mariah W. 350
Clarke, Nancy E. 159
Clasky, Jane Gunn, 214
Claunch, Elizabeth, 192
Claunch, Felix, 282
Claunch, James, 234
Claunch, Jennetta, 26
Claunch, Jesse, 263

Colleta, David H. 340
Collier, Charles M. 171
Collier, Sarah, 81
Collins, A. M. 280
Collins, Asder, 121
Collins, Alex. F. 173
Collins, Harriett, 251
Collins, Isaac, 7
Collins, John, 123,317
Collins, Louisa J. 323
Collins, Mary F. 82
Collins, Mitchell, 195
Collins, Musouri A. 106
Collins, Nancy, 71
Collins, Nancy M. 318
Collins, Robert T. 281
Collins, William N. 116
Collins, William F. 189
Collins, Wright P. 25
Colter, F. M. 305
Colvit, Owen, 64
Colvit, Richard, 139
Colvit, Susan, 62
Commons, Belinda, 47
Commons, Benjamin, 218
Commons, Carrol, 343
Commons, Henry S. 334
Commons, Hiram, 250
Commons, John, 336
Commons, John M. 54
Commons, Mary, 17
Commons, Mary E. 290
Commons, Samuel V. 247
Commons, Sarah, 109,276
Commons, Sarah E. 348
Commons, Sarah L. 217
Commons, William G. 116
Compton, Tabitha J. 286
Conally, Drury M. 16
Conally, Nathaniel, 45
Conaway, F. A. 297
Conaway, Jodia, 319
Conaway, Judith L. 132
Conaway, Morgan H. 258
Conaway, Susanna, 282
Core, Charlotta, 27
Cone, William, 27
Conepland, Elizabeth, 280
Conger, Isaac, 3,50,53,64,107
Conger, S. M. 365
Connelly, Willie, 298
Connelly, Thos. 372
Conner, Jas. S. 369
Cook, Elizabeth, 231
Cook, Emily A. 235
Cook, Felix M. 169
Cook, John M. 297

Cook, Lucinda, 142
Cook, Malinda, 202
Cook, Moses, 37
Cook, Norbourne, 44
Cook, Robert, 21
Cook, William M. T. 209
Cook, James T. 376
Cooper, Durrel M. 129
Cooper, D. R. 186,189,190,192,194
    195
Cooper, David R. 8
Cooper, David P. 210
Cooper, Elizabeth, 291
Cooper, James A. 187
Cooper, James D. 244
Cooper, Noah N. 217
Cooper, Phillip, 36,291
Cooper, Phillips, 204
Cooper, Samuel M. 111
Cooper, Sarah, 197
Cooper, William, 56
Cooper, William S. 119
Copelan, William, 276
Copeland, George, 19
Copeland, Jno. B. 175
Copeland, John, 17,48,72,82,103
    108,140,179,245,257,263,268,270
    288,300,302,319,322,324,329,340
    349,352,353,354
Copeland, Mary, 55
Copeland, Massey, 79,153
Copeland, Nichlas, 274
Copland, George, 20
Copland, Nicholas, 230
Cordal, David M. 97
Corder, David, 62
Corder, Jacob B. 177
Corder, James, 341
Corder, Jno. 188,193,195,200,212
    216,245,255,263,302,316,321
Corder, John C. 17
Corder, Rachel, 157
Corder, T. S. 163,352,353,354,359
    360,368
Corley, Mary, 58
Cossling, Malinda, 167
Cotton, Elizabeth, 204
Cotton, Hardy H. 207
Cotton, Thomas J. 82
Cottrell, Richard, 49
Couch, Almyra, 144
Couch, Benjamin, 21
Couch, Delila, 70
Couch, F. M. 309
Couch, Ibby, 42
Couch, Jane, 49
Couch, Jonathan, 32

Couch, Linley, 139
Couch, Linney, 9
Couch, Louisa J. 95
Couch, Margaret, 10
Couch, Milossa M. 327
Couch, Nancy, 38
Couch, Sarah Ann E. 65
Coulter, Elvira, 286
Counts, David, 96
Counts, Jane, 302
Counts, Phenas Ann, 245
Couser, Alsa, 353
Couser, Sarah Ann, 347
Coutler, Sarah Ann E. 177
Cowan, George R. 143
Cowan, Henry C. 75
Cowan, Joseph V. 147
Cowan, Margaret A. 169
Cowan, Mary C. 299
Cowan, S. M. 307,312
Cowan, Sam'l M. 43,44,249,251,256
    260,264,270,277,284,289,292,294
    298,300,309,314,343
Cowden, Martha Jane, 274
Cowen, Coladonia, 261
Cowen, H. C. 114,124,126,142,191
    192,207,237,258,261,263
Cowley, James, 9
Cowley, Mathew M. 165
Cowley, T. Benjamin, 19
Cowsen, John F. 42
Cowson, Nancy, 48
Cox, Andrew J. 158
Cox, Elizabeth, 330
Cox, Emelen, 232
Cox, Francis E. 187
Cox, James, 245
Cox, John H. 360
Cox, M. Ann, 367
Cox, Mandana E. 271
Cox, Margaret A. 361
Cox, Marilda, 317
Cox, Mary Jane, 361
Cox, Nancy M. 304
Cox, Richard L. 44
Cox, Sarah, 198
Cox, Sarah C. 178
Cox, Susan E. 219
Crabtree, John C. 347
Crabtree, Martha, 37
Crabtree, Nancy, 172
Crabtree, Samuel, 85,272
Crabtree, Susan, 87
Crabtree, William, 52,244
Cragg, Elizabeth, 208
Craig, David C. 265
Craig, George, 130

Craig, George A. 245
Craig, Martha, 363
Craig, William, 28
Crane, Caroline, 76
Crane, Jane, 281
Crane, Mary A. 229
Crane, Spartin G. 80
Crane, T. R. W. 255
Crawford, Anthony, 170
Crawford, Carter T. 63
Crawford, Charles M. 40
Crawford, E. M. 191
Crawford, Elizabeth A. 71
Crawford, Ellen, 204
Crawford, Emily E. 192
Crawford, Felix McP. 171
Crawford, George A. 133
Crawford, Henryetta, 31
Crawford, John, 129
Crawford, John G. 65
Crawford, Margaret A. 347
Crawford, Martha A. 174
Crawford, Martha L. 217
Crawford, Rebecca K. 235
Crawford, Sarah E. 340
Crawford, Sarah S. 46
Crawford, William, 89
Crawley, Nicey J. 364
Creacks, Nancy C. 315
Creacy, Elizabeth, 227
Creason, Elizabeth, 243
Creasy, Mary, 68
Crenshaw, Mary, 122
Crenshaw, Mary J. 259
Crenshaw, Sam L. T. 4
Crenshaw, William T. 64
Creson, Mary M. 378
Cretchet, John, 47
Criner, Thomas, 2
Critchet, Elephia, 118
Crofford, Elizabeth, 146
Crofford, James M. 99
Crofford, Margaret, 96
Crofford, Robt. 186
Cross, William, 284
Crossland, John V. 162
Crosthwait, James M. 146
Crowder, Elizabeth Jane, 111
Crowder, Mary, 12
Crowder, Mary A. 14
Crowder, Mildred, 77
Crownover, William, 150
Crows, Mary L. 47
Cruise, Jacob, 231
Cruise, Moses, 24
Crump, Charles G. 205
Crunk, George W. 125

Daves, James. 224
Davidson, Andrew, 99
Davidson, Andrew J. 200
Davidson, Carleton, 72
Davidson, Elizabeth, 376
Davidson, Elizabeth M. 348
Davidson, George W. 101
Davidson, James, 70
Davidson, Julia, 290
Davidson, Lucinda, 205
Davidson, Martha Jane, 165,215
Davidson, Mary, 151
Davidson, Mary J. 292
Davidson, Mildred, 218
Davidson, Thomas, 11
Davidson, W. H. 307
Davidson, W. T. 380
Davidson, William, 57
Davis, Albin P. 125
Davis, Allen, 43,237
Davis, Anderson, 170
Davis, Ann E. 57
Davis, Archabald, 357
Davis, Charlotte, 152
Davis, Darinda, 29
Davis, David G. 113
Davis, Dotia Ann, 127
Davis, Elizabeth, 25
Davis, Gabiel, 203
Davis, Giles, 240,241
Davis, H. S. 320
Davis, J. B. 339
Davis, J. S. 169,186,327,329,355
    361
Davis, Jackson C. 2
Davis, James J. 222
Davis, James M. 115,250
Davis, James S. 5,214
Davis, James W. 108
Davis, Jane, 214
Davis, John, 125
Davis, Jonathan N. 87
Davis, Josephine, 265
Davis, Louisa B. 189
Davis, Margaret E. 156
Davis, Martha, 145
Davis, Mary A. 58
Davis, Mary C. 191
Davis, Nancy C. 338
Davis, Narcissa, 8
Davis, Narcissa N. 116
Davis, Racheal, 337
Davis, Robert, 257
Davis, Robert C. 192
Davis, Sally, 11
Davis, Sarah A. 132
Davis, Sarah Ann, 66
Davis, Sisly Ann, 247

Davis, Thatetha J. 179
Davis, Tilman, 234
Davis, Washington, 126
Davis, William, 34,100
Davis, Wm. M. 11,23
Dawers, Nancy Ann, 127
Deal, John S. 257
Deal, Riney Ann, 91
Dean, Alvin M. 39
Dean, Anne, 66
Dean, Eliza, 84
Dean, Hannah, 237
Dean, J. M. 25
Dean, Jane, 368
Dean, Jeremiah, 129,142,143,146
    160,228,254,263,284,289,291,318
    323,340,361
Deavers, Henry L. 130
Deck, Ann G. 13
Deford, James H. 264
Deimer, C. A. 310
Delana, Eliza, 165
Delancy, Mary E. 321
Deldem, Manerva, 254
Delemon, Jas. O. 200
Dellender, Charles, 88
Deloney, A. T. 343
Demaster, Mary L. 297
Dempsey, Dicey Pricilla Nancy
    Adeline, 373
Dempsey, George, 138
Dempsey, Mary Jane Elizabeth Rebecca,
    365
Denham, Margret E. 380
Denml, Margarett, 325
Dennis, A. A. 287
Dennis, B. F. 223
Dennis, Emeline, 9
Dennis, George W. 7,8,41,42,56,57,64
    144
Dennis, Helen M. 299
Dennis, Henry T. 36
Dennis, Irail F. 200
Dennis, James, 159
Dennis, Lemuel P. M. 194
Dennis, Louisa, 325
Dennis, Manerva E. 376
Dennis, Mary, 11
Dennis, Mary Ann, 236
Dennis, Parthena Ann, 231
Derick, John B. 337
Deshager, Eliza, 185
Devns, Elijah, 17
Dewitt, M. B. 363,364,371,372,380
Dewoody, John A. 20
Dickerson, F. A. 163
Dickey, Caroline, 344
Dickey, Elizabeth, 75

Duckworth, Joseph, 267
Dudley, Elizabeth, 158
Dudley, Virgil A. 284
Duke, Amanda M. 262
Duke, Andrew, 77
Duke, Berry, 107
Duke, Caroline, 344
Duke, Eliza, 188
Duke, Elizabeth Ann, 209
Duke, Elvira, 323
Duke, Green B. 114
Duke, Jefferson, 18
Duke, Mariah, 9
Duke, Mary Ann, 139
Duke, Sarah Jane, 191
Duke, William R. 200
Duncan, Rebecca A. 257
Duncan, Susan C. 324
Duncan, William, 192
Dunham, William C. 223
Dunkin, Martha Ann, 291
Dunlap, James, 50
Dunlap, Mary Jane, 223
Dunlap, R. M. 356
Dunlap, W. C. 127,131,133,142,149
    150,157,159,162,163,182,184,209
    217,219,229,249
Dunn, George W. 343
Dunn, Henry H. 226
Dunn, Matilda, 294
Dunn, Mary Ann, 343
Dunphney, Catherine A. 245
Dunson, Partheny, 99
Dunson, Sandford, 2
Durham, Rachel, 119
Durham, Robert, 40
Durham, Sally, 22
Durham, Samuel D. 132
Durham, Sarah, 163
Durn, Edward B. 338
Dusenberry, H. F. 268
Dusenberry, John S. 240
Dusenberry, Mahuldah M. 69
Duval, A. S. 251
Dyer, Amanda, 132
Dyer, Elizabeth, 19
Dyer, James L. 343
Dyer, James W. 317
Dyer, John, 56
Dyer, John H. 379
Dyer, Martha A. 238
Dyer, Sarah M. 370
Dyer, W. M. 113
Dyer, William, 172,174,176,185,200
    201,202,203,206,212,213,227,239
    241,242,252,255,260,263
Dyer, Wm. 193

E

Each, Elizabeth, 150
Eadens, Mary, 253
Eagan, Eliza, 76
Eagleton, G. 379
Eagleton, G. E. 349,356
Eakes, William, 242
Eakin, Allison, 211
Ealicke, Caroline, 118
Early, N. B. 92
Easley, Henry, 145
Easlick, Austin, 262
Easlick, Isaac N. 303
Easlick, Rhoda, 153,230
Easlick, Sarah, 108
Easlick, Thomas, 206
Eastland, Ann T. 34
Eastland, Cyrus, 122
Eastland, Thomas, 13,46,221
Easton, Robert T. 128
Eaton, Almeda E. 230
Eaton, C. C. 277
Eaton, Cyntha, 218
Eaton, James M. 110
Eaton, Jesse, 198
Eaton, Minirva, 82
Eaton, Samuel, 289
Eaton, Sarah, 218
Eaton, William W. 263
Echols, Augustus T. 119
Echols, Elizabeth J. 246
Echols, Malinda E. 38
Echols, Martha A. 96
Echols, Mary, 148
Echols, Obidiah C. 114
Echols, Reubin, 328
Echols, Willis H. 191
Edde, Candess C. 129
Edde, Delila, 297
Edde, Elizabeth, 288
Eddens, Benjamin M. 181
Eddens, William, 286
Eddings, Mary Jane, 183
Eddington, Charles D. 32
Eddington, Elizabeth E. 210
Eddins, Amanda, 248
Eddins, Mary Ann, 20
Ede, Patience, 26
Edens, Elizabeth A. 241
Edens, Emely Jane, 352
Edens, Frances M. 285
Edens, James, 199
Edens, Jane, 335
Edens, John M. 121
Edmaston, John, 160
Edmindson, C. H. 81,91,112,118

Edminson, Robert, 19
Edminston, Martha J. 212
Edminston, W. C. 73
Edmison, George, 268
Edmiston, Josephine, 270
Edmiston, Martha, 256
Edmiston, Milton A. 44
Edmiston, Robert, 29
Edmiston, Rossannah M. 41
Edmiston, Samuel, 242
Edmiston, Sarah M. 69
Edmiston, William, 255
Edmiston, G. W. C. 4,32,47,55
Edmondsen, Mary M. 150
Edmondson, C. N. 139
Edmondson, Campbell, 197
Edmondson, Catharine, 97
Edmondson, Issabella, 68
Edmondson, J. A. 357,361
Edmondson, M. A. 359
Edmondson, Milton A. 83
Edmondson, Susan A. 123
Edmondson, Susannah, 47
Edmundsen, Charles, 103
Edmunson, Alexander, 270
Edwards, Eliza M. J. 180
Eislick, Rhoda, 317
Elliott, C. D. 317
Elliott, James C. 278,282,293,316
    350
Elliott, S. E. W. 269
Ellis, Cleabery, 61
Ellis, Delila, 294
Ellis, Elizabeth, 184,336
Ellis, Iren A. 13
Ellis, James, 13
Ellis, James C. 299
Ellis, Jasper, 237
Ellis, Josiah, 163
Ellis, Margaret Ann, 147
Ellis, Mary, 125
Ellis, Mary F. 250
Ellis, Nancy, 103
Ellis, Narcissa, 69
Ellis, R. 54,70
Ellis, S. D. 290

Ellis, Sarah Ann, 262
Ellis, Sarah E. C. 158
Ellis, Stacy, 277
Ellis, Wiley C. 1
Ellis, William H. 255
Ellis, Wm. R. 367
Ellison, Joseph, 10
Elston, Allen, 328
Elston, Labra, 42
Eltoll, Willie E. 373
Elum, Nancy A. 145

Elvells, Martha, 284
Ely, James, A. G. 4
Emery, Mary, 323
Emmens, Catherine, 148
Emmon, John, 9
Emmons, E. A. 351
Emmons, J. M. 280
Emmons, James J. 221
Emmons, S. M. 240,251,256,270,275
    287,292,293,307,310,322,332,336
    365,369
Emmons, Sophia S. F. 240
Endsley, Alexander M. 119
Endsley, Margaret E. 196
English, James E. 156
English, Montgomery, 12
English, Samuel L. 112
Ennis, F. 251
Enochs, Caroline A. P. 119
Enochs, David S. 68
Enochs, Jane, 146
Enochs, John G. 23,234
Enochs, Mary M. 16
Enochs, Rebecca E. 156
Enochs, Sarah S. 117
Enochs, Susan (Sarah?) E. E. 374
Enochs, Susan G. 23
Ensley, J. P. 360
Epps, Elizabeth, 23,283
Epps, Frances D. 349
Epps, Hiram, 28
Epps, Hugh M. C. 23
Epps, James C. 381
Epps, James N. 381
Epps, Louisa J. 118
Epps, Margaret Jane, 32
Epps, William, 346
Ervin, John F. 117
Ervin, Milton, 333
Ervin, Nancy, 106
Eslick, Austin, 207
Eslick, Harvey, 92
Eslick, J. H. 304,305,317,320,325
    332,335,336,343,361,362,369,370
    371,372,373,378
Eslick, John G. 57
Eslick, Mahalla, 79
Eslick, Nancy, 75
Eslick, Newton, 164
Eslick, Polly, 2
Eslick, Rhoda, 117
Eslick, William, 140
Estill, Ann R. 61
Eurin, Lucinda, 101
Evans, Alfred, 23
Evans, Carrol, 112
Evans, Decy, 330

Evans, Dessy, 49
Evans, Eli, 209,269
Evans, Harriet, 34
Evans, Isaac, 334
Evans, James, 293
Evans, John, 116
Evans, Lucinda, 43
Evans, Malissa, 122
Evans, Martha, 208
Evans, Mary E. 296
Evans, Nicholas, 334
Evans, Nicholas M. 165
Evans, R. F. 297
Evans, Salina, 43
Evans, Sarah, 193
Evans, Sebron, 249
Evans, William S. 74
Evens, James D. 325
Evens, Mary Ann, 337
Evens, Mary E. 352
Evens, Nancy E. 342
Evens, William, 285
Evins, Elizabeth, 53
Evins, John C. 162
Ewing, Eliza M. 245
Ewing, Elizabeth Jane, 293
Ewing, J. C. 316
Ewing, Martha J. 278
Ewing, Y. C. 315
Ezell, Ellender J. 83
Ezell, F. L. 307,365,382
Ezell, Manerva A. 174
Ezell, Micajah, 153
Ezell, Z. T. 372,373
* Easlick, Sophronia, 270
F

Fackender, Robt. 291
Fackener, Margaret C. 141
Fackenter, Amanda, 203
Fackenton, Sarah, 92
Fankaley, Amand, 94
Fanning, George, 204
Fanning, Jno. W. 193
Fanning, Martha J. 215
Fanning, Samuel, 144
Fanning, William C. 164
Fannon, America, 249
Fannon, Andrew J. 265
Fannon, Benj. F. 301,343
Fannon, Delpha Ann, 266
Fannon, Elizabeth, 23
Fannon, Francis M. 246
Fannon, Phebe, 119
Fannon, Samuel, 13
Farguharson, R. 246,247,305,306
    320,324,339,345,373

Farguharson, Robert, 344
Farkner, Jas. H. 289
Farmer, Stephen M. 114
Farrar, Daniel, 12,133,134,139
    143,146,152,162,168,169,200,227
    242
Farrar, Jane, 75
Farrar, Mary E. 351
Farrar, Mary Jane, 223
Farrar, Nancy Jane, 369
Farris, C. B. 75
Farris, Samuel P. 112
Farrow, Elnyra A. E. 99
Farson, Henry T. 258
Fartner, L. H. 289
Faulkenberry, Sarah E. 246
Faulkenberry, Wm. P. 268
Faulkener, Anna, 212
Faulkner, Mary, 56
Faulkner, Mary Jane, 194
Faulkner, William, 70,237
Fauster, Eliza, 207
Fautner, William W. 228
Fauttenbury, Jerih M. 219
Felps, Alexander, 48
Felps, Alfred, 44
Felps, Caroline, 326
Felps, Elizabeth, 28,226
Felps, Jane, 62,160
Felps, Jasper N. 166
Felps, John, 153,259
Felps, Sarah, 62
Ferbes, Mary, 39
Ferguson, Alexander D. 218
Fernault, William W. 17
Fields, George W. 305
Fife, Samuel, 104
Fife, William, 41
Figg, James I. 18
Fincher, Mary, 100
Fincher, Sarah J. 356
Fincher, William C. 287
Findlay, Martin, 24
Findley, Jas. S. 183
Findley, Rachael, 144
Findly, Newton W. 364
Findly, Wm. A. 271
Finly, Jackson C. 227
Finney, David C. 118
Finney, James J. 162
Fisher, Jonathan, 47
Fist, Moses, 379
Fitch, A. J. 360
Fitch, Anderson, 65,172
Fitch, John, 97
Fitch, Mary Jane, 346
Fitch, Richard A. 91

Flack, Alvis, 124
Flack, Lavina, 81
Flack, Susan, 312
Flannagan, Sarah A. 81
Flask, Loucinda, 72
Fleming, F. E. 309
Fleming, John W. 17
Fleming, Lewis F. 281
Fleming, Martha, 66
Fleming, Vitilee, 348
Flemings, Andrew, 161
Flint, Norman, 207
Flippo, Jefferson, 381
Floyd, Elijah, 261
Floyd, Jno. F. 186
Floyd, Mary C. 228
Floyd, Sally T. 258
Floyd, Watson, 137
Fluty, George W. 182
Fly, John F. 381
Flynt, Amasa, 350
Flynt, H. E. 328
Flynt, James C. 339
Flynt, Martin, 61
Flynt, Navis, 270
Flynt, Tarply, 2
Foman, Rachael, 52
Fonvill, William, 294
Forbes, Alsalom, 114
Forbes, Elizabeth, 103
Forbes, Kauzetty, 225
Forbes, Martha Ann, 2
Forbes, Montgomery C. 154
Forbus, Gilina, 91
Forbus, Richard, 183
Ford, James N. 224
Ford, Mary Jane, 332
Ford, Tandy W. 222
Forehand, Martin L. 174
Foreman, John, 15
Forester, Alexander, 82
Forester, Elizabeth, 246
Forester, James, 254
Forester, Nancy, 227
Forester, Owen, 135
Forester, Tempe, 268
Forrester, John, 126
Forrester, Nancy J. 213
Forrester, Sarrah, 177
Forrester, Tabitha, 110
Forrister, C. 354
Forsyth, J. W. 353
Forsythe, Ann, 305
Forsythe, James P. 245
Fortune, Charles V. 227
Fortune, Elizabeth, 20
Fose, Catharine, 96

Foster, Alsey, 342
Foster, Caroline, 262
Foster, Charlotta A. 359
Foster, Elizabeth J. 99
Foster, James, 326
Foster, John B. 43
Foster, Maria, 76
Foster, Mary A. 52
Foster, Nancy, 244
Foster, Rachael, 49
Foster, Rogin, 275
Foster, S. W. 363
Foster, Sarah, 98
Foster, Sarah Ann, 114,308
Foster, Washington, 123
Foster, William V. 124
Foster, Willis H. 214
Fouville, William B. 238
Fowler, Caladena, 250
Fowler, Charles, 351
Fowler, Dennis, 275
Fowler, Vina, 347
Fox, Ann, 64
Fox, Benjamin, 373
Fox, Elizabeth, 269,343
Fox, John H. 62
Fox, Marilla F. 252
Fox, Nancy Ann, 251
Fox, Rebecca J. 134
Fox, Robert F. 324
Fox, Susan, 68
Fox, Susan W. 69
Fraley, Jesse, 228
Frame, Elizabeth Ann, 37
Frame, John H. 11
Frame, Minerva, 6
Frame, Robert, 106
Frame, Sarah Caroline, 114
Franklen, Samantha E. 154
Franklin, A. A. 372
Franklin, Arabella J. 316
Franklin, Elizabeth C. 60
Franklin, Harmen, 119
Franklin, Hiram, 104
Franklin, Jas A. 280
Franklin, John, 25
Franklin, John W. 266,344
Franklin, Louisa J. 189
Franklin, M. L. 356
Franklin, Macon, 127
Franklin, Mary Ann, 181
Franklin, May, 187
Franklin, Sarah Ann, 172
Franklin, Sarah L. 278
Franklin, Sarah M. 51
Franklin, Sina, 238
Franklin, Thomas, 103,179

Franklin, Westly, 191
Franklin, Wm. W. 297
Frazier, Johnathan, 132
Freeley, Jesse, 146
Freeman, A. C. 305
Freeman, Abner, 60
Freeman, Belinda, 308
Freeman, Daniel F. 61
Freeman, Egletine, 299
Freeman, Francis, 111
Freeman, George, 202
Freeman, Letha, 47
Freeman, Mary A. 250
Freeman, Mary N. 138
Freeman, Moses C. 340
Freeman, Nancy Jane, 296
Freeman, S. V. 355
Freeman, Sarah, 93,127
Freeman, Stephen, 129
Freeman, T. H. 251,252,253,262,278
    283,290,316,320,321,330,332,344
    345,347,348,350
Freeman, Thomas H. 52
Freeman, William M. 249
French, C. A. 119
Fritts, Joseph, 132
Frost, John, 65,157
Frost, Lucinda, 341
Frost, William C. 71
Fucher, F. A. 268
Fulerton, James R. 238
Fulgham, Amanda J. 243
Fulgham, Sarah A. 222
Fuller, Hasea, 8
Fuller, Letha B. 136
Fuller, Nancy, 91
Fuller, Sarah, 211
Fullerton, Elizabeth C. 24
Fullerton, Margaret A. E. 224
Fullerton, Mary E. 160
Fullerton, Robert, 191
Fulton, Eliza Jane, 121
Fulton, Francis F. 256
Fulton, Martha A. 264
Fulton, Mary M. 70
Furgerson, Augustus, 49

G

Gabble, Edward, 85
Gabner, Elizabeth M. 194
Gaddis, George F. 314
Gaddy, Elizabeth, 339
Gaddy, George, 18
Gaddy, Mary, 10
Gaddy, Samuel, 99
Gaddy, Thomas J. 333

Gaddy, William, 32
Galvey, Nathan, 373
Gale, L. W. 366
Gale, Mary Ann, 283
Gale, W. M. 154
Gallaway, A. M. 241
Gallaway, Alex M. 2
Gallaway, Mary K. 17
Gallaway, Samuel B. 254
Gallaway, W. J. 160
Galoway, James C. 338
Gamble, Elizabeth, 161
Gamblen, John H. 107
Gander, J. T. 320
Ganel, Liney, 193
Gant, George, 78,174
Garin, William W. 95
Garman, Ann, 126
Carman, Harret, 130
Garman, Robert P. 85,238
Garner, Eliza Ann, 78
Garner, Harriett P. 108
Garrett, Michael, 149
Gassaway, John T. 194
Gatlen, Mary, 126
Gatlen, William, 301
Catlin, Frances M. 337
Gattis, Amanda M. 242
Gattis, Berry, 373
Gattis, Elizabeth, 17
Gattis, Emely, 132
Gattis, George W. 267
Gattis, Green C. 76
Gattis, Isaac N. 34
Gattis, James, 90
Gattis, Martha Ann, 345
Gattis, Martha Jane, 346
Gattis, Nancy C. 76
Gattis, Robt. F. 281
Gattis, Sally Ann, 116
Gattis, Sarah Catherine, 297
Gattis, Susan E. 300
Gattis, Thomas. 111
Gattis, W. M. 23,28,36,45,46,56,58
    60,73,76,86,106,107,111,113,114
    115,118,120,122,128,144,146,151
    152,156
Gattis, William, 19,49,76,108,260
    267,279,288,297,323,331,337,345
    367
Gattis, Willie, 86
Gattis, Wm. H. 239
Gault, James J. 138
Gault, Henry C. 38,139
Gault, Hugh C. 139
Gaung, Mary Ann, 18
Gavin, Matilda, 94

Gray, Wilson, 33
Grayham, Ewing, 116
Grayham, John J. 325
Green, Elvena J. 242
Green, Emely, 153
Green, G. 69
Green, Henry, 153
Green, Isaac, 29
Green, James E. 371
Green, Jas. C. 200
Green, John A. 218
Green, Mary E. 16
Green, Mildred H. F. 347
Green, N. O. 264
Green, Sally S. 224
Green, Susan F. 281
Greer, Alexander A. 133
Greer, Angeline, 282
Greer, Drucilla, 61
Greer, Jane C. 26
Greer, Joanna E. 211
Greer, Joseph N. 150
Greer, Julia E. 297
Greer, Martha P. 265
Greer, Rebecca J. 310
Greer, Thomas V. 131
Gregory, William T. 136
Gregg, John W. 70
Gregg, Marget, 14
Gregory, Brown, 62
Gregory, Elizabeth, 144
Gregory, Ruth A. 301
Gregory, John, 10
Gregory, John F. 350
Gregory, Louisa, 144
Gregory, Martha, 274
Gregory, Mary, 63
Gregory, Sarah, 57
Gregory, William D. 135
Griffen, Nancy, 235
Griffin, Elizabeth, 99
Griffin, L. V. 115
Griffin, Louisa Jane, 274
Griffin, Pallis, 376
Griffin, Sarah, 109
Griffin, T. V. 43
Griffin, Wm. B. 187
Griffis, Elizabeth, 349
Griffis, Jane, 334
Griffis, Martha C. 127
Griffis, Nancy, 88
Griffis, Oliver P. 49
Griffis, Susan, 69
Griffis, William, 53
Grigg, Henry A. 191
Grigg, Samuel B. 191
Griggard, Willie A. 68

Grills, Elizabeth V. 232
Grills, Eveline P. 352
Grills, James A. 213
Grills, Mary A. 218
Grills, Sarah C. 228
Grills, W. T. 314
Grills, Wm. J. 216,237,291,297,367
Grisard, Margret V. 353
Grisard, Susan E. 249
Grizard, Mary C. 287
Grizard, Sarah F. 123
Groce, E. F. M. 365
Groce, Mary, 331
Groce, Thomas, 378
Gross, Mary Jane, 215
Grubbs, Eliza J. 348
Grubbs, Sarah F. 333
Grubbs, Nancy C. 316
Guilliams, Farry A. 68
Guin, Elizabeth, 135
Guinn, David B. 38
Gullett, James, 306
Gulley, A. J. 286
Gulley, Bardin J. 298
Gulley, J. J. 311
Gulley, Lucinda, 286
Gully, Mary A. C. 368
Gully, Mary F. 375
Gully, Nancy E. 292
Gully, Sarah, 332,362
Gunter, Alvessa, 137
Gunter, Eliza, 108
Gunter, Franklin, 111
Gunter, James P. 323
Gunter, John W. 122
Gunter, Martha, 27
Gunter, Mary D. 368
Gunter, Rebecca, 112
Gunter, Sarah Ann, 233
Gunter, W. M. 14
Guthrie, Samantha J. 348
Guy, Abner, 17
Guy, Margaret Ann, 64

H

Haffy, T. M. 253
Hagen, Margret Ann, 120
Haggard, Robt. M. 263,329,361,362
367
Haggard, Wm. 46
Hagis, Rebecca, 6
Hague, Cathrine L. 93
Hague, Eugine C. 295
Hague, John P. 272
Hague, Keziah M. 123
Hague, Mary C. 95

Irvin, Robert A. 179
Isaacs, Adiliza, 85
Isaacs, Agatha, 5
Isaacs, Samuel. 4
Isaacs, Samuel J. 56
Isham, Caroline, 224
Isham, Claborn, 78
Isham, Malinda Ann, 37
Isham, Martha Ann, 128
Isom, Eliza, 200
Isom, Elizabeth, 332
Isom, G. T. 267
Isom, Mary B. 326
Isom, Rachael, 74
Isom, Sarah, 217
Isom, Volentine C. 151
Ivy, A. J. 284

J

Jacks, D. 89
Jacks, D. M. 71,93,138,156,158
    173,214,219,236,240,269,275,277
    287,291,296,301,320,361,364
Jackson, Ann, 61
Jackson, E. A. 356
Jackson, Benj. 325
Jackson, Elizabeth, 368
Jackson, Elizabeth A. 100
Jackson, Isabella, 93
Jackson, Isaiah R. 39
Jackson, Mary, 294
Jackson, Wiley Ann, 325
Jackson, Priscilla, 367
Jackson, Rosariah A. 223
Jackson, Sarah Ann, 228
Jackson, Vincy E. 289
Jackson, William C. 154
Jacobs, Henry, 203,255
Jacobs, Robert, 206
James, A. C. 296
James, Abraham, 156
James, Ambros, 162
James, Ann, 268
James, Jane B. 3
James, Lewis G. 358
James, Malinda, 241
James, Martha E. 142
James, Newberry, 26
James, R. M. 369
James, Susan J. 240
James, W. W. 355
James, William L. 204
James, William M. 67
Jannett, Elizabeth D. 78
Jared, Wm. F. 218

Jarnett, James B. 47
January, Hiram, 6
January, William A. 166
Jean, David, 329
Jean, David C. 305
Jean, Elizabeth, 360
Jean, John, 136,323
Jean, John W. 148
Jean, Mary Ann Elizabeth, 358
Jean, Sarah, 359
Jean, Thomas, 296
Jean, Wiley, 323
Jean, William, 12
Jean, Wyatt, 354
Jeans, Calvin, 183
Jeans, Francis M. 47
Jeans, Jesse L. 173,371
Jeans, Joseph, 282,320
Jeans, Martha A. 194
Jeans, Mary, 234
Jeans, Nancy, 241
Jeffers, Benjamin, 53
Jefferson, Loisa A. 282
Jeffiers, Leah A. 350
Jeffries, William J. 238
Jening, Martha Jane, 337
Jenkins, Eliza J. 181
Jenkins, Elizabeth, 240
Jenkins, John, 167
Jenkins, Lucinda J. 306
Jenkins, Martha Ann, 369
Jenkins, Mary, 265,270
Jenkins, Thomas, 46
Jenkins, W. 67,74,77,78
Jenning, Elizabeth, 74
Jennings, Charlotta M. 186
Jennings, Jane M. 189
Jennings, Sarah Ann, 207
Jennings, Susannah F. 5
Jennings, W. C. 40,42,44,60,61,70
    77,78,79,93,111,112,113,139,144
    157,179,180,184,203,208,215,216
    219,231,236,248,266,296,340
Jennings, W. M. C. 34
Jennings, W. Z. 366
Jester, John R. 285
Jeter, Emeline F. 366
Jewel, Caroline, 144
Jewell, James, 232
Jewell, Martha A. 205
Jewell, Marcy Jane, 212
Jewell, W. E. 355
Jewell, Walter, 16
Jiffers, William, 91
Jinkins, N. M. 312
Jinkins, Sarah, 329

Parker, John, 43
Parker, Mariah, 56
Parker, Martha F. 351
Parker, Mary E. 105
Parker, Parthana E. 137
Parker, Sarah Jane, 220
Parker, Susan C. 144
Parker, William A. 187
Parker, Woodroof, 179
Parkerson, John, 136
Parkerson, Thomas W. 150
Parkes, A. W. 9,15,16,21,23,25,30
   33,40,42,45,48,63,67,68,83,85
   108,123,129,130,132,133,136,137
   140,146,147
Parkes, Ambrose L. 180
Parkes, Anice N. 189
Parkes, Felix G. 120
Parkes, Frances A. 46
Parkes, Henry, 116
Parkes, Isaac, 42,82
Parkes, Louisa S. 171
Parkes, Martha D. 80
Parkes, Martin L. 180
Parkes, Mary, 68
Parkes, Mary C. 67
Parkes, Nancy, 146
Parkes, Parthena, 78
Parkes, S. W. 110
Parkes, Susan F. 130,231
Parkes, Thos. L. D. (Jr) 159
Parkes, W. W. 164,167,192,198,200
Parkes, William W. 112
Parkes, Woodroof, 22,27,29,78,79
   91,148,151,152,161,166,167,174
   182,191,194,197,205,207,212,215
   225,239,249,253
Parkes, Woodruff, 22,24,95,105,113
   122,144,146
Parkinson, Brown, 282
Parkinson, Hugh, 132,135,281,346
   362,366
Parkinson, Hugh P. 43,155
Parkinson, James, 355
Parkinson, T. W. 238,254,264,291
   294,297,299
Parks, Aaron, 376
Parks, Allen, 63
Parks, Amanda, 67
Parks, Ann, 374
Parks, Ann S. 30
Parks, Benjamin T. 8
Parks, Catharine, 242
Parks, Elizabeth, 186
Parks, Emily, 79
Parks, Jesse W. 255
Parks, Martha J. 244

Parks, Martin L. 241
Parks, Milton, 222
Parks, Moses, 58
Parks, William, 181
Parks, Woodruff, 12,38,48,61,63,67
   86
Parr, F. P. L. 278
Parr, J. C. 300
Parr, Jane, 48
Parr, William M. 242
Parr, Zebulon, 304,318
Parrish, Emaline, 14,296
Parrish, Emily, 140
Parrish, James, 69,90
Parrish, Lydia A. 99
Parrish, May Ann, 81
Parrish, Milley, 190
Parrish, Sarah, 6
Parrish, Susanah, 222
Patillo, T. A. 378
Patrick, Andrew J. 316
Patrick, Margaret E. 17
Patrick, Marsset R. 377
Patrick, Sarah E. 200
Patrick, W. M. 280
Patterson, D. C. 300
Patterson, D. M. 326
Patterson, D. S. 273,275,285,297,333
   337,355
Patterson, Elizabeth S. 330
Patterson, Gilliam, 213
Patterson, Hannah, 31
Patterson, John, 57
Patterson, John M. 22
Patterson, L. M. 310
Patterson, Martha E. 202
Patterson, Nancy, 55
Patterson, Sally, 1
Patterson, Sarah, 334,381
Patterson, Stephen, 213
Patterson, Susan, 160
Patton, E. L. 363
Patton, Mary L. 334
Patton, Mary M. 220
Payne, Caroline, 322
Payne, Deauna, 16
Payne, Maria, 369
Payne, Susan, 56
Paysinger, Bashaby, 132
Paysinger, Henry, 74
Paysinger, Julian, 162
Paysinger, Martha J. 357
Paysinger, Mary, 118
Paysinger, Rhody, 275
Paysinger, Thomas A. 73
Pearce, James, 214
Pearce, Jesse, 149

Pearce, John A. 33
Pearce, Malinda, 196
Pearce, Milley, 112
Pearce, Polly, 374
Pearce, Simon A. 210
Pearce, William, 237
Pearson, Bettie L. 343
Pearson, Mannon C. 48
Pearson, Meredth, 20
Pearson, Milton, 164
Pearson, Sarah, 221
Pearson, S. J. 335
Pebby, Mahulda, 67
Pegram, Martha C. 271
Pelepoe, Allen W. 129
Pemberton, Eliza A. 213
Penick, Keriah Jane, 13
Penn, Margaret, 24
Penney, Hugh P. 131,143
Penney, N. P. 150
Pennington, Emely, 30,316
People, Prissilla, 374
Pepper, Theopulus, 351
Perkins, Drury M. 13,238
Perry, Eveline, 166
Perry, George, 188
Perry, Isham, 20
Perry, J. W. 283
Perry, James W. 116
Perry, Jasper, 333
Perry, Martha J. 237
Perry, Mary, 207
Perry, Mary Ann, 305
Perry, Nancy, 42,144
Perry, Nathan, 9
Perry, Rhodica, 190
Perry, Samuel, 201
Perry, William, 69
Peter, Ellis, 246
Pettes, Martha Jane, 289
Petty, Elizabeth, 279
Petty, Emeline, 308
Petty, Hannah Retta, 7
Petty, Jane M. 20
Petty, Joseph, 114
Petty, Louise J. 362
Petty, Lyddia, 361
Petty, Narcissa, 54
Petty, Nathan, 172
Petty, Ralph, 73
Petty, William, 161
Petty, Wm. 202
Petway, T. S. 306
Pewet, Jas. N. 191
Peyton, Nancy E. 233
Peyton, William H. 223
Phagan, Elizabeth A. 103

Phagan, James H. 330
Phagan, Margaret, 51
Phagan, Mary G. 79
Phagan, Philips T. 160
Phagan, William M. 375
Pheleps, Cintha A. 99
Pheleps, Jefferson, 242
Pheleps, Nancy, 310
Philips, Arena, 50
Philips, Cressy, 73
Philips, Fereby, 7
Philips, H. 100,102,103,123,134
    138
Philips, Herman, 115
Philips, Hiram, 117,121
Philips, Letty, 52
Philips, Martha A. 102
Philips, William A. 196
Phillips, B. U. G. 159
Phillips, E. J. 303
Phillips, Elizabeth, 181,237
Phillips, George W. 127
Phillips, James, 230
Phillips, John T. 284
Phillips, Joshua, 224
Phillips, Martha E. D. 261
Phillips, Mary M. 186
Phillips, Nancy J. 175
Phillips, W. M. 161
Philpot, Alexander, 41
Philpot, Elizabeth, 213
Philpot, Jas. 293
Philpot, Margaret M. 250
Philpot, William, 176
Pibus, Sarah, 93
Pickens, A. M. 57,60,81,83,91,100
    108,123,126
Pickett, Andrew J. 65
Pickett, Ebenzer, 65
Pickett, Henson, 107
Pickett, Louisa, 28
Pickett, Louisa J. 317
Pickett, Mark H. 42
Pickett, Mary E. 298
Pickett, Theordore, 293
Pickle, Nancy Ann, 251
Pickle, Nancy J. 315
Pierce, Ambrose H. 71
Pierce, Martha, 165
Pierce, N. B. 269
Pigg, Ann, 13
Pigg, Delia E. 163
Pigg, Elizabeth, 295
Pigg, James, 330,336
Pigg, James B. 309
Pigg, Jennett, 255
Pigg, Joel T. 362

Prickett, G. W. 29
Frickle, Squire, 40
Prince, Gidien, 160
Prince, Jeremiah, 331
Pritchard, Levi, 49
Pritchett, Drury, 3
Pritchett, Jamamce, 179
* Procter, Robert L. 159
Prosser, A. M. 203
Prosser, Frances, 353
Prosser, Hepsey, 381
Prosser, J. A. 317,372
Prosser, J. G. 267
Prosser, James A. 163
Prosser, Jesse, 294
Prosser, Jonathan E. 102
Prosser, Louisa, 175
Prosser, N. A. 355
Prosser, Martha Jane, 340
Prosser, Mary E. 356
Prosser, P. G. 240
Prosser, Peggy Jane, 11
Prosser, Priss, 218
Prosser, Sarah, 227
Prosser, William, 248
Prosser, William D. 213
Pruett, America, 240
Pruett, Lucillar, 225
Pruett, Nancy O. 242
Pruett, Samuel D. 245
Pruitt, Emily, 179
Pruitt, William A. 36
Pruitt, William W. 18
Pruitt, Wilson C. 66
Pruvitt, Folly, 21
Pryor, W. M. 65,73,80,85,87,89,90
    106,108,130,135
Pryor, William, 197,232,248,252
    264,268,275,277,279,295,299,300
    314,320,356
Puckett, B. G. W. 230,258,263,268
Puckett, G. W. 20,44,47,51,55,96
    103,104,111,120,121,124,125,128
    129,156,158,161,220,267,286,333
    360,371
Puckett, George W. 142
Puckett, Mary J. 330
Pucleeled, G. W. 305
Pullam, Frances, 223
Pullam, Margret, 210
Pulliam, John W. 49
Pulliam, Nandana M. 54
Pulliam, W. P. 6,12,24,33,37,38,50
    54,60

* Priwitt, Catharine, 90

Pullin, Joseph G. 238
Pullin, W. M. 30,35
Pully, Celia, 156
Pully, Elizabeth, 111
Pully, Leaply, 106
Pully, Mary, 251
Purdom, Mark, 254
Puryear, Elizabeth, 9
Putman, J. C. 365
Pwight, William P. 14
Pylant, Casey Ann, 371
Pylant, Gabriel, 98
Pylant, Gray J. 322
Pylant, Green A. 143
Pylant, James C. 251
Pylant, Jno. L. 214
Pylant, Penera, 85
Pylant, Rebecca, 300
Pylant, William G. 295

Q

Qualls, 98
Quarles, Irena L. 86
Quarles, Jemina, 54
Quinn, Josiah O. 33
Qunn, Elizabeth O. 30
Qush, Malaciah, 21

R

Radegar, Sarah Ann, 346
Radican, Mary, 111
Raiborn, Mathew, 172
Rainey, Benjamin, 24
Rainey, Deshasen, 98
Rainey, Elizabeth, 171
Rainey, Febe Jane, 203
Rainey, James, 203
Rainey, Jane, 175
Rainey, Martha I. 83
Rainey, Nancy, 115,155
Rainey, William J. 206
Rains, Baily, 193
Rains, Earle, 40
Rains, Emily A. 222
Rains, Frances, 335
Ralekid, Permelea, 353
Ralston, Samuel S. 22,23,38
Ralty, John, 306
Rambo, R. M. 368
Ramsey, Anne, 283
Ramsey, David, 14
Ramsey, Eliza Jane, 40
Ramsey, Elizabeth, 18,158
Ramsey, Ellen, 375
Ramsey, Elzina, 88

Reese, Minerva, 291
Reese, Nancy K. 197
Reese, Nancy N. 242
Reese, Perlivia Ann, 209
Reese, R. E. 310
Reese, Robert, 330
Reese, Thos. J. 209
Reese, Virginia, 223
Reese, W. L. 274,276,298,335,346
    351,353,367,368,370
Reese, Wilkerson, 280
Reese, William W. 103,113
Reese, Wm. H. 237
Reeves, Eliza, 200
Reeves, Jane, 245
Reeves, John C. 179,188,190,193
    196,208,217,221,236,242
Reeves, Margaret, 53
Reeves, Martha Ann, 32
Reeves, Miles J. 332
Reeves, Nancy, 228
Reeves, P. H. 326
Reeves, Sally, 18
Reeves, Susanah, 4,8,115
Reid, Abzolom M. 7
Reid, George, 50
Reid, S. E. 269
Relakin, Perneler, 353
Remells, J. E. 360
Remington, C. H. 249,250
Renarger, John, 336
Renegar, A. J. 261
Renegar, Belinda, 69
Renegar, Catharin, 36
Renegar, Davidson, 244
Renegar, Ellis, 107
Renegar, George F. 82
Renegar, H. J. 331
Renegar, Jacob, 266
Renegar, Jasper, 296
Renegar, John M. 172
Renegar, Joseph H. 177
Renegar, Martha, 298
Renegar, Mary, 5,41,69
Renegar, Mary Jane, 297
Renegar, Nicholas, 117
Renegar, Sanferd, 151
Renfro, Indiana, 285
Renfrow, James F. 184
Rennegar, Sarah, 245
Revis, David J. 249
Rew, James O. 296
Reynolds, Jesse, 320
Reynolds, S. R. 373
Rhea, Elizabeth Ann, 158
Rhea, James H. 240
Rhea, Jefferson L. 187

Rhea, John J. 346
Rhea, M. B. 68,91
Rhea, Margret, 105
Rhea, Margret Jane, 194
Rhea, Mary M. B. 51
Rhea, Pheban, 108
Rhea, W. B. 65,66,80,81,101,111
    112,121,122,124,125,128,141,149
    150,177,181,194,201,206,236,242
    244
Rheah, Nancy E. 271
Rhoads, Wm. A. 374
Rhodes, Ann Maleir, 65
Rhodes, Eliza, 277
Rhodes, Jane, 353
Rhodes, Lemuel, 52
Rhodes, Rebecca, 17
Rhodes, Sarah, 77
Rhodes, Simeon, 39
Rhone, Samuel H. 301
Rhoten, Elizabeth A. 79
Rhoton, Mary Ann, 230
Rhyne, V. M. 46,267
Rice, Creek T. 266
Rice, Green P. 153
Rice, Mary Elizabeth, 375
Rice, Othniel, 60
Rice, Palina, 62
Rich, Henry J. 190
Rich, Jane, 55
Rich, Joseph M. 275
Rich, Thos. J. 367
Rich, Williamsen, 166
Richard, William, 155
Richardson, Druory, 251
Richardson, Jackson, 324
Richardson, Martha, 153
Richardson, Pitta C. 31
Richardson, Rolin M. 3
Richerson, Frances, 346
Richey, Sarah C. 352
Richisen, James, 300
Rickets, Diana, 246
Rickets, Martha, 237
Ricks, Ann Roberta, 161
Ricks, Martha Ann, 277
Riddle, Alexander, 368
Riddle, Betsey, 24
Riddle, Ephrain, 22
Riddle, Harmun, 22
Riddle, M. V. 322
Riddle, Martha P. 379
Riddle, Mary, 323
Riddle, P. P. 197
Riddle, Stephen, 31
Riddle, William, 76
Riggan, Wm. H. 308

Simmons, Susan Ann Jane, 301
Simmons, William, 13
Simmons, Zachariah, 24
Simpson, Joseph, 345
Simpson, Rachel M. 182
Simpson, Sarah J. 179
Simpson, William R. 46
Sims, David, 282
Sims, George W. 248
Sims, James M. 211
Sims, John, 162,300
Sims, Mary, 8
Sims, Mary Ann, 318
Sims, Rachel, 65
Sinkton, Sarah, 145
Sisco, Fleming J. 348
Sisk, Solomar B. 139
Sivley, Mary Frances, 361
Sixton, Eliza P. 320
Slack, Francis N. 152
Slain, James B. 217
Slaughter, Samuel A. 187,270
Sloan, A. S. 164,174,175,176,188
 189,192,226,229,232,238,247,255
 258,282,321,323,326,330,341,342
 344,349,352,355,363,368,374,376
Sloan, Amanda, 303
Sloan, Ann Jane, 128
Sloan, Elizabeth J. 174
Sloan, Grissilda B. 150
Sloan, Lucinda E. 155
Sloan, Rachael, 225
Sloan, Samuel H. 113
Sloan, Sarah J. 152
Sloan, Wm. A. 368
Slone, M. L. 278
Small, A. C. 39
Small, Amos, 86,104,108,118,123,135
 136,143,154,171,188,193,227,233
 235,238,255,261,312,318,357,359
 378
Small, Cisa Ann, 102
Small, Elizabeth H. 88
Small, George, 89
Small, Lucy E. 12
Small, Susannah T. 8
Smallman, William, 240
Smith, A. D. 364
Smith, A. G. 144,148,167,171,176
 180,183,194,196,198,202,204,205
 206,207,208,217,221,224,228,233
 236,250,269,270,272,278,288,292
 294,310,312,314,319,322,328,329
 330,336
Smith, A. T. 190,191
Smith, Adaliza T. 124
Smith, Alex, 26,227,274,310

Smith, Alexander, 257
Smith, Alexander F. 126
Smith, Alfred, 51
Smith, Alfred R. 226
Smith, Alfred W. 226
Smith, Allen, 11,206
Smith, Amanda A. 288
Smith, Amanda J. 163
Smith, Andrew J. 62
Smith, Arviller, 104
Smith, Asa, 42,190,237
Smith, Auston C. 29
Smith, B. F. 248
Smith, C. 124,155
Smith, Caleb, 131,342
Smith, Calvin, 265
Smith, Carey P. 41
Smith, Ceton, 382
Smith, Champion, 355
Smith, Charles, 332
Smith, Charles L. 40,342
Smith, Charles W. 343
Smith, Clerissa, 329
Smith, Cytha A. 265
Smith, D. F. 255
Smith, David, 227
Smith, David R. 2
Smith, David G. 303
Smith, David L. 247
Smith, David M. 274
Smith, Davis, 2,4,7,8,11,14,25,37
 41,45,51,57,67,75,77,82,86,87
 94,109,113,114,116,125,128,148
 157,273,376,377,380
Smith, Drury J. 66
Smith, Edward, 266
Smith, Eliza, 46,144,146
Smith, Eliza Ann, 76
Smith, Elizabeth, 142,205,237,273
 277,312
Smith, Elizabeth A. 330
Smith, Elizabeth C. 231
Smith, Elizabeth U. 191
Smith, Emily, 13
Smith, Fernette T. 48
Smith, Frances A. 314
Smith, Frances E. 206,322,355
Smith, Frances M. 358
Smith, Geo F. 180
Smith, George W. 20,124
Smith, Green D. 7
Smith, Hardy H. 53
Smith, Harriett M. 336
Smith, Harrison, 72
Smith, Henretta, 228
Smith, Henry, 137
Smith, Henry L. 10,261

Stedman, E. H. 281
Stedman, John H. 325
Steed, Augustine, 32
Steed, Mary Ann, 182
Steed, Naonn, 89
Steed, Nathaniel, 3
Steed, Syntha, 85
Steed, William F. 184
Steel, A. J. 258,291,365
Steel, G. M. 302,363
Steel, G. U. 23
Steelman, Cyntha Ann, 217
Steelman, Elizabeth, 161,259
Steelman, George W. 348
Steelman, Halifax A. 212
Steelman, James R. 233
Steelman, Jane, 80
Steelman, Joel, 308
Steelman, John, 372
Steelman, John H. 286,300,302,305
    326,335,342,346,347,365
Steelman, Mary, 372
Steelman, Sarah, 279
Steelman, W. M. 197,251
Stegall, Margaret, 27
Stegall, Matilda, 244
Stegall, Sarah Jane, 159
Stephens, Cyntha, 368
Stephens, Elizabeth E. 341
Stephens, Elsira, 161
Stephens, Ervin, 8
Stephens, John, 120
Stephens, Joseph C. 381
Stephens, Mary Ann, 204
Stephens, Nancy, 214
Stephens, Nancy Jane, 255
Stephens, Richard, 34
Stephens, William, 1
Stephens, William J. 210
Stephens, Willis, 368
Stephenson, Charlotte, 272
Stephenson, Dulsena, 212
Stephenson, Frances A. 360
Stephenson, G. W. 283,380
Stephenson, George P. 272
Stephenson, J. 329
Stephenson, James M. 196
Stephenson, John C. 137
Stephenson, Sarah A. 109,329
Stephenson, Silas, 221
Stephenson, T. W. 96
Stephenson, Wm. H. 212
Steteer, Nancy M. 106
Stevenson, F. E. B. 356
Stevenson, James, 99
Stevenson, James C. 134,135,138,174
    202,223,227,244,324,325,327,342

Stevenson, Robert, 241
Stevinson, Franklin, 185
Steunett, Ruffin C. 81
Stewart, A. J. 135
Stewart, Angaline, 350
Stewart, Ann D. 92
Stewart, Avery, 58
Stewart, Cathrine, 150
Stewart, Eliza E. 157
Stewart, Harriet F. 41
Stewart, Heatarpas, 349
Stewart, James C. 377
Stewart, John, 27
Stewart, John D. 95
Stewart, John H. 161
Stewart, John P. 368
Stewart, Joseph, 15
Stewart, Margaret, 54
Stewart, Martha, 335,336
Stewart, Martha F. 312
Stewart, Mary A. 352
Stewart, Nancy L. 309
Stewart, Sarah Ann, 265
Stewart, Sarah Jane, 302
Stewart, Sopia A. E. 58
Stewman, Allen, 183
Stiles, Elizabeth E. 171
Stiles, J. A. 369
Stiles, Margaret A. 366
Stiles, Naomi E. J. 349
Stiles, Samuel, 54,342
Stiles, Sarah, 105
Stockstill, Eliza, 360
Stockstill, W. F. 354
Stockton, Thomas J. 81
Stone, A. F. 293
Stone, A. S. 205
Stone, Abegail, 173
Stone, America F. 236
Stone, Awna, 296
Stone, Calvin, 43
Stone, Dolphus A. 199
Stone, E. W. 331
Stone, Eliza, 93
Stone, Elizabeth, 156
Stone, Emily, 169
Stone, I. L. 5,10,22
Stone, James A. 14
Stone, Maronda, 79
Stone, Mary, 158
Stone, Narcissa, 274
Stone, Reubin J. 336
Stone, Sarah L. 196
Stone, Sarah P. 301
Stone, Selina, 117
Stone, William, 195

Summers, McHenry, 159,231
Summers, T. P. 169
Summers, William, 241
Summons, Thomas P. 82
Sumners, Nancy M. 183
Sumners, T. T. 233,234
Sumners, T. P. 182,209,226,255
Sumners, Thomas P. 380
Sumners, Ths. P. 248
Sumoore, Epomtas, 138
Surber, Joseph, 235
Surber, Rachel P. 52
Surber, Julia A. 294
Surler, John, 109
Surney, Sarah, 83
Surreen, McKinney, 167
Surrels, Isham, 85
Sutleff, A. 366
Suttle, Frances, 73
Suttrell, James, 72
Suttrell, Louise, 79
Swan, Elizabeth, 278
Swauner, Mary, 8
Swauner, Mary E. 188
Swauner, Obediah, 101
Swenea, John, 31
Swinebrand, Henry Green, 272
Swinebroad, Amanda M. 228
Swinebroad, Dona, E. D. 304
Swinebroad, George W. 119
Swinebroad, Manerva, 282
Swinebroad, Mary, 139
Swinebroad, Parthena C. 281
Swinford, Amanda J. 142
Swinford, John, 32
Swinford, Lydia, 100
Swinford, Martha Cathrine, 369
Swinford, Susan C. 147
Sykes, A. J. 276

T

Taft, David M. 352
Tafts, William, 299
Tanbelerster, Amanda Jane, 378
Tankersly, Oliver D. 42
Tanner, Nancy, 5
Tapley, William J. A. 138
Tarant, J. W. 247,249
Tate, A. A. 338
Tate, A. J. 299
Tate, Agness Y. 285
Tate, James J. 75
Tate, Lavina G. 174
Tate, Manica, 112
Tate, Mary E. 248
Tate, Robert J. 40

Tate, Sarah, 310
Tate, Tursey A. 203
Tate, William V. 319
Tatum, Elizabeth F. 87
Tatum, Sarah B. 117
Taukersby, Jasper, 246
Taukersby, Stephen G. 199
Taukesby, George N. 260
Taylor, Adaline, 39
Taylor, Bryant, 195
Taylor, C. L. 9
Taylor, Charles G. 275
Taylor, Edward, 207
Taylor, Eliza Jane, 369
Taylor, Elizabeth B. 106
Taylor, Elizabeth J. 344
Taylor, Erastus, 342
Taylor, Frances, 72
Taylor, H. C. 337
Taylor, Harrison C. 29
Taylor, Henry, 208
Taylor, Huldy Jane, 236
Taylor, J. C. 89
Taylor, J. H. 64,65,66,69,70,71,74
    77,79,80,81,84,93,106,113,131
Taylor, James, 15
Taylor, James B. 233
Taylor, James H. 94
Taylor, Jas. M. 293
Taylor, John H. 335
Taylor, John N. 92
Taylor, Jonathan A. 14
Taylor, Joseph, 80
Taylor, Julia Ann, 189,381
Taylor, Louisa F. 106
Taylor, Lucinda, 100
Taylor, Malinda, 19
Taylor, Marcus C. 255
Taylor, Margret R. 215
Taylor, Martha, 136,368
Taylor, Martha Ann, 160
Taylor, Martha F. 303
Taylor, Martha J. 285
Taylor, Martha K. 349
Taylor, Mary, 52,210
Taylor, Nancy E. 177
Taylor, Nathaniel, 258
Taylor, Peter C. 100
Taylor, Phebe, 208
Taylor, Polly, 82
Taylor, R. M. 312
Taylor, Rebecca, 254
Taylor, Redrick P. 173
Taylor, Robert, 329
Taylor, Robert A. 108
Taylor, Sanders, 184
Taylor, Sarah, 133,206

Taylor, Sarah A. 290
Taylor, Sarah B. 354
Taylor, Sarah C. 266
Taylor, Sirah, 9
Taylor, Sytha Ann, 358
Taylor, Temple, 163
Taylor, Thomas, 120
Taylor, W. C. 360
Taylor, W. M. 369
Taylor, William F. 230
Taylor, William H. 264
Taylor, Wm. B. 336
Taylor, Wm. Y. 231
Taylor, Young A. 171
Taylor, Young S. 38
Taylor, Young T. 103,164,171,177
    191,196,199,201,204,209,210,217
    246,255,257,260,265
Tayts, David M. 221
Teems, Martha Ann, 124
Tell, Elizabeth, 249
Tempelton, Alfred L. 231
Tempelton, Evelen, 228
Tempelton, Jas. A. 236
Tempelton, M. P. 339
Tempelton, Margaret, 317
Templeton, Manerva, 115
Templeton, Nancy, 123
Templeton, Robert, 154
Templeton, Robert L. 140
Templeton, Sarah E. 296
Templeton, Sarah L. 216
Templeton, W. W. 232
Temples, Elizabeth, 138
Temples, Moses, 200
Temples, Rosanna, 17
Tennison, Elizabeth, 201,333
Tennison, John L. 316
Terry, Hugh T. 264
Tetty, Susan D. 264
Thomas, Cornelius, 109
Thomas, Edwin T. 81
Thomas, Elize, 15
Thomas, H. D. A. 333
Thomas, Margaret L. 159
Thomas, Mary, 151
Thomas, William L. 356
Thomeson, Martha, 8
Thomison, Ann, 341
Thomison, Hugh, 325,360
Thomison, Julia A. 143
Thomison, Martha J. 350
Thomison, Mary E. 324
Thomison, William, 9
Thomison, 120,133
Thompson, Adeline, 133
Thompson, Alexander, 356

Thompson, Daniel, 377
Thompson, David, 45
Thompson, Eleanor C. 68
Thompson, Elizabeth, 1
Thompson, Francis A. 322
Thompson, Francis W. 146
Thompson, George, 106
Thompson, Hugh W. 164
Thompson, Huldah, 346
Thompson, J. L. 224,245
Thompson, James L. 321,359
Thompson, John, 14
Thompson, Jonathan C. 6
Thompson, Josiah S. 212
Thompson, Loucinda E. 284
Thompson, Louisa, 358,380
Thompson, Martha J. 261
Thompson, Mary A. 195
Thompson, Nancy R. 283
Thompson, Nathan J. 246
Thompson, Patrick, 251
Thompson, Rachel, 380
Thompson, Ruth K. 373
Thompson, Samuel A. 312
Thompson, Syntha, 343
Thompson, Tabitha, 112
Thompson, W. H. 376
Thompson, William, 113,251
Thompson, William J. 83
Thompson, William M. 220
Thompson, Wilson, 222
Thompson, Wm. H. 279
Thornton, H. L. 317
Thornton, William, 48
Thorp, Martha J. 283
Thurman, Harah, 381
Thurman, Rebecca, 46
Thurman, Rebecca A. 236
Tigert, J. B. 347,357
Tiller, B. F. 380
Tiller, Beckwith J. 48
Tiller, Catharine E. 39
Tillery, John W. 379
Tillery, William, 282,376
Tilly, Wm. 289
Timmins, Jno. H. 241
Timmins, Martha A. 75
Timmins, Mary, 5
Timmins, Materia, 45
Timmins, W. M. 1,3,7,16,25,30,52
Timmins, William, 32
Timmons, Alexander, 244
Timmons, Candis C. 181
Timmons, Charles W. 120
Timmons, George W. 129
Timmons, Susan A. 259
Timmons, Thomas, 261

White, Thadeus, 314
White, Thomas, 274
White, William C. 83
White, William P. 315
White, William V. 66
White, Willie, 319
White, Wm. C. 23
White, Wm. M. 235
White, Wm. P. 347
Whiteside, Manerva Ann, 169
Whitlock, Nancy F. E. 140
Whitlock, Octava, 98
Whitman, Mary E. 226
Whitman, R. M. 224,249,271,374
Whitman, Robert M. 165
Whitman, Robt. M. 5,14,45,70,66
Whitman, Root M. 66
Whitt, David, 267
Whittenbery, Norman, 167
Whittington, A. H. 303
Whittington, Daniel S. 50
Whittington, Lucinda V. 126
Whittington, Nancy, 127
Whitworth, A. M. 370
Whitworth, George W. 373
Whitworth, Hannah, 65
Whitworth, John, 84
Whitworth, Martha J. 290
Whitworth, R. L. 364
Whitworth, Sarah E. 268
Whitworth, Taily, 196
Whitworth, Thos. B. 304
Whitworth, Thos. J. 290
Wicker, James M. 185
Wicker, Martha, 99
Wicker, Robert F. 341
Wicks, Mary S. 191
Wiegart, George Ann, 327
Wiggins, Catharine B. 297
Wila, Rachel, 101
Wilburn, Daniel T. 248
Wilburn, James, 248
Wilburn, Wade, 172
Wilch, Nicholas N. 23
Wiles, Celea, 26
Wiles, Charles, 65
Wiles, Nancy J. 207
Wiles, Rosanah, 147
Wiles, Stephen L. 173
Wiley, James, 17
Wiley, Joseph C. 225
Wiley, L. B. 321
Wiley, Margaret, 34,231
Wiley, Martha J. 321
Wiley, Mary E. 264
Wiley, Mary T. 157
Wiley, Mirah L. 233

Wiley, Nancy, 2
Wiley, Susannah J. 176
Wilkerson, Caroline, 164
Wilkerson, Eliza, 83,234
Wilkerson, Margaret, 65
Wilkerson, Sarah, 1
Wilkerson, Temperance, 68
Wilkins, Caroline, 219
Wilkins, Edy, 6
Wilkins, Elizabeth, 107
Wilkins, George W. 145
Wilkins, Jane, 249
Wilkins, John F. 200
Wilkins, Martha, 90,312
Wilkinson, Sarah Ann, 5
Willer, Emily, 197
Willet, Eliza L. 12
Willet, Sarah Ann, 8
Williams, Alexander, 76
Williams, Alfred W. 214
Williams, Amon A. 188
Williams, Clarinda, 141
Williams, Carrell, 365
Williams, David W. 9
Williams, Eldredge S. 176
Williams, Eliza J. 176
Williams, Elizabeth, 69
Williams, Elizah T. 106
Williams, Francis M. 304
Williams, Henry, 318
Williams, J. P. 231,245
Williams, James, 62
Williams, James F. 242
Williams, Jasper, 302
Williams, Jerome B. 376
Williams, Jo. P. 303
Williams, John, 10
Williams, John R. 340
Williams, Joseph F. 69,71,94
Williams, Louisa Ann, 363
Williams, Louisana, 237
Williams, Lucinda, 75,309
Williams, M. G. 233
Williams, M. P. 94
Williams, Margaret, 71,86
Williams, Margaret A. 125
Williams, Mary, 180
Williams, Mary A. 83
Williams, Mary Ann Adaline, 237
Williams, Minerva, 241
Williams, Nancy A. 128
Williams, Nancy Ann E. 185
Williams, P. J. 259
Williams, Penina E. 195
Williams, Rac, 303
Williams, Reece, 319
Williams, Sarah, 6,30,71

MARRIAGE RECORDS
1838-1860

A record of Marriage Licenses issued by the Clerk of Lincoln County
Court Tennessee After the 1st day of February 1838.

(p 1)
Thomas Kirkland to Sally Patterson, Feby 3, 1838
                    February 4, 1838 A. W. Parks

Wiley C. Ellis to Peggy Ann Wagoner, Feby 3, 1838
                    February 4, 1838 Wm Timmins, J.P.

William Warren to Sarah Wilkerson, Feby 5, 1838
                    February 6, 1838 John King

Robert Wood to Mary Mallard, Feby 5, 1838
                    February 8, 1838 Joel Reece

William W. Moores to Jane M. Browning, Feby 5, 1838
                    February 8, 1838 A. B. Gilbert

William Stephens to Jane Berry, Feby 6, 1838
                    February 7, 1838 Samuel J. Bland

William G. Hamilton to Caroline McGaugh, Feby 6, 1838
                    --   Thomas Chiles, M.G.

John Webb to Rebuah Cumberland, Feby 6, 1838
                    February 28, 1838 John Moorehead, J.P.

John Bearden to Mary Warren, Feby 13, 1838

Micajah Clark to Jemima Murrell, Feby 14, 1838
                    February 15, 1838 John Webb, M.G.

David Tipps to Elizabeth Thompson, Feby 15, 1838

Samuel M. Rosebrough to Lucy Brandon, Feby 18, 1838

James Grant to Caroline Hinkle, Feby 24, 1838

(p 2)
Benjamin D. Hancock to Fenetta Lyon, Feby 22, 1838
                    February 22, 1838 Henry Turney, J.P.

Wiley Ware to Fanny R. Carithers, March 7, 1838
                    --   Davis Smith, J.P.

Thomas Criner to Sarah Walker, March 5, 1838
                    March 5, 1838 Robert Monday

Alex M. Gallaway to Nancy Wiley, March 11, 1838

David B. Smith to Martha Gunter, March 12, 1838
                March 14, 1838 By Thomas Chiles, M.G.

Sanford Dunson to Martha Ann Forbes, March 12, 1838
                March 12, 1838 I. N. Flair. J.P.

Henry Snow to Polly Eslick, March 13, 1838

John A. Tuley to Sally McGauch, March 15, 1838

Lewis Wamack to Ellenor Campbell, March 15, 1838
                February 14, 1838 John Gilbert

Abram Cunningham to Mary Miles, March 17, 1838
                March 22, 1838 Samuel Boone, J.P.

Tarply Flynt to Eliza M. Claiborn, March 22, 1838

Jackson C. David to Caladoni Husbands, March 22, 1838

Hugh Watson to Ellen McMillen, March 22, 1838
                March 22, 1838 John Lanier, J.P.

(p 3)
John Michael to Elizabeth McClure, March 24, 1838
                March 25, 1838 Wiley C. Newman, J.P.

Arnold Brine to Parthena Colberson, March 26, 1838
                March 27, 1838 C. W. McGuire, J.P.

William G. Spain to Mary E. Logan, March 27, 1838

Alexander Brady to Polly Milstead, March 28, 1838
                April 3, 1838 Isaac Conger (Seal)

William B. Sanders to Martha Driver, March 29, 1838
                March 29, 1838 Wm Timmins, J.P.

Archibald Baxter to Jane B. James, March 29, 1838

Richard M. Rolin to Eliza Ann Holman, April 1, 1838

Nathaniel Steed to Martha Brady, April 2, 1838
                April 12, 1838 Samuel Boone, J.P.

Jonas Byons to Malinda Hall, April 3, 1838
                April 3, 1838 Stephen Walker, J.P.

William Tripp to Drury Tritchett, April 4, 1838

James D. Morris to Sarah Robinson, April 4, 1838
                April 2, 1838 Wm Timmins, J.P.

Armstead Pamplin to Cynthia Ann Haney, April 5, 1838
                April 5, 1838 By Benj F. Clark, J.P.

Singleton Sikes to Margaret Hilton, April 10, 1838
                    April 10, 1838   Wm Timmins, J.P.

William H. Tuley to Adaline Buchanan, April 12, 1838

(p 4)
Henry Coble to Sarah Brady, May 3, 1838
                    --   By Davis Smith, J.P.

A. J. Clark to Ellenor B. Clift, May 3, 1838
                    May 3, 1838   G. W. C. Edmiston, J.P.

John F. Walker to Elizabeth Pack, May 3, 1838
                    May 15, 1838   G. B. Allison, J.P.

Manual Alstead to Micey Hogue, May 13, 1838

James Carba to Betsey Nicholas, May 17, 1838
                    May 23, 1838   John King, J.P.

George C. McClain to Louisa Smith, May 19, 1838
                    May 20, 1838   Jefferson Keiso, J.P.

William Lyles to Eliza Christian, May 20, 1838
                    May 20, 1838   By John Walker, J.P.

Curral Lee to Elizabeth Latham, May 23, 1838
                    May 24, 1838   Jno C. Year, M.G.

Saml T. Crenshaw to Milley Watson, May 31, 1838
                    May 31, 1838   John Lanier, J.P.

Hampton Sims to Mary Ann Brown, June 6, 1838

Samuel Isaacs to Rebecca Aleon, June 12, 1838
                    June 24, 1838   Wm Spencer, J.P.

Manuel Robert to Caroline Calhoon, June 18, 1838

Isham Smith to Elney Oliver, June 21, 1838

William S. Bowers to Cynthia Winters, June 23, 1838
                    June 24, 1838   By Samuel J. Bland, J.P.

(p 5)
James A. G. Ely to Eliza Batie, June 27, 1838
                    July 28, 1838   J. R. Brown

Henry Waggoner to Frances Hulsey, July 11, 1838
                    July 12, 1838   G. B. Allison, J.P.

Felix Grundy McGaugh to Minerva Jane Whitaker, July 16, 1838

James S. Culberson to Abigail Kennedy, July 16, 1838
                    July 17, 1838   C. T. McGuire, J.P.

Jermiah Sulivan to Lucinda Leach, July 16, 1838
               July 17, 1838 By Samuel Boone, J.P.

William N. Reece to Frances J. Holbert, July 19, 1838
               July 19, 1838 Pleasant Holbert, J.P.

James S. Davis to Nancy E. Tanner, July 21, 1838
               July 21, 1838 John Lanier, J.P.

William W. Tucker to Martha Marler, July 21, 1838
               July 26, 1838 A. B. Gilbert

Richard McNatt to Sophia McNatt, July 21, 1838
               July 22, 1838 Robt M. Whitman

Thomas H. Glidewell to Lethe A. Simmons, July 23, 1838

Leroy Lukev to Susannah P. Jennings, July 24, 1838
               July 31, 1838 By David Crook, M.G.

Martin Wright to Frances Massey, July 25, 1838
               July 26, 1838 J. L. Stone, J.P.

John Caldwell to Mary Timmins, August 4, 1838
               August 7, 1838 Henry Turney, J.P.

Poling Smith to Elizabeth Henry, August 9, 1838

(p 6)
Thomas L. Sanson to Mary Renegar, August 9, 1838

David Rorex to Sarah Ann Wilkinson, August 14, 1838

Bluford P. Nowlin to Margaret Phagan, August 15, 1838

John M. Van Hoozer to Agatha Isaacs, August 15, 1838
               August 17, 1838 Wm Anderson, J.P. for L. C.

Hiram January to Sarah Williams, August 18, 1838
               August 19, 1838 Wm Spencer, J.P.

James Sorrells to Minerva Frame, --

Isham G. Bailey to Susan B. Smith, August 21, 1838
               --   A. W. Parks, J.P.

Moses Bradley to Jenny Boren, August 22, 1838

James Vincent to Sarah Parrish, August 23, 1838
               August 23, 1838 Stephen Walker, J.P.

John Bethum to Polly Ann Cole, August 25, 1838
               August 26, 1838 W. P. Pulliam, J.P.

Edward G.G. Reanland to Mary L. Moores, August 27, 1838
               August 30, 1838 John Bell, M.G.

Hugh Fandalph to Loucinda Milan, August 29, 1838
                    August 30, 1838 Samuel J. Bland, J.P. for L.C.

John Abbot to Rebecca Hagis, August 29, 1838

Littleton N. Stovale to Emily Gray, August 30, 1838
                    September 2, 1838 Samuel J. Bland, J.P. for L.C.

(p 7)
Samuel Hawkins to Edy Wilkins, September 1, 1838
                    September 3, 1838 Samuel J. Bland, J.P. for L.C.

Jonothan O. Thompson to Loucinda Hall, September 3, 1838
                    September 3, 1839 James R. Brown

Wiley C. Newman to Polly Bethany, September 3, 1838

Green D. Smith to Martha Holbert, September 5, 1838
                    --   By Davis Smith, J.P.

Harrison Wells to Mary Bryant, September 10, 1838

Absolom M. Reid to Sabry Lemmons, September 10, 1838
                    --   Davis Smith, J.P.

William H. Rees to Mary M. Whitaker, September 12, 1838
                    September 13, 1838 A. B. Gilbert

Moses Seveaton to Julia Ann Gray, September 12, 1838
                    September 16, 1838 By George W. Dinnis, J.P.

Preston Hampton to Rachael Maliex, September 13, 1838
                    September 13, 1838 B. F. Clark, J.P.

Preston Burke to Rhoda Dallas, September 14, 1838
                    --   By Wm Timmins, J.P.

Asa Jones to Fereby Philips, September 15, 1838
                    September 18, 1838 By Samuel J. Bland, J.P.

Isaac Collins to Mary Frances Brown, September 15, 1838

Matthews T. Cole to Hannah Ritta Petty, September 17, 1838

Jacob Hasch to Martha Caroline Rowel, September 18, 1838
                    September 18, 1838 J. K. Blair, J.P.

(p 8)
John Hamilton to Nancy Van Hoozer, September 18, 1838
                    September 18, 1838
            Certified September 19, 1838 Wm Anderson, J.P. for T.C. (Seal)

Jas. D. Smith to Narcissa Davis, September 18, 1838
                    --   Davis Smith, J.P.

Morris Carpenter to Mary Swauner, September 18, 1838
                    September 20, 1838 Pleasant Holbert, J.P.

E. Blankenship to E. Blankenship, September 19, 1838
                    September 20, 1838 Samuel J. Bland, J.P.

Hasea Fuller to Sarah Ann Willet, September 20, 1838
                    September 20, 1838 A. B. Gilbert

Wilson Woodard to Sally Polk, September 21, 1838

John W. Dobbs to Naimi Bowman, September 22, 1838
                    September 26, 1838. By Samuel Bland, J.P.

David B. Cooper to Mary A. Mitchel, September 24, 1838

James G. Harrison to Susannah J. Small, September 24, 1838
                    September 27, 1838 A. B. Gilbert

Peter Weaver to Priscilla Driver, September 26, 1838

Ervin Stephens to Emily Wheeler, September 27, 1838
                    October 2, 1838 S. I. Bland, J.P.

Preslley Ruckers to Margagt Cunningham, September 29, 1838
                    September 30, 1838 Herry Larney, J.P.

William Clark to Elizabeth Ruth, October 1, 1838
                    October 1, 1839 B. Wilson, J.P.

A. Vincent to Mary Ann Parrish, October 1, 1838

Benjamin T. Parks to Martha Thomeson, October 3, 1838
                    October 4, 1838 By George W. Dennis, J.P.

William H. Sims to Mary Sims, October 4, 1838

(p 9)
John Emmons to Delila Robinson, October 6, 1838

G. L. Taylor to Peggy Hindman, October 9, 1838
                    October 9, 1838 T. C. Williams, J.P of L.C.

I. L. Bedford to Emeline Ruter, October 12, 1838
                    October 16, 1838 Joseph Smith

Wm Bedford to Mary Jones, October 13, 1838
              —   By A. W. Parks, J.P.

Nathan Perry to Everline Mitchel, October 13, 1838
                    October 14, 1838 John Lanier, J.P.

James E. Curry to Matilda Massey, October 18, 1838
              —   By A. W. Parks, J.P.

Wm Merrill to Charlotte Grant, October 18, 1838
                    October 18, 1838 C. W. McGuire, J.P.

Sirah Taylor to Elizabeth Puryear, October 23, 1838

Byrd Douglas to Martha E. Bright, October 23, 1838

October 23, 1838 M. Marshall

Israel Morris to Linney Couch, October 29, 1838

October 29, 1838 T. S. Williams, J.P.

Pedford Hopkins to Nancy Neely, November 2, 1838

November 4, 1838 S. I. Bland, J.P.

Benjamin Mabers to Rebecca A. Mason, —

(p 10)

William W. David to Margaret Johnston, November 6, 1838

November 8, 1839 John Gilbert

William Thomison to Jane Daily, November 13, 1838

November 15, 1838 By Thomas Chiles, M.G.

James Cowley to Mariah Duke, November 13, 1838

Mark McClure to Charlotte Lynn

Isaac S. Porter to Emeline Dennis, November 15, 1838

John Williams to Martha Buchanan, November 20, 1838

November 20, 1838 By B. F. Clark, J.P.

James Campbell to Mahala Hambrick, November 21, 1838

Joseph Ellison to Margaret Couch, November 23, 1838

November 25, 1838 Wiley C. Newman, J.P.

Erasmus Ward to Mary Wing, November 23, 1838

Nathan P. Hardin to Martha Jane Wells, November 24, 1838

November 25, 1838 J. L. Stone, J.P.

Henry L. Smith to Elizabeth A. Wanslow, November 24, 1838

50 Pd   William Abbot to Margaret MCalister, November 26, 1838

November 26, 1838 Robert Drennon, J.P.

18¾ Ct   Jarrel J. Burrow to Matilda Madison, November 29, 1838

Due

William Wright to Mary McNatt, November 30, 1838

December 11, 1838 I. H. Leptewich

(p 11)

John Grigory to Mary Gaddy, December 4, 1838

James Rutledge to Mary Ann Ready, December 5, 1838

December 6, 1838 A. B. Gilbert

Alexander Peard to Nancy Clark, December 5, 1838

Joseph Clark to Jane E. Massy, December 8, 1838

December 8, 1838 B. F. Clark, J.P.

Thomas Davidson to Margaret Jane Hudson, December 11, 1838
                    December 13, 1838   John Gilbert
Moses Howell to Pay 31. only having Paid 31.

John H. Frame to Mary Dennis, December 11, 1838
                    December 13, 1838   By William Spencer, J.P. for L.C.

Allen Smith to Milisa Lock, December 12, 1838
                    December 13, 1838   J. K. Blair, J.P.

William M. David to Sally Davis, December 13, 1838
                    December 16, 1838   Davis Smith, J.P.

Wilbourn Beck to Dorcas Allsup, December 17, 1838
                    December 20, 1838   Phasant Holbert, J.P.

Lodowick Archer to Sally Ann Goff, December 18, 1838
                    December 18, 1838   Robert Drennan, J.P.

Joel Wright to Peggy Jane Prosser, December 18, 1838
                    December 18, 18, 1839   A. B. Gilbert

(p 12)
Montgomery English to Sarah Bell, December 19, 1838

Perry Wells to Eliza L. Willet, December 19, 1838

Daniel Farrar to Nancy C. Shipp, December 22, 1838
                    December 25, 1838   C. W. McGuire, J.P.

L. B. Cole to Assena H. Stovall, December 25, 1838
                    December 25, 1838   S. I. Bland, J.P.

Joseph Row to Susan Wagoner, December 25, 1838
                    December 27, 1838   By Samuel Boone, J.P.

Jesse Norman to Martha King, December 30, 1838
                    February 30; 1839   By John Moorehead, J.P.

A. D. Summerford to Lucy E. Small, January 1, 1839
                    January 8, 1839   A. B. Gilbert

William Jean to Susan Tarran, January 2, 1839
                    January 3, 1839   T. S. Williams, J.P.

Wm D. Moorehead to Mariah Cunningham, January 3, 1839
                    January 3, 1839   Woodruff Parkes, Eqr.

John Mays to Pamila Anthony, January 4, 1839
                    January 4, 1839   John Walker, J.P.

Jackson Berry to Frances Carson, January 5, 1839
                    January 6, 1839   John King, J.P.

Calvin Beck to Mary Crawder, January 9, 1839

John Rodgers to Martha Hancock January 9, 1839
                    January 9, 1839 By Wm P. Pullian, J.P.

John George to Perbna Stanfield, January 9, 1839

(p 13)
Jackson Bramion to Nancy A. Rivers January 12, 1839

S. D. Buchanan to Celia A. Kennon, January 12, 1839

Alexander Hayes to Mary Strong, January 14, 1839

David N. Wise to Emily Smith, January 14, 1839
                    January 15, 1839 A. B. Gilbert

John McCown to Tibitha Coleman, January 14, 1839
                    February 9, 1839 By Samuel J. Bland, J.P.

Drury M. Perkins to Sarah H. Bonner, January 15, 1839
                    January 15, 1839 Pleasant Holbert, J.P.

James Harrison to Anna Pigg, January 17, 1839
                    January 17, 1839 Henry Turney

James Ellis to Irsn A. Ellis, January 17, 1839

E. T. Cashin to Mary Shelton, January 19, 1839
                    January 22, 1839 W. C. Newman, Esq.

James B. Dillenon to Mary Brewer, January 22, 1839
                    --   By C. W. McGuire, J.P.

Joseph Johnson to Keriah Jane Penick, January 23, 1839

Green B. Rossell to Margaret Brannon, January 26, 1839
                    February 3, 1839 Boone Wilson, J.P.

Samuel Fannon to Elizabeth Gray, January 30, 1839
                    January 31, 1839 By John King, J.P.

Lamuel Todd to Ann G. Deck, January 31, 1839
                    --   Wall - Marshall
(p 14)
Robert Harwell to Parthena P. Smith, February 2, 1839

James A. Stone to Milly Reese, February 2, 1839
                    February 3, 1839 By Robert M. Whitman

William Hale to Amanda Staton, February 3, 1839
                    February 3, 1839 John Walker, J.P.

John H. Reed to Marget Gregg, February 4, 1839

James Darnell to Nancy Merrill, February 5, 1839
                    --   By Wm Anderson, J.P.

William Kidd to Sarah Dale, February 6, 1839

John Thompson to Lousenda Easlick, February 6, 1839

Burrel Hale to MayyAnn Murry, February 7, 1839
--   A. B. Gilbert, M.G.

David Allen to Sarah Martin, February 13, 1839
                February 14, 1839 Joel Reese

David Ramsey to Mary Ann Cunningham, February 14, 1839

Jonathan A. Taylor to Betsey A. Wilson, February 18, 1839
                February --, 1839 Davis Smith, J.P.

William I. Hopkins to Marget Neely, February 18, 1839
                February 12, 1839 By Samuel O. Bland, J.P.

William P. Dwight to Amanda M. Medcalfe, February 20, 1839
                February 21, 1839 By M. Marshall

(p 15)
Andrew J. King to Ibby Mitchell, February 26, 1839

Morgan W. Hinkle to Cyntha Dowthet, February 26, 1839
                February 27, 1839 By J. W. Holman, J.P.

Wm F. Smith to Mary Jane Todd, Febfuary 26, 1839
                February 26, 1839 By M. Marshall

Wm Gunter to Mary A. Crowder, February 27, 1839
                February 28, 1839 By Boone Wilson, J.P.

Joseph Stewart to Martha Williamson, February 28, 1839

S. A. N. Hart to E. G. Motlow, February 28, 1839
--   By A. W. Parks

Wm A. Morgan to Mary Davidson, March 2, 1839
                March 8, 1839 By L. H. Leftwick, M.G.

John Foreman to Prudence Mansfield, March 6, 1839
                March 7, 1839 By John Moorehead

Josiah M. Norwood to Sarah A. Ramsey, March 7, 1839

James Taylor to -- Brow, March 7, 1839

Hollis T. Allen to Eliza Sharp, February 11, 1839
                March 11, 1839 By John Walker, J.P.

Joseph Burt to Elize Thomas, February 11, 1839

Moses H. Bonner to Ann F. Robertson, February 12, 1839

Eliphas Shelton to Mary Hardin, February 19, 1839
                March 19, 1839 W. C. Newman, J.P.

(p 16)
Richmond P. Reed to Polly Marlow, March 27, 1839
                    March 28, 1839 By Ira McKiney, J.P.

Eli Moores to Agnes Broadway, March 29, 1839
                    March 30, 1839 By Tho Childs

Walker E. Jewell to Francis A. Broadway, March 30, 1839
                    March 31, 1839 By Stephen Walker, J.P.

Martin K. Shofner to Martha Burnett, March 30, 1839
                    March 31, 1839 By W. C. Newman, J.P.

Williamson Matney to Sarah Frances Bedford, April 1, 1839
                    April 2, 1839 By Wm Timmins, J.P.

Thomas Atwood to Nancy Kean, April 1, 1839
                    April 3, 1839 Tho Childs

Isaac J. Curry to Mary M. Enoch, April 13, 1839
                    --   By Wm Timmins, J.P.

Robert C. McEouen to Mary E. Greer, April 16, 1839
                    April 16, 1839 By M. Marshall

Drury M. Connally to Deauna Payne, April 16, 1839
                    April 17, 1839 By John Moorehead, J.P.

Wm T. Wilson to Rebeccah I McCormack, April 18, 1839

James Wright to Eliza J. McLemore, April 24, 1839
                    April 24, 1839 By J. H. Leftwick, M.G.

(p 17)
Elisha Bagley to Elizabeth Todd, May 7, 1839
                    May 7, 1839 By M. Marshall

Allen Pool to Rebecca Rhodes, May 9, 1839
                    May 9, 1839 By Saml I. Bland, J.P.

Abner Guy to Bodine F. King, May 13, 1839
                    May 15, 1839 By Stephen Walker, J.P.

John C. Corder to Sarah Mangum, May 15, 1839

William W. Fernault to Mary Commons, May 22, 1839
                    May 22, 1839 By John Lanier, J.P.

James B. Gray to Mary E. Russell, May 30, 1839

Daniel E. George to Julia Snoddy, June 5, 1839
                    June 7, 1839 John Copeland

Moses Buchanan to Judith Moffett, June 18, 1839
                    June 18, 1839 By John Lanier, J.P.

W. H. Neece to Margaret Carns, June 22, 1839
June 24, 1839 By J. H. Leftwick, M.G.

A. C. Ogoltree to Melisia Monday, June 22, 1839
June 23, 1839 By A. Alexander, J.P.

John W. Fleming to Polly Moore, June 24, 1839

James A. Burnet to Matilda Shofner, June 25, 1839
--   By Wm C. Newman, J.P.

James W. McClung to Margaret E. Patrick, June 25, 1839
June 25, 1839 M. Marshall

Elijah Devns to Rosanna Temple, June 26, 1839
June 26, 1839 B. Wilson, J.P.

James I. Burnett to Matilda H. Shofner, June 26, 1839

James Wiley to Mary N. Gallaway, July 3, 1839

F. R. Moore to E. W. Wynn, July 4, 1839
July 4, 1839 Tho Whitaker, J.P.

Miles H. McCowan to Mary L. Rowland, July 6, 1839
July 8, 1839 I. K. Blair, J.P.

Wm Cashin to Elizabeth Gattis, July 8, 1839
July 9, 1839 By John Moorehead, J.P.

(p 18)
John H. Mills to Louisa Buntley, July 10, 1839
--   Samuel Boone, J.P.

Charles Merrell to Lydia Massay, July 13, 1839
--   By John Webb

George Gaddy to Sally Reeves, July 13, 1839

Jefferson Duke to Elizabeth Ramsey, July 15, 1839
July 16, 1839 Tho Whitaker, J.P.

Willis H. Holman to Jane P. Moore, July 15, 1839

George Milstead to Ruth Rutledge, July 16, 1839
--   Samuel Boone, J.P.

Wm H. Moores to Elizabeth H. Sugg, July 17, 1839
July 18, 1839 By Plasant Holbert, J.P.

Wm W. Pruitt to Mary Ann Gaung, July 19, 1839
July 19, 1839 By Stephen Walker, J.P.

(p 19)
Wm McCormack to Mary Hughey, July 23, 1839

Mr. A. Murry to Parthena Hall, July 27, 1839
                    July 20, 1839 By A. P. Gilbert

James I. Figg to Mary I. Mason, July 30, 1839
                    July 30, 1839 Jno. Moore, J.P.

A. I. Carloss to Mary Ann Franklin, July 30, 1839
                    July 30, 1839 By M. Marshall

Robert Edminson to Sophia Blackamore, July 31, 1839

John Mayfield to Jauntha Watson, August 1, 1839
                    August 1, 1839 By William Cattis, J.P.

I. W. Martin to Mary Johnston, August 1, 1839
                    --   Saml. Boone, J.P.

William H. Bossell to Elizabeth Dyer, August 3, 1839
                    August 8, 1839 B. Wilson, J.P.

Ridley B. Wynn to Rebecah R. Hopkins, August 3, 1839

Benjamin T. Cowley to Margart Elizabeth Ann Hicks, August 7, 1839

John Mills to Malinda Taylor, August 9, 1839
                    August 10, 1839 By John King, J.P.

J. B. Bristow to Sarah Mathew, August 12, 1839
                    August 18, 1839 By Joel Reese, J.P.

Nichalos Burns to Mary Warren, August 13, 1839
                    August 13, 1839 By J. H. Leftwich, M.G.

Alfred West to Eunicey Robinson, August 14, 1839

Grove Copeland to Nancy Braden, --
                    September 15, 1839 John King, J.P.

(p 20)
Meredth Pearson to Ann I. Moore, August 14, 1839

Isham Perry to Sarah Hodges, August 17, 1839

Milton Buchanan to Sinah A. Marrs, August 27, 1839
                    --   J. Iarnir, J.P.

John F. Black to Jane M. Petty, August 27, 1839
                    August 27, 1839 By G. W. Puckett

Alfred Blythe to Nancy Wedd, September 2, 1839
                    --   By Wm Martin, M.G.

George Webb to Sarah Jones, September 2, 1839
                    --   By Wm Martin, M.G.

Andrew Hendrick to Tempey Williams, September 9, 1839

John A. Dewoody to Mary T. Tool, September 11, 1839
       --   By John Bell, M.G.

Thomas Justice to Nancy Blades, September 12, 1839

George Copland to Nancy Braden, September 14, 1839

George W. Smith to Elizabeth Fortune, September 14, 1839

Jacob Vance to Mary Ann Eddins, September 16, 1839
       September 23, 1839 I. N. Blair, J.P.

Robert R. Graves to Esther Hinkle, September 16, 1839

Eli Barnes to Teletha Owden, September 17, 1839
       September 25, 1839 Ira McKinney, J.P.

(p 21)
Demsey Pace to Polly Pruvitt, September 19, 1839

Benjamin Couch to Rebucah Casey, September 23, 1839

Daniel M. Tucker to Nancy Y. Higgins, September 25, 1839
       September --, 1839 By J. H. Leftwich, M.G.

Edward Butler to Cardine McDaniel, September 26, 1839
       September 26, 1839 Ira McKinney, J.P.

Robert Cook to Rachael Long, September 28, 1839
       September 29, 1839 Wm C. Timmins, J.P.

Malaciah Qush to Sarah McDugal, September 30, 1839

John T. Balch to Sarah R. Blakemoore, October 2, 1839

Loderick Robertson to Nancy Waggoner, October 5, 1839

Hial S. Woodard to Martha Haley, October 8, 1839
       October 9, 1839 Plasant Holbert, J.P.

Jacob A. Keller to Lourut Walker, October 10, 1839
       November 4, 1839 By A. W. Parks, J.P.

John Litch to Susannah W. Miller, October 10, 1839
       October 10, 1839 By Levi Vickory, J.P.

Wm Bearden to Nancy Hobbs, October 14, 1839
       November 7, 1839 By H. Turney, J.P.

Lewis Sexton to Rachael Moore, --
       --   By Wm Anderson, J.P.

Thomas Manifee to Catherine Bowers, October 16, 1839
       December 16, 1839 By Stephen Walker, J.P.

(p 22)

John W. Blair to Eliza J. Howell, October 17, 1839
October 17, 1839 I. K. Blair, J.P.

John Rigg to Sally Durham, October 19, 1839

Gilbert K. Adams to Caroline McKinney, October 21, 1839

Andrew Waggoner to Betsey Hulsey, October 21, 1839
October 22, 1839 Woodruff Parks, J.P.

Ephraim Riddle to Racheal Smith, October 23, 1839

Harmon Riddle to Marget Hunt, October 24, 1839

Tho. McAfee to Martha Posson, October 26, 1839
October 27, 1839 John Gilbert

David S. Gray to Mary Moorhead, October 31, 1839
October 31, 1839 Woodruff Parks, J.P.

Alex'l Waggoner to Cyntha Foo, November 8, 1839
November 10, 1839 Samuel Boone, J.P.

James M. Bell to Catherine K. McDaniel, November 12, 1839
November 12, 1839 W. H. Baldrige, M.

Joel P. Bryant to Susan Alexander, November 13, 1839

John M. Patterson to Ruth K. Browning, November 13, 1839
November 13, 1839 W. L. Baldrige, M.

Jonathan Harden to Mariah Wilson, November 15, 1839
--   By I. L. Stone, J.P.

Jefferson Parkam to Betsey Leavers, November 18, 1839

(p 23)

John B. Tucker to Nancy a. Townson, November 20, 1839
November 26, 1839 By W. H. Holcumbe

Lewis B. Morgan to Bernette Hart, November 23, 1839
April 24, 1839 By Joel Rees, J.P.

James I. Blackemore to Martha L. Hays, November 29, 1839
--   By John Bell

Wm C. White to Polly M. Nixon, December 6, 1839
December 12, 1839 By Wm Gattis, J.P.

Joshua Stroud to Nancy Mills, December 6, 1839

Nicholas N. Wilch to Asena Beavers, December 10, 1839

Wm Gleghorn to E. H. Wilson, December 11, 1839
December 12, 1839 Samuel S. Ralstom

Elijah Cleghorn to G. G. Wilson, December 11, 1839
December 12, 1839 Samuel G. Ralston, M.G.

Richard Hill to Louisa Litterill, December 12, 1839

Wm M. Davis to Amelia A. Turney, December 12, 1839

John G. Enochs to Susan C. Enochs, December 13, 1839
December 15, 1839 Joseah Smith, M.G.

Hugh M.C. Epps to Elizabeth Epps, December 14, 1839
December 18, 1840 A. B. Gilbert

Benjamin G. Benson to Adaline Wright, December 16, 1839
December 19, 1839 David Crook

Allen Jones to Mary Ann Sanders, December 18, 1839
December 19, 1839 By Stephens Walker, J.P.

John Hurt to Parthena Ann Dennis, December 21, 1839
December 23, 1839 Tho Whitaker, J.P.

William E. Gibbs to Anna Majors, December 23, 1839

Alford Nixon to Elizabeth Fannon, December 23, 1839
December 24, 1839 Tho G. Williams, J.P.

Alfred Evans to Sady Hilton, December 23, 1839
--   By A. W. Parks, J.P.

G. U. Steel to Mary Robertson, December 24, 1839
(p 24)
Allen L. Anderson to Elizabeth C. Fullerton, December 25, 1839

Martin Findlay to Mary Meek, December 25, 1839
December 26, 1839 J. K. Blair, J.P.

James Burton to Nancy Moss, December 23, 1839
December 31, 1839 By William F. Pulliam, J.P.

Zachariah Simons to Betsey Fiddle, December 28, 1839

Mathew Harty to Charlotte Jones, December 28, 1839

Moses Cruise to Catherine Johnston, December 30, 1839
December 31, 1839 James Rorex, J.P.

John Harper to Malinda Norman, January 1, 1840
--   By John King, J.P.

Robert S. Strong to Margaret Penny, January 2, 1840
January 2, 1840 J. K. Blair, J.P.

John F. Shelton to Martha T. Milam, January 2, 1840

Benjamin Rainey to Elizabeth Parker, January 3, 1840

17

Andrew King to Elizabeth Hobbs, January 4, 1840
January 5, 1840 W. C. Newman, J.P.

(p 25)
J. M. Dean to Ann Roundtree, January 6, 1840
January --, 1840 By A. W. Parks, J.P.

Wright P. Collins to Elizabeth Davis, January 6, 1840
January 7, 1840 By Davis Smith, J.P.

David Polly to Lucinda Simmons, January 7, 1840

William Price to Rebecah Gore, January 8, 1840
January 9, 1840 Wm C. Timmons, J.P.

John Franklin to Elizabeth Neely, January 8, 1840
January 9, 1840 I. K. Blair, J.P.

James Woodard to Rebecah Roane, January 13, 1840

(p 26)
Greenwood Nichols to Rebecah Nix, January 13, 1840

Isaac C. Hall to Marget S. Campbell, January 15, 1840
January 16, 1840 Woodruff Parks, J.P.

Joel Peese to Patience Ede, January 15, 1840
January 16, 1840 By Joseph Smith

Jonathan B. Dildine to Malinda Hunts, January 18, 1840

Newberry James to Catherine Wright, January 18, 1840
January 19, 1840 By A. B. Gilbert

William Pilant to Nancy Campbell, January 18, 1840
January 20, 1840 Levi Vickory, J.P.

Joshua Smith to Jennetta Claunch, January 22, 1840

David R. Smyth to Jane C. Greer, January 23, 1840
--   By M. Marshall

Elias McDaniel to Mary George, January 24, 1840
A. Smith to pay 2/3 a bal not Pd.

Henry Sulivan to Celea Wiles, January 25, 1840
January 30, 1840 A. B. Gilbert

James McCowley to Mary Beggorby, January 27, 1840
February --, 1840 By Stephen Walker, J.P.

(p 27)
James Seaton to Mary Ann Mims, January 28, 1840

Soloman Mason to Elizabeth Land, January 29, 1840

John Stewart to Nancy Abernathy, January 29, 1840

William Cone to Elizabeth Wright, February 1, 1840
                    February 11, 1840 John Gilbert

John A. Johnson to Eliza Moffett, February 3, 1840
                    --   James Rorex, J.P.

Edmond Boaze to Elizabeth Hoots, February 3, 1840
                    February 4, 1840 James Rorex, J.P.

Campbell Douthet to Margaret M. Stegall, February 4, 1840
                    February 11, 1840 J. W. Holman, J.P.

Bolin Clark to Sarah Blyth, February 6, 1840

Isaoh King to Catharine Hullsey, February 6, 1840
                    February 6, 1840 Woodruff Parks, J.P.

Thomas H. Armstrong to Charlotta Cone, February 12, 1840
                    February 13, 1840 John Gilbert

Wm D. Lackey to Mary W. Hinkle, February 13, 1840

Thomas W. Bell to Mary Damron, February 17, 1840
                    February 20, 1840 By Aarron Alexander

(p 28)
Willis B. Stovall to Elizabeth Felps, February 18, 1840
                    February 18, 1840 By Stephen Walker, J.P.

Jesse Shelton to Betsey Shaw, February 19, 1840
                    February 20, 1840 Robert Drennan, J.P.

James Clark to Susan Williams, February 22, 1840
                    February 23, 1840 By Wm. R. Jones, J.P.

David Hines to Eliza Ann Kymes, February 24, 1840
                    February 27, 1840 By Joseph Smith

William McKinney to Elizabeth Wakefield, February 29, 1840
                    March 1, 1840 Henry Turney, J.P.

Leonard H. McKinney to Elzera Woodard, February 29, 1840
                    March 5, 1840 By B. F. Clark, J.P.

William Craig to Louisa Pickett, March 5, 1840
                    March 5, 1840 T. S. Williams, J.P.

Richard W. West to Ruth Sulivan, March 5, 1840
                    March 5, 1840 By Ira McKinney, J.P.

Hiram Epps to Fenetta Weaver, March 9, 1840
                    March 10, 1840 John Weaver, M.G.

Jacob Eayes to Prudence Hamilton, March 9, 1840
                    March 11, 1840   Ira McKinney, J.P.

John McRee to Francis M. Hayes, --
                    March 12, 1840   Henry Turney, J.P.

(p 29)
Daniel B. Ward to Elizabeth Lard, March 10, 1840
                    March 11, 1840   By Wm Gattis, J.P.

Robert Edmiston to Martha Wise, March 10, 1840

Isaac Green to Mary Beasley, March 11, 1840
                    March 12, 1840   Tho S. Williams, J.P.

James C. Pace to Amanda Clanton, March 11, 1840

John Reese to Darinda Davis, March 16, 1840
                    March 17, 1840   By H. Birmingham, J.P.

Harrison C. Taylor to Candass D. McCoy, March 19, 1840
                    March 19, 1840   By H. Turney, J.P.

Austin G. Smith to Mary E. Clanton, March 19, 1840

William Dollar to Eliza Ann Levar, --, 1840
                    March 15, 1840   By G. W. Prichett

William Watson to Sarah McAfee, March 21, 1840

Berry Hobbs to Nancy Owens, March 25, 1840
                    March 25, 1840   By Pleasant Holbert, J.P.

James M. Birmingham to Mary A. Cooks, March 25, 1840
                    --   By H. Birmingham, J.P.

Samuel C. Miles to Martha White, March 26, 1840
                    March 26, 1840   Woodruff Parks, J.P.

(p 30)
Isaac N. Wright to Jane T. Downing, March 26, 1840
                    March 26, 1840   By Ira McKinney, J.P.

Eppey Harden to Minerva Reese, April 1, 1840
                    --   By D. Birmingham, J.P.

James Towery to Drusilla Moss, April 2, 1840
                    April 2, 1840   By Wm P. Pullen, J.P.

Abraham Washburn to Sarah Ann M. Gray, April 4, 1840
                    April 2, 1840   By M. Marshall

Hezekiah Smith to Sarah King, April 8, 1840
                    April 12, 1840   By Wiley C. Newman, Esq.

Thomas Childs to Sarah Williams, April 9, 1840
                    April 9, 1840   B. F. Clark, J.P.

William P. Loyd to Thursay Ann Martin, April 11, 1840
                    April 12, 1340 John Moorehead, J.P.

John S. Baggett to Elizabeth Mahala Jones, April 18, 1840

Robert Honey to Emeline White, April 22, 1840
                    April --, 1840 A. W. Parks, J.P.

Jeremiah Sullivan to Catharine O. Qunn, April 22, 1840
                    April 23, 1840 By Samuel Boone, J.P.

Leander Speck to Polly Mason, --, 1840

William S. Woodward to Nancy R. Bruce, May 2, 1840
                    May 2, 1840 By C. W. McGuire, J.P.
(p 31)
Stephen Riddle to Jinsey Tucker, May 5, 1840

George Colman to Hannah Patterson, May 11, 1840

Benjamin Haword to Esther H. George, May 13, 1840
                    May 14, 1840 By John Moorehead, J.P.

Alexr. H. Gill to Nancy Leftwick, May 21, 1840

Joseph Donaldson to Susannah W. Brown, May 26, 1840
                    --   By John Lanier, J.P.

Marsel Bartlet to Ritta C. Richardson, May 27, 1840
                    --   By J. H. Leftwick, M.G.

Wm Turley to Martha Mitchell, May 27, 1840
                    May 28, 1840 T. T. Williams, J.P.

John Swensa to Betsey Oliver, May 30, 1840

Oliver C. Holmes to Henryetta Crawford, June 3, 1840

(p 32)
William Gaddy to Martha Ann Reevis, June 6, 1840
                    May 11, 1840 By Pleasant Holbert, J.P.

Jonathan Couch to Sarah Nowall, June 15, 1840
                    June 18, 1840 By David Snoddy, J.P.

John Ray to Margaret Jane Epps, June 16, 1840
                    June 21, 1840 By G. W. C. Edmiston, J.P.

Augustin Steed to Mary Brady, June 17, 1840
                    June 18, 1840 By Joseph Smith

James T. Childress to Elizabeth D. Hughey, July 7, 1840
                    July 7, 1840 By C. W. McGuire, J.P.

Charles D. Eddington to Mary Ledbetter, July 8, 1840

Wiley Hill to Malinda King, July 10, 1840
                    July 16, 1840 A. B. Gilbert

James D. Hays to Rebeca Hays, July 10, 1840
                    July 21, 1840 Henry Turney, J.P.

John Swinford to Arena Abbott, July 14, 1840

William Timmins to Martha Inhan Martin, July 16, 1840
                    July 16, 1840 By Rev. Joseph Smith

William H. Gibson to Elizabeth Freeman, July 21, 1840

(p 33)
Henry Waggoner to Julian Johnston, August 3, 1840
                    August 4, 1840 By James Rorex, J.P. for L.C.

Joel Halbert to Lethe Harrison, August 5, 1840

William T. Hamlin to Eliza McLin, August 5, 1840
                    August 6, 1840 By M. Marshall

Linville P. Shephard to Rutha Broadaway, August 6, 1840
                    August 6, 1840 By Thos Chiles

Wilson Gray to Rosannah Clark, August 19, 1840
                    August 20, 1840 By A. W. Parkes, J.P.

John A. Pearce to Emily Sanderson, August 21, 1840
                    August 26, 1840 By Stephen Walker, J.P.

William W. Delany to Eliza Jane Martin, August 21, 1840
                    August 26, 1840 By Wm. P. Pullim, J.P. for L.C.

Haslip Goforth to Labrary Bland, August 26, 1840
                    August 26, 1840 C. W. McGowan, J.P.

Josiah O. Quinn to Louisa Lane, August 29, 1840
                    September 17, 1840 By Samuel Boone, J.P. (Seal)

Hugh P. Mooney to Caroline T. Roan, September 3, 1840
                    September 3, 1840 By C. W. McGuire, J.P.

Michael Lincoln to Mary Ann Marshall, September 3, 1840
                    September 3, 1840 T. S. Williams, J.P.

(p 34)
Isaac N. Gattis to Leuticie Cashin, September 9, 1840
                    September 10, 1840 T. S. Williams, J.P.

Richard Stephens to Lucinda Frost, September 9, 1840
                    September 10, 1840 J. W. Holman, J.P.

William Givens to Margaret Wiley, September 9, 1840
                    September 16, 1840 By James Pressley

Charles H. Whitaker to Harriet Evans, September 9, 1840

Isham I. Walker to Polly Arnold, September 14, 1840
                September 17, 1840 By Wm C. Jenning, J.P.

Shaddrick A. King to Mary McAdams, September 16, 1840

David D. Fosbrough to Ann T. Eastland, September 23, 1840
                September 24, 1840 By Benj. F. Clark, J.P.

John Neive to Nancy Landess, September 23, 1840
                September 23, 1840 By Stephen Walker, J.P.

Joel L. Peese to Mary L. Soloman, September 28, 1840
                September 28, 1840 By John Bell

William Davis to Nancy Gavin, September 28, 1840

Benjamin McClusky to Sarah Howard, September 28, 1840
                --   By Stephen Walker, J.P.

(p 35)
Silas C. Ross to Matilda Ayers, September 30, 1840
                October 1, 1840 C. W. McGuire, J.P.

William W. Vaughn to Fanny Pool, October 1, 1840
                October 4, 1840 By Wm P. Pullem, J.P. L.C.

Samuel C. McCay to Susan E. Hampton, October 1, 1840
                October 1, 1840 By C. W. McGuire, J.P.

Matthew H. Campbell to Mary A. Hampton, October 1, 1840
                October 1, 1840 By C. W. McGuire, J.P.

Henry Warren to Mary Bright, October 5, 1840

(p 36)
William A. Pruitt to Mary McDougal, October 14, 1840
                October 14, 1840 J. Kelso, J.P.

James Hamilton to Elizabeth S. McGaugh, October 14, 1840
                October 14, 1840 Benjm F. Clark, J.P. for L.C.

Alexander McAdams to Nancy A. Nelson, October 14, 1840

Joseph Wright to Hetty Goode, October 15, 1840

John McCullough to Ducinda Bynum, October 15, 1840
                October 15, 1840 By Thomas Chiles, M.P.

Thomas Holman to Permelia Johnson, October 17, 1840
                October 18, 1840 By James Rorex, J.P. for L.C.

James G. Hays to Martha S. Raymond, October 24, 1840
                October 24, 1840 By Wm R. Jones, J.P. for L.C.

Henry T. Dennis to Martha Caroline Hobbs, October 24, 1840
                October 25, 1840 By John King, J.P.

Andrew Cashin to Catharin Tennager, October 28, 1840
                    October 29, 1840 By Wm Cattis, J.P.

Philip Cooper to Nancy Sanders, October 27, 1840
                    October 29, 1840 Jno. Moore, J.P.

Peter Cunningham to Sarah Mills, October 28, 1840
                    October 29, 1840 John Weaver, G.M.

(p 37)
Lewis C. McCowan to Caesena Blair, October 29, 1840
                    October 29, 1840 By J. K. Blair, J.P. L.C.

Charles Price to Elizabeth Ann Frame, November 4, 1840
                    November 12, 1840 By David Sneddy, J.P.

Pleasant Oliver to Lucinda Smith, November 5, 1840
                    November 5, 1840 By W. P. Pulliam, J.P. for L.C.

Umstead George to Cena West, November 6, 1840
                    November 10, 1840 By Thos. Chiles, M.G.

Constant T. McMillen to Malinda Ann Ishan, November 11, 1840

William H. Bryant to Martha Crabtree, November 12, 1840

Lewis H. Little to Nancy A. Randolph, November 17, 1840
                    November 18, 1840 By W. P. Pulliam, J.P. for L.C.

Moses Cook to Martha Beard, November 21, 1840
                    November 22, 1840 By Davis Smith, J.P. for L.C.
                                                    (Seal)
Samuel M. Rowell to Matilda W. Lay, November 25, 1840
                    November 26, 1840 J. K. Blair, J.P. L.C.

John Wood to Jane J. Dobbins, November 25, 1840
                    November 26, 1840 Henry Turney, J.P.

(p 38)
David B. Guinn to Narcissa Owen, November 26, 1840
                    November 26, 1840 By Pleasant Holbert, J.P.

Anderson Tucker to Nancy Story, November 26, 1840

Jesse Preston to Mary Aldridge, November 27, 1840
                    November 27, 1840 W. C. Newman, J.P.

Argyle Wells to Sarah Oliver, December 1, 1840
                    December 1, 1840 By W. P. Pulliam, J.P. of L.C.

John A. Browning to Mary Ann Ruth Dollins, December 2, 1840
                    --   By John Bell, (Min.)

Thomas Huff to Nancy Couch, December 2, 1840
                    December 3, 1840 Wiley C. Newman, J.P.

Young S. Taylor to Caroline Marshall, December 3, 1840
        December 3, 1840 By Woodroof Parks, Esqr.

Henry C. Gault to Mary Ann Cleghorn, December 5, 1840
        December 8, 1840 By Samuel S. Ralston, M.G.

Newton Harris to Theodosia Hampton, December 8, 1840
        December 8, 1840 By R. F. Clark, J.P.

Franklin A. Campbele to Elvira Husbands, December 10, 1840
        --   By John Bell, M.G.

(p 39)
A. C. Small to Vijiah A. George, December 14, 1840

Alvin M. Dean to Ann S. Parkes, December 14, 1840

James Caughran to Jane Wilson, December 16, 1840

Alexander G. Dickson to Sarah Hinkle, December 16, 1840
        December 17, 1840 H. S. Porter, M.G.

Isaiah R. Jackson to Adaline Taylor, December 18, 1840

Joseph W. Trigg to Nancy Robertson, December 19, 1840
        December 24, 1840 By Aaron Alexander

Simeon Rhodes to Mary Ferbes, December 21, 1840
        December 23, 1840 By J. K. Blair, J.P. L.C.

Wm Norman to Sarah Leonard, December 22, 1840
        December 24, 1840 By John King, J.P.

James R. Rogers to Catharine F. Tiller, December 22, 1840
        December 22, 1840 T. S. Williams, J.P.

John P. Cole to Susan M. C. Leonard, December 23, 1840

James E. Seymore to Matilda Graig, December 24, 1840
        December 24, 1840 By C. W. McGuire, J.P.

(p 40)
William Ashby to Nancy Ashby, December--, 1840
        February 4, 1841 John Weaver, G.M.

James M. Arnold to Elizabeth Walker, December 28, 1840
        January 11, 1841 W. C. Jennings, J.P. for L.C.

Charles M. Crawford to Mary Brown, January 1, 1841
        January 9, 1840 A. W. Parkes, J.P.

Starkie Robertson to Catharine Robertson, January 4, 1841
        January 5, 1841 By Stephen Walker, J.P.

George Oliver to Jane Campbell, January 5, 1841
        January 7, 1841 By M. Marshall, V.D.M.

Charles L. Smith to Mary Stanley, January 6, 1841
January 7, 1841 By Benj. F. Clarke, J.P. for L.C.

Jarle Pains to Tera Smith, January 6, 1841
January 8, 1841 By Wm Spencer, J.P. for L.C.

Robert J. Tate to Eliza Jane Ramsey, January 7, 1841
January 8, 1841 By Thomas Chiles, M.G.

William J. Toagey to Emily J. Chambless, January 8, 1841
January 11, 1841 A. F. Driskill, M.G.

Squire Prickle to Martha Harris, January 11, 1841
January 14, 1841 By Benj. F. Clark, J.P.

Robert Durham to Elizabeth Riggs, January 13, 1841

(p 41)
Samuel Hogan to Elzira Robinson, January 13, 1841
January 14, 1841 Davis Smith, J.P. for L.C. (Seal)

James R. McKinney to Lydia Ann Watson, January 14, 1841
January 14, 1841 By Benj. F. Clark, J.P.

William Hamilton to Emiline Hobbs, January 16, 1841
January 17, 1841 By John King, J.P.

Joseph G. Smith to Rosannah M. Edmiston, January 19, 1841
-- By M. Marshall, V.D.M.

Alexander Philpot to Mary Renegar, January 20, 1841

William Fife to Elizabeth Caughran, January 20, 1841
January 21, 1841 By Robert Drennan, J.P. for L.C.

James R. Hallam to Clarence M. Bailey, January 21, 1841
January 21, 1841 By M. Marshall, V.D.M.

John Hopper to Martha Dooley, January 25, 1841
January 26, 1841 By Thomas Chiles, M.G.

John Hobbs to Elly Michael, January 25, 1841
January 28, 1841 Wiley C. Newman, J.P.

Carey P. Smith to Cynthia M. Walker, January 27, 1841
January 28, 1841 By George W. Dennis, J.P.

William R. Warren to Harriet E. Stuart, January 28, 1841
January 28, 1841 Samuel Boone, J.P. (Seal)

(p 42)
John G. McClellan to Eliza J. McClellan, January 28, 1841
January 28, 1841 By George W. Dennis, J.P.

Price D. Shelton to Jane Stylen, February 1, 1841
February 2, 1841 By W. C. Jennings, J.P.

Asa Smith to Nancy Terry, February 4, 1841
            February 4, 1841 By Wm Spencer, J.P. for L.C.

William P. Koeld to Mary Smith, February 6, 1841
            February 7, 1841 By M. Marshall, V.D.M.

John F. Cowsen to Elizabeth Price, February 8, 1841

Isaac Parkes to Viannus Mullins, February 8, 1841
            February 8, 1841 By A. W. Parkes, J.P.

John B. Hays to Labra Elston, February 9, 1841

John Smith to Ibby Couch, February 11, 1841
            February 14, 1841 By T. S. Williams, J.P.

Oliver D. Tankesly to Malessa Arnold, February 13, 1841
            February 18, 1841 W. C. Newman, J.P.

John S. West to Elizabeth Rayburn, February 13, 1841
            February 14, 1841 By Thomas Chiles, M.G.

Mark H. Pickett to Catharine Shelton, February 14, 1841
            February 15, 1841 W. C. Newman, J.P.

(p 43)
John B. Foster to Sarah L. Bryant, February 15, 1841
            February 16, 1841 Henry Turney, J.P.

Allen Davis to Lucy Lagenby, February 16, 1841

Calvin Stone to Elizabeth Kiger, February 18, 1841
            February 23, 1841 By T. V. Griffin, E.C.C.

Archbald D. King to Seeny Morris, February 20, 1841
            February 25, 1841 T. S. Williams, J.P.

William J. Gill to Salina Evans, February 22, 1841
            February 25, 1841 By S. M. Cowan, Minister of the
                                                        Gospel

Jackson Champion to Angelina Upton, February 23, 1841
            February 25, 1841 By Stephen Walker, J.P.

John Parker to Matilda Hawkins, February 24, 1841
            February 24, 1841 By J. K. Blair, J.P. L.C.

Daniel Hawkins to Margaret Ables, February 24, 1841
            February 24, 1841 By J. K. Blair, J.P. L.C.

William Wiseman to Lucinda Evans, February 24, 1841
            February 25, 1841 Py J. W. Eolman, J.P.

Hugh Parkinson to Martha Morton, February 27, 1841

(p 44)

Richard L. Cox to Sarah C. Burningham, March 1, 1841
                    March 4, 1841 By G. W. Puckett

William D. McKinney to Sarah N. Weak, March 3, 1841
                    March 4, 1841 By S. M. Cowan, Minister

James E. Travis to Elizabeth Ann Scivally, March 4, 1841
                    March 4, 1841 By W. Jenkins, V.D.M.

Alfred Felps to Jane Spray, March 6, 1841
                    March 7, 1841 By Joel Rees, J.P.

Norbourne Cook to Amanda Clayton, March 8, 1841
                    March 9, 1841 By A. G. Gibson, M.G.

Lewis G. Sanderson to Eliza Jane Maloney, March 8, 1841
                    March 9, 1841 By C. W. McGuire, J.P.

Holloway Powers to Narcissa Bales, March 9, 1841
                    March 9, 1841 By W. C. Jennings, J.P.

John Crabtree to Nancy Figg, March 11, 1841
                    March 11, 1841 By Henry Turney, J.P.

James Russ to Margaret E. Laird, March 11, 1841

Milton A. Edmiston to Minerva L. Kimes, March 13, 1841

(p 45)

George W. Tuck to Materia Timmins, March 15, 1841
                    April 18, 1841 A. W. Parks, J.P.

Nathaniel Conally to Virginia A. Chewning, March 22, 1841
                    March 25, 1841 Wiley C. Newman, J.P.

Thomas George to Mary Colbert, March 27, 1841
                    March 27, 1841 By T. S. Williams, J.P.

William H. Hall to Elizabeth Marbery, March 29, 1841
                    March 29, 1841 By Jno. Moore, J.P.

Miles R. Sherrell to Elizabeth H. Sharp, March --, 1841
                    April 1, 1841 By M. Marshall, V.D.M.

David Thompson to Lucinda Tucker, March 30, 1841
                    March 31, 1841 By Wm Gattis, J.P.

Wm H. Moores to Margaret M. Bell, March 30, 1841
                    March 30, 1841 By Aaron Alexander

Henry C. Dickson to Eveline Reed, March 31, 1841
                    April 1, 1841 Davis Smith, J.P. for L.C. (Seal)

Robert S. McDonald to Maria McDaniel, April 3, 1841
                    April 4, 1841 By Stephen Walker, J.P.

Charles Martin to Hetty West, April 7, 1841
                    April 7, 1841 By Robt. M. Whitman

(p 46)
William Wamack to Rebecca Thurman, April 9, 1841
                    April 9, 1841 Robert Drennan, J.P. for L.C.

Thomas Jenkins to Nancy Adcock, April 9, 1841

Nathaniel Bradford to Anna Blackshear, April 16, 1841

Allen Johnston to Sooly D. Browning, April 19, 1841
                    April 22, 1841 By Samuel Boone, J.P. (Seal)

William C. Bryant to Sarah Buchanan, April 19, 1841
                    April 19, 1841 By C. W. McGuire, J.P.

William K. Simpson to Eliza Smith, April 22, 1841

Davidson Holly to Sally Roe, April 28, 1841
                    April 29, 1841 By Joel Rees, J.P.

Thos. B. Eastland to Sarah S. Crawford, April 29, 1841
                    May 2, 1841 By Benj. F. Clark, J.P. for L.C.

Allen G. Waggoner to Catharine Call, May 7, 1841
                    May 13, 1841 By Wm Gattis, J.P.

WmSon Haggard to Frances A. Parkes, May 12, 1841

Vardy M. Rhyne to Mary Trailer, May 15, 1841
                    May 16, 1841 By Pleasant Bearden, J.P. for L.C.
                                                        (Seal
(p 47)
Jonathan Fisher to Anr Tucker, May 19, 1841

John L. Gobbele to Elizabeth Riley, May 22, 1841
                    May 25, 1841 By T. L. Young, M.G.

Mial Ramsey to Belinda Commons, May 27, 1841

James D. Jarnett to Susannah Edmondson, May 29, 1841
                    May 29, 1841 By Pleasant Holbert, J.P.

H. L. Todd to Mary L. Crows, May 31, 1841
                    June 1, 1841 By J. A. Simmons, (J.P.)

John Cretchet to Letha Freeman, June 11, 1841

Abner Scoggins to Elizabeth McCardy, June 15, 1841
                    June 15, 1841 By Wm R. Jones, J.P.

Elijah Dollar to Elizabeth C. Haley, June 16, 1841
                    June 16, 1841 By G. W. Puckett

Francis M. Jeans to Elizabeth Nixon, June 22, 1841
                    June 24, 1841 By David Snoddy, J.P.

Enoch D. Fox to Sarah F. Moorehead, June 23, 1841
               July 1, 1841 By J. V. Holman, J.P.

John Bandy to Harriet Withers, June 24, 1841
               June 24, 1841 By G. W. C. Edmiston, J.P.

(p 48)
Mannon G. Pearson to Nancy Cowson, July 7, 1841

Alexander Felps to America Spry, July 13, 1841
               July 13, 1841 By Joel Rees, J.P.

Peter J. Hamilton to Cordela Mary Whitaker, July 19, 1841
               July 22, 1841 By Pleasant Holbert, J.P.

Reddin B. Mattox to Susannah L. Reeves, July 19, 1841
               July 19, 1841 By C. W. McGuire, J.P.

Peter Shelton to Sarah Keith, July 19, 1841
               --   By J. Copeland, M.G.

Beckwith J. Tiller to Sarah Ramsey, July 20, 1841
               July 20, 1841 By Woodroof Parks, Esqr.

John Washburn to Sarah M. Bell, July 27, 1841
               July 29, 1841 A. G. Gibson, M.

Benjamin B. Bryant to Jane Parr, July 27, 1841

Milton Walker to Fevnette T. Smith, July 27, 1841

William Springer to Rachael Wells, July 27, 1841
               July 29, 1841 By Major M. Bedwell, M.G.

William Thornton to Lucinda McBride, July 28, 1841

(p 49)
Richard Cottrell to Jane Crouch, July 28, 1841
               July 28, 1841 By Jno. Moore, J.P.

William Stafford to Mary Robertson, July 31, 1841
               August 1, 1841 By A. W. Parkes, J.P.

Isham Hambrick to Martha Walker, July 31, 1841
               August 10, 1841 By Wm R. Jones, J.P.

Duncan Dollar to Rachael Jones, July 31, 1841
               October 27, 1841 By William R. Jones, J.P.

James M. Mathews to Rachael Foster, August 2, 1841
               August 3, 1841 By M. M. Bedwell, M.G.

Augustus Forgerson to Mary Lope, August --, 1841
               August 12, 1841 By A. G. Gibson, M.

Levi Pritchard to Jeminna Oliver, August 9, 1841
               August 11, 1841 By William Cattis, J.P. L.C.

Oliver P. Griffis to Dessy Evans, August 11, 1841
August 16, 1841 By Robert Brennan, J.P. For L.C.

John W. Pulliam to Martha R. Marshall, August 14, 1841
August 19, 1841 By Wm R. Jones, J.P.

Green Miles to Elizabeth McWhorter, August 14, 1841
August 15, 1841 By John Moorehead, J.P.
(p 50)
Daniel J. Whittington to Caroline J. Beaty, August 17, 1841
August 17, 1841 By Henry Turney, J.P.

George Reid to Jane White, August 21, 1841
August 24, 1841 By H. Birmingham, J.P.

Aquilla Arnold to Elmira Laugston, August 21, 1841
August 27, 1841 W. C. Newman, J.P.

William Pamplin to Lucy Hanks, August 28, 1841
September 1, 1841 By Isaac Conger

William M. McMillen to Lucinda McDaniel, August 28, 1841
August 29, 1841 By Ira McKinney, J.P.

James Hightower to Polly Jones, August 30, 1841
September 13, 1841 Samuel Boone, J.P. (Seal)

Samuel Jones to Arena Philips, August 30, 1841
September 2, 1841 By Wm. R. Jones, J.P. for L.C.

Mitchel Pool to Anna S. Wallace, September 1, 1841
September 9, 1841 By W. P. Pulliam, J.P.

James Dunlap to Elizabeth Pollard, September 2, 1841
September 2, 1841 By

(p 51)
Alfred Smith to Mary M. B. Rhea, September 2, 1841

Stephen M. Lewis to Sarah M. Franklin, September 4, 1841

Robert B. Southern to Mary Van Hooxer, September 4, 1841
September 12, 1841 By G. W. Puckett

David F. Hobbs to Sarah Shipp, September 7, 1841
September 9, 1841 By C. W. McGuire, J.P.

Daniel E. Gowen to Mary Ann Myrick, September 8, 1841
September 10, 1841 By Jno. Moore, J.P.

Richard Hill to Sarah Hobbs, September 13, 1841
September 13, 1841 By John Lanier, J.P.

Frances Wells to Louisa G. Drake, September 13, 1841
September 14, 1841 Jno. Moore, J.P.

George McWhorter to Fanny Ledford, September 14, 1841
                    September 16, 1841 By John Moorehead, J.P. for L.C.

Hezekiah Brown to Elizabeth Mallard, September 15, 1841
                    September 19, 1841 By M. M. Bedwell, M.G.

Jesse Malone to Penina Robertson, September 16, 1841

John N. Owen to Nancy P. Noah, September 16, 1841
                    September 16, 1841 Davis Smith, J.P.

(p 52)
Robert Lauderdale to Rachael P. Surber, September 16, 1841

John D. Hall to Prescious C. Smith, September 18, 1841

William C. Andrews to Mary Ann Darnell, September 23, 1841
                    September 16, 1841 By Thomas Chiles, M.G.

William Crabtree to Mary A. Foster, September 23, 1841

John McGee to Mary Taylor, September 29, 1841
                    September 30, 1841 By Samuel Boone, J.P. (Seal)

Joseph B. Hodge to Rachael Foman, September 30, 1841
                    September 30, 1841 By Wm C. Timmins, J.P.

John J. Sexton to Angeline E. Yeager, October 2, 1841
                    October 4, 1841 By Wm R. Jones, J.P.

Thomas H. Freeman to Martha A. Whitaker, October 4, 1841
                    October 14, 1841 By Wm C. Timmins, J.P.

Harrison H. Hughey to Elizabeth B. Hampton. October 5, 1841
                    October 5, 1841 By Pleasant Holbert, J.P.

Lemuel Rhodes to Jane McCan, October 7, 1841

(p 53)
Benjamin Jeffers to Clarrissa Jones, October 8, 1841
                    October 8, 1841 By Isaac Conger, (Preacher)
            Certified October 30, 1841, Isaac Conger (Seal)

John Satterfield to Letty Philips, October 11, 1841
                    October 12, 1841 By Wm. R. Jones, J.P.

John A. McPhail to Mary E. Gilliland, October 13, 1841
                    October 13, 1841 By Matt Marshall, V.D.M.

Isaac N. Hedgpeth to Margaret Reeves, October 13, 1841
                    October 14, 1841 By Pleasant Holbert, J.P.

Robert A. Hamilton to Mary J. McMullen, October 19, 1841

William H. Griffis to Elizabeth Evins, October 19, 1841

Ephrain F. Christie to Sarah A. Saunders, October 20, 1841

William B. Smith to Catharine Brandon, October 20, 1841
                    October 21, 1841 By J. W. Holman, J.P.

Hardy H. Smith to Susan A. Young, October 22, 1841

Sterling McLemore to Margaret Ward, October 26, 1841

Lewis Shipp to Elizabeth McElroy, October 26, 1841
                    October 26, 1841 By Pleasant Holbert, J.P.

(p 54)
Elijah Majors to Mandana M. Pulliam, October 29, 1841
                    October 29, 1841 By W. P. Pulliam, J.P. for L.C.

Job K. Boles to Martha Power, October 29, 1841
                    October 31, 1841 By Levi Vickey, J.P. for L.C.

James S. George to Margaret Stewart, November 1, 1841
                    November 2, 1841 By C. W. McGuire, J.P.

John M. Commons to Mary McElroy, November 2, 1841
                    November 2, 1841 By Benjm. F. Clark, J.P. for L.C.

Stephen Porter to Jemina Quarles, November 4, 1841
                    November 4, 1841 By R. Ellis, M.G.

John L. Ashby to Eliza Mills, November 6, 1841
                    November 11, 1841 John Weaver, M.G..

Samuel Underwood to Louisa McGehee, October 6, 1841
                    --   7, --   By John Moorhead, J.P.

Willford Nickson to Narcissa Pettey, October 6, 1841
                    November 7, 1841 T. S. Williams, J.P.

Charles McIntosh to Margaret Land, October 6, 1841
                    November 9, 1841 By John Lanier, J.P.

Samuel Stiles to Mary Cashin, October 20, 1841
                    November 21, 1841 John Moorhead, J.P.

(p 55)
Reid Hopper to Jane Rich, November 21, 1841
                    November 21, 1841 By Ira McKinney, J.P.

Benjamin F. Beardeh to Susan M. Blake, November 23, 1841

King David Bradford to Winney McCoy, November 23, 1841
                    November 24, 1841 By Jno. Moore, J.P.

George W. Beasley to Sarah Stanley, November 24, 1841
                    November 25, 1841 By G.W.C. Edmiston, J.P.

James M. Spencer to Mary Copeland, November 25, 1841
                    November 25, 1841 By J. W. Holman, J.P.

Thomas W. Brents to Angiline Scott, November 25, 1841
November 25, 1841 By J. W. Holman, J.P.

William Kennon to Nancy Pack, November 30, 1841

Pleasant M. Ellis to Nancy Patterson, December 1, 1841

John Barnes to Polly Ann Mellekin, December --, 1841
December 9, 1841 By Ira McKinny, J.P.

Anderson Billings to Feby Melson, December 4, 1841
December 5, 1841 By J. A. Simmons, J.P.

(p 56)
Samuel M. Hedgepeth to Sarah Wilson, December 4, 1841
December 16, 1841 By C. W. McGuire, J.P.

Joel Wooley to Mariah Parker, December 4, 1841
December 9, 1841 By G. W. Puckett

Jacob Vanhoozar to Nancy Majors, December 8, 1841
December 10, 1841 Wm. Anderson, J.P. for L.C.

Samuel J. Isaacs to Amanda J. Robertson, December 9, 1841

Ezekiel McAfee to Mary Faulkner, December 11, 1841
January 19, 1843 John Weaver, G.M.

John Dyer to Susan Payne, December 15, 1841
December 21, 1841 By Wm Cattis,(J.P.) L.C.

Calvin Koonce to Sarah Clounch, December 15, 1841
December 16, 1841 By George W. Dennis, J.P.

Jesse Blacksher to Sally Massey, December 15, 1841

William Cooper to Susannah McClure, December 18, 1841
December 18, 1841 W. C. Newman, J.P.

Miles Gibbs to Jane Meeks, December 18, 1841
December 21, 1841 By Wm. Anderson, J.P. for L.C.

(p 57)
John M. Clark to Catharine Raney, December 18, 1841
December 21, 1841 By Joseph H. Holloway, M.G.

John Patterson to Eliza Hinds, December 20, 1841
December 23, 1841 By A. M. Pickens, M.G.

Harry C. Coleman to Margaret J. Hodge, December 22, 1841
December 22, 1841 By Robert Drennan, J.P.

Andrew J. Berry to Nancy Shelton, December 22, 1841
December 22, 1841 By John Moorhead, J.P.

Tempsey Pace to Delila Hanks, December 23, 1841
                    December 23, 1841 By Thos. C. Young, M.G.

John T. Wilson to Ann E. Davis, December 23, 1841
                    December 23, 1841 Davis Smith, J.P. for L.C.

John G. Eslick to Sarah Gregory, December 23, 1841
                    December 23, 1841 By George W. Dennis, J.P.

Sample Orr to Patience B. Houston, December 25, 1841

William Davidson to Martha Brandon, December 28, 1841
                    December 28, 1841 By T. L. Young, M.G.

(p 58)
Matthew Carter to Cynthia Noles, January 1, 1842
                    January 2, 1842 By Wm Gattis, J.P. - L.C.

William F. Saunders to Martha Houston, January 2, 1842
                    January 2, 1842 By T. S. Williams, J.P.

Albert Speck to Nancy Ward, January 4, 1842
                    January 5, 1842 By Wm Gattis, (J.P.) L.C.

Avery Stewart to Sophia A. E. Stewart, January 6, 1842
                    January 6, 1842 By C. W. McGuire, J.P.

Samuel Morris to Nancy Massey, January 7, 1842
                    January 9, 1842 By Wm Martin, C.M.

James Harris to Louisa Buchanan, January 8, 1842
                    January 13, 1842 By A. G. Gibson, C. M.

Daniel Boren to Clementina Bradley, January 8, 1842
                    January 9, 1842 By John King, J.P.

John W. Kenedy to Mary A. E. Corley, January 8, 1842
                    January 11, 1842 By Wm Anderson, J.P.

Coleman Wells to Eliza Tucker, January 8, 1842

Moses Park to Mary A. Davis, January 11, 1842
                    January 13, 1842 By Pleasant Bearden (Seal)
                                        J.P. for L.C.

Russell Hughes to Elmina Staten, January 11, 1842
                    January 11, 1842 By Benjamin F. Clark, J.P. L.C.

(p 59) Omitted

(p 60)
John Kimes to Margaret Millard, January 12, 1842
                    January 13, 1842 A. M. Pickens, M.G.

Edward McBay to Jane Cumberland, January 13, 1842
                    January 13, 1842 By Wm Gattis, J.P. L.C.

Robert Ross to Julia Copic, January 13, 1842
        January 13, 1842 By Wm Noild, J.P.

William D. Roper to Mary E. Harris, January 15, 1842

Samuel T. Nicks to Malinda C. Gilbert, January 18, 1842
        January 20, 1842 By J. A. Simmons, J.P.

Abner Freeman to Drucilla Glidewell, January 19, 1842
        January 20, 1842 By J. A. Simmons, J.P.

John to Curtis to Elizabeth C. Franklin, January 19, 1842

Othniel Rice to Mary Mooney, January 19, 1842
        January 20, 1842 By Jno. Moore, J.P.

Ruffie Stricklin to Mary Ann Butler, January 23, 1842
        January 24, 1842 By Stephen Walker, J.P.

William Rees to Susan Burrow, January 24, 1842
        January 25, 1842 By J. H. Leftwick, M.G.

James Mills to Elenor Weldes, January 24, 1842
        January 27, 1842 By Samuel Boone, J.P.

(p 61)
Martin Flynt to Ann R. Estill, January 25, 1842

Napoleon B. Clayton to Mary Trenthan, January 26, 1842

Daniel Holman to Mary Anderson, January 27, 1842
        January 27, 1842 By Woodruff Parks, Esqr.

William Hall to Sarah Leonard, January 27, 1842
        January 27, 1842 W. C. Jennings, J.P.

Daniel F. Freeman to Catharine J. Simmons, January 29, 1842

James Gerelds to Druicilla Greer, January 31, 1842

Jackson Rogers to Maholy Gray, February 1, 1842
        February 2, 1842 By John King, J.P.

John Huey to Elija J. Graham, February 2, 1842
        February 2, 1842 By Matt Marshall

Clesbey Ellis to Nancy Snow, February 5, 1842
        February 10, 1842 By Thomas Chiles, M.P.

Arnold Blades to Ann Jackson, February 5, 1842

John G. Wells to Susan Harris, February 7, 1842
        February 13, 1842 By A. G. Gibson, M.G.

(p 62)
Brown Gregory to Mary Ann McClellan, February 7, 1842

Derry Cole to Melissa Coleman. February 7, 1842
                    September 26, 1842, Henry Turney, J.P.

Thomas McClure to Mary M. Dickson, February 11, 1842
                    February 13, 1842 W. C. Newman. J.P.

Alexander S. Rivers to Jane Felps, February 21, 1842

Byars Logan to Sarah Felps, February 21, 1842
                    February 22, 1842 Joel Rees. J.P. (Seal)

Davis Blackshear to Elizabeth Curtis, February 22, 1842

Edwin S. Douglass to Louisa M. Bell, February 24, 1842

James Williams to Caroline Neal, February 24, 1842

John H. Fox to Mary Wagoner, February 26, 1842
                    March 1, 1842 By Thomas S. Young, M.G.

David Corner to Susan Colvit, March 1, 1842
                    March 3, 1842 By George W. Jones, J.P.

Andrew J. Smith to Elizabeth Oliver, March 9, 1842
                    March 7, 1842 By W. P. Pulliam, J.P. for L.C.

(p 63)
Hiram W. King to Susan McAdams, March 9, 1842

Carter T. Crawford to Elizabeth Hill, March 10, 1842
                    --   By A. W. Parks. J.P.

Coleman Runneles to Martha Runneles, March 11, 1842

William Curtis to Margaret McAfee, March 12, 1842

Peter Gilley to Eliza Witt, March 13, 1842
                    March 14, 1842 By Levi Vickory, J.P.

John Craumer to Mary Sewell, March 15, 1842
                    March 15, 1842 By Wm Weeld, J.P.

Thomas H. Moore to Mana E. Bright, March 17, 1842
                    March 17, 1842 By M. Marshall, V.D.M.

William McAfee to Lydia E. Hedgepeth, March 19, 1842
                    March 24, 1842 By Ira McKinney, J.P.

John A. Silvertooth to Mahala L. D. Gibson, March 19, 1842
                    --   By A. W. Parks, J.P.

Allen Parks to Mary Gregory, March 28, 1842
                    March 31, 1842 By Woodruff Parks, Esqr.

William Preston to Unice Morris, March 31, 1842

(p 64)
Thomas Moore to Ann Fox, April 2, 1842
April 3, 1842 By J. W. Holman, J.P.

Charles L. Walker to Mary B. Smith, April 2, 1842
April 3, 1842 By George W. Dennis, J.P.

Albert Bryant to Mary Street, April 7, 1842
April 7, 1842 David Snoddy, J.P.

Samuel McCulla to Elizabeth Brown, April 9, 1842
April 9, 1842 By John H. Taylor, J.P. (Seal)

Patrick H. Wanslow to Elizabeth C. Brown, April 9, 1842

John Crane to Rebecca Wade, April 12, 1842
April 16, 1842 By Isaac Conger

Owen Colvut to Malinda Saunders, April 12, 1842
April 12, 1842 T. S. Williams, J.P.

Daniel Leatherman to Sally Dobbins, April 13, 1842

William Marshall to Margaret Ann Guy, April 21, 1842
April 21, 1842 By Stephen Walker, J.P. for L.C.

William T. Crenshaw to Esther Wright, May 4, 1842
May 10, 1842 John Weaver, M.G.

John Mullins to Julie Ann Gray, May 5, 1842
May 5, 1842 By David J. Powell, J.P.

(p 65)
Charles Wiles to Hannah Mills, May 9, 1842
May 15, 1842 John Weaver, M.G.

Michael Seagraves to Sarah Ann B. Couch, May 10, 1842
May 10, 1842 By Wm Fryor, J.P.

Ebenzer Pickett to Mary Graham, May 10, 1842
May 19, 1842 T. S. Williams, J.P.

Andrew J. Picket to Margaret Wilkerson, May 14, 1842
May 19, 1842 T. S. Williams, J.P.

John Frost to Hannah Whitworth, May 21, 1842
May 21, 1842 By John H. Taylor, J.P.

Jasper P. Hammonds to Mary F. Jones, May 22, 1842
May 22, 1842 By W. B. Rhea, J.P.

John G. Crawford to Rhoda Anne Maleir, June 3, 1842
June 3, 1842 By A. G. Gibson, M.G.

William Wright to Elizabeth Mitchell, June --, 1842
June 7, 1842 James B. Chilcoat, J.P.

William Morton to Eliza Jane Morton, June 2, 1842

Anderson Fitch to Elizabeth Roch, June 13, 1842
June 16, 1842   T. S. Williams, J.P.

Aaron McDugal to Rachael Sims, June 14, 1842
June 15, 1842   Hiram Buchanan, J.P.

(p 66)
Edward G. Johnson to Sarah Ann Davis, June 20, 1842
June 21, 1842   By W. B. Rhea, J.P.

Wilson C. Pruitt to Elizabeth K. Brown, June 21, 1842
June 21, 1842   By J. H. Taylor, J.P.

Samuel Soloman to Martha Fleming, June 25, 1842
June 30, 1842   By Robt M. Whitman

Drury J. Smith to Siambra Westerman, July 2, 1842

William V. White to Delitha Korne, July 4, 1842
July 4, 1842   By S. Leatherwood, J.P.

Elisha E. Dismukes to Sarah C. Lay, July 6, 1842
July 6, 1842   By A. G. Gibson, M.G.

Vincent Mullins to Mary McCan, July 12, 1842
July 13, 1842   By Samuel J. Eland, J.P.

Benjamin H. Berry to Anne Dean, July 15, 1842

John Harbin to Margaret Lincoln, July 18, 1842
July 21, 1842   By David Snoddy, J.P.

Jonathon W. Butler to Rosalin M. Ayers, July 20, 1842
July 21, 1842   By Benjamin Butler

Nimrod W. Watson to Mary B. Randolph, July 21, 1842

(p 67)
Jesse McClure to Jane McClure, July 25, 1842
July 26, 1842   W. C. Jennings, J.P.

Jeptha Yarbough to Julia A. Campbell, July 26, 1842
July 26, 1842   T. S. Williams, J.P.

Samuel Little to Jane Jones, July 26, 1842
July 28, 1842   By Stanford Lasater
Certified July 19, 1842   Stanford Laster

Hardy H. Logan to Harriet Motlow, July 27, 1842
July 28, 1842   By Joel Rees, J.P.

William M. James to Julia Ann Soloman, July 30, 1842

John Somerford to Mary C. Parks, August 1, 1842
                    August 4, 1842 Woodruff Parks, Esqr.

William T. Childress to Mahulda Bobby, August 2, 1842
                    December 16, 1842 James P. Chilcoat, J.P. for L.C.

Samuel D. Collins to Rebecca J. McMillen, August 2, 1842
                    August 4, 1842 Davis Smith, J.P.

William Dooley to Sarah Massey, August 2, 1842
                    August 4, 1842 By Thomas Childs

Jesse W. Hobbs to Louis A. George, August 4, 1842
                    August 11, 1842 By C. W. McGuire, J.P.

Amg' Anthony to Amanda Parks, August 4, 1842
                    August 7, 1042 By A. W. Parks, J.P.

(p 68)
Harvey Damrol to Mary Parks, August 4, 1842
                    August 7, 1842 By A. W. Parks, J.P.

James L. Camper to Issabella Edmondson, August 8, 1842
                    August 9, 1842 By Pleasant Holbert, J.P.

William R. Akin to Mary Creasy, August 9, 1842
                    August 14, 1842 By Cornelius McGuire, Minister of
                    the Methodist Episcopal Church

David C. Enochs to Martha A. C. Dance, August 10, 1842
                    August 12, 1842 T. L. Young, M.G.

Harry A. Guilliams to Susan Nelson, August 14, 1842
                    August 15, 1842 By P. M. G. Allsop, J.P. for L.C.

Michael Holt to Matilda Long, August 19, 1842
                    August 21, 1842 By A. W. Parkes, J.P.

John D. Mitchel to Susan Fox, August 20, 1842

Robert Warren to Temperance Wilkerson, August 23, 1842
                    August 30, 1842 By Lewis Newson, J.P.

William Warren to Elizabeth Burnes, August 23, 1842
                    August 25, 1842 By Lewis Newson, J.P.

James B. Maloney to Eleanor C. Thompson, August 25, 1842
                    August 30, 1842 By C. W. McGuire, J.P.

Willie A. Griggard to Susan F. Whitaker, August 29, 1842
                    September 1, 1842 By Joel Fees J. P. (Seal)

(p 69
Felix Waggoner to Mahuldah M. Dusenberry, August 30, 1842
                    September 1, 1842 W. Jenkins, V.D.M.

William Perry to Elizabeth M. Allen, August 30, 1842
                    September 1, 1842 By J. H. Taylor, J.P.

Wiley K. Hardin to Sarah M. Edmiston, August 31, 1842
                    September 1, 1842 By J. G. Greene, M.G.

James Parrish to Sarah Vincent, September 1, 1842
                    September 2, 1842 By W. R. Jones J.P. L.C.

Charles S. Howell to Julia Ann McKinney, September 5, 1842

David G. Weaver to Belinda Renegar, September 6, 1842
                    September 6, 1842 By John Moorehead J.P. for L.C.

Joel B. Kaar to Mary Renegar, September 6, 1842
                    September 8, 1842 By John Moorhead J.P. for L.C.

William B. Walker to Narcissa Ellis, September 8, 1842
                    September 8, 1842 By Saml. M. Cowan, M.G.

Benjamin Whitaker to Susan W. Fox, September 10, 1842
                    September 11, 1842 By J. W. Holman, J.P.

James Cunningham to Susan D. Griffis, September 10, 1842
                    September 11, 1842 By A. S. Randolph, J.P. for L.C.

Joseph P. Williams to Elizabeth Williams, September 12, 1842
                    September 15, 1842 J. B. Hollis, M.G.
(p 70)
Lenzy C. Harper to Cassa Cobble, September 13, 1842
                    September 15, 1842 John H. Taylor, J.P.

John W. C. Cunningham to Mary A. Buchanan, September 13, 1842
                    September 13, 1842 By William Harris, J.P.

James Davidson to Mary M. Fulton, September 14, 1842
                    September 14, 1842 Wm Neeld, J.P. for L.C.

James Nees to Ermin Leftwich, September 14, 1842
                    September --, 1842 By Robt. M. Whitman

Charles H. Bethany to Delila Couch, September 14, 1842
                    September 14, 1842 W. C. Jennings, J.P.

John T. Gordon to Louisa Buchanan, September 14, 1842

John W. Gregg to Martha J. Reed, September 15, 1842

William Faukener to Elizabeth Bandy, September 16, 1842
                    September 17, 1842 John Weaver, M.G.

Hawley Williamson to Elizabeth Beachboard, September 19, 1842
                    October 4, 1842 By Hiram Buchanan, J.P.

Michael Lincoln to Mary Jane Cooper, September 26, 1842
                    September 27, 1842 T. S. Williams, J.P.

Thomas H. Bledsoe to Permelia Nelson, September 26, 1842
　　　　　　　　September 29, 1842 By R. Ellis

(p 71)
Samuel D. Brown to Phebe Rutledge, September 27, 1842
　　　　　　　　October 6, 1842 John Weaver, G.M.

Ambrose H. Pierce to Sarah Williams, September 29, 1842
　　　　　　　　October 3, 1842 By J. W. Holman, J.P.

Charles Bethune to Elizabeth Cole, September 29, 1842
　　　　　　　　September 29, 1842 Wm Neeld, J.P. for L.C.

Joseph Sexton to Margaret Williams, October 5, 1842
　　　　　　　　October --, 1842 Joseph P. Williams, G.P.

John M. Buchanan to Elizabeth A. Crawford, October 6, 1842
　　　　　　　　October 6, 1842 By A. G. Gibson, M.G.

Moses Curtis to Elizabeth Blacksher, October 8, 1842

Elisha M. Brewer to Mary Ann Ryals, October 12, 1842
　　　　　　　　October 13, 1842 By J. Kimes, J.P.

James Monks to Tabitha Brown, October 17, 1842
　　　　　　　　October 20, 1842 By D. Jacks, M.G.

William Wood to Nancy Collins, October 18, 1842
　　　　　　　　October 20, 1842 By Ira McKinney, J.P. (Seal)

William C. Frost to Angeline Bert, October 18, 1842
　　　　　　　　October 20, 1842 By J. H. Taylor, J.P.

Jacob Barnes to Salina J. Merrell, October 18, 1842
　　　　　　　　October 18, 1842 By Spencer Leatherwood, J.P.

(p 72)
William Allbright to Mary Arrendale, October 19, 1842
　　　　　　　　October 19, 1842 By Robert Drennan, J.P. for L.C.

Emory M. Posey to Susan P. Smith, October 20, 1842
　　　　　　　　October 20, 1842 Wm B. McLaughlin, J.P. for L.C.

James Suttrell to Frances Taylor, October 27, 1842
　　　　　　　　October 27, 1842 Wiley M. Newman, J.P.

Harrison Smith to Margaret McWhorter, November 1, 1842

Isaac Rutledge to Martha J. Waggoner, November 1, 1842
　　　　　　　　November 3, 1842 By John Copeland, M.G.

William Bullock to Mary M. Bridges, November 4, 1842
　　　　　　　　November 22, 1842 By E. B. King, J.P.

Carleton Davidson to Loucinda Flask, November 7, 1842
　　　　　　　　November 8, 1842 By J. H. Leftwick, M.G.

42

Alfred Douthet to Amanda Dillender, November 7, 1842
           November 13, 1842 By Pleasant Holbert, J.P.

John L. Scott to Harriet Chapman, November 8, 1842
           November 10, 1842 By William Harris

John R. Toole to Matilda G. Kennon, November 9, 1842
           November 10, 1842 By A. G. Gibson, M.G.

Thomas McAfee to Elizabeth McFee, November 10, 1842
           November 10, 1842 Henry Turney, J.P.

(p 73)
Thomas M. Newman to Rinah McGehee, November 13, 1842
           December 10, 1842 By John King, J.P.

John M. McFerrin to Margaret Hughey, November 15, 1842
           November 17, 1842 By Wm. R. Jones, J.P. L.C.

General W. C. Edminston to Sally Dobbins, November 16, 1842
           November 16, 1842 By M. Marshall, V.D.M.

Thomas A. Paysinger to Mary A. McRee, November 17, 1842
           November 17, 1842 Henry Turney, J.P.

Francis Suttle to Frances A. Wilson, November 22, 1842
           November 24, 1842 Thos. L. Young, M.G.

Daniel Ortner to Hannah Harris, November 23, 1842
           November 24, 1842 By Joel Rees, J.P. (Seal)

Douglas Harper to Martha J. Brown, November 25, 1842
           November 27, 1842 By Wm Gattis, J.P.

Ralph Petty to Minerva Myrick, November 26, 1842
           November 26, 1842 By Wm Pryor, J.P. for L.C.

Benjamin Bryan to Mary Ann Hicks, November 26, 1842
           November 27, 1842 By David J. Rowell, J.P.

Cornelius Johnson to Cressy Philips, November 28, 1842

William Lathan to Mary Ann Campbell, November 30, 1842

(p 74)
Joseph Gibson to Sarah Kelson, December 1, 1842
           December 1, 1842, By Wm R. Jones, J.P. (Seal)

William Smith to Susannah Beachborad, December 5, 1842
           December 8, 1842 By Ses Walker, J.P.

Erice P. Gray to Elizabeth Jenning, December 7, 1842
           December 8, 1842 Jno. Morehead, J.P.

Henry Paysinger to Elizabeth Leatherwood, December 8, 1842
           December 8, 1842 By David J. Rowell, J.P.

James Hill to Majesary Abbott, December 8, 1842
                    December 8, 1842 Robert Drenran, J.P.

Ezekiel Baker to Susan Carrie, December 12, 1842
                    December 12, 1842 John H. Taylor, J.P.

Robert B. Burton to Sarah Murphy, December 14, 1842
                    December 15, 1842 By Samuel J. Bland, J.P.

John W. Wright to Sarah Elizabeth Lenard, December 15, 1842
                    December 15, 1842 By E. B. King, J.P.

William S. Evans to Elizabeth Waggoner, December 15, 1842
                    December 22, 1842 By W. Jenkins, V.D.M.

John Marberry to Rachael Isom, December 16, 1842
                    December 16, 1842 By David J. Rowel, J.P.

Arthur A. Goodin to Martha B. Wilson, December 19, 1842
                    December 20, 1842 By H. B. Warren, M.G.

(p 75)
Andrew Roberts to Elizabeth Dickey, December 19, 1842

Reubin B. Ramsey to Matilda B. Kennedy, December 20, 1842

James B. Gill to Tallafar Robertson, December 21, 1842
                    January 22, 1842 By C. W. McGuire, J.P.

Harvey C. Cowan to Agness B. McDaniel, December 21, 1842
                    December 22, 1842 By C. B. Farris, M.G.

James J. Tate to Issabella Carey, December 22, 1842

William Tucker to Nancy Eslick, December 22, 1842
                    December 23, 1842 By John King, J.P.

William S. Bachman to Martha A. Timmins, December 22, 1842
                    December 22, 1842 By Stanford Laster
              Certified April 25, 1843 Stanford Laster

William W. McNelly to Lucinda C. McKinney, December 22, 1842
                    December 22, 1842 By A. G. Gibson, M.G.

Benjamin B. Brandon to Lucinda Williams, December 23, 1842
                    December 25, 1842 By S. S. Woodward, J.P. (Seal)

Robert S. Woodward to Mary McKinney, December 24, 1842
                    December 29, 1842 Davis Smith, J.P. for L.C.

James N. George to Jane Farrar, December 26, 1842
                    December 27, 1842 By C. W. McGuire, J.P.

(p 76)
James C. Birmingham to Eliza Eagan, December 26, 1842
                    December 27, 1842 By Spencer Leatherwood, J.P.

Green C. Gattis to Mary Ann Marshall, December 27, 1842
January 3, 1843 By William Gattis, J.P. L.C.

Charles Wiles to Emeline Wade, December 27, 1842
December 29, 1842 John Weaver, G. M.

Elijah F. Wade to Caroline Crane, December 28, 1842
January 1, 1843 John Weaver, G.M.

Alexander Williams to Maria Foster, December 29, 1842
December 29, 1842 T. S. Williams, J.P.

William Riddle to Nancy C. Gattis, December 29, 1842
January 1, 1843 By Wm Gattis J.P. for L.C.

Hugh M. Smith to Eliza Ann Smith, December 29, 1842
December 29, 1842 By Wm B. McLaughlin, J.P.

194 Licenses Issued in 1842

(p 77)
John E. McWhorter to Sarah E. Noe, January 4, 1843
January 4, 1843 By Robert Drennan, J.P.

William A. Moore to Elizabeth Waggoner, January 6, 1843
January 12, 1843 By Samuel Boon, J.P.

Daniel Bethune to Louesnda Rowles, January 9, 1843
January 10, 1843 By Samuel J. Bland, J.P.

Daniel Blakemore to Ann M. Chitwood, January 11, 1843
January 12, 1843 By John W. McDaniel, Preacher
of the Gospel of Christ

Andrew A. Stroud to Sarah Rhodes, January 11, 1843
January 12, 1843 By Sam'l J. Bland, J.P.

Daniel Smoot to Ann Shaw, January 12, 1843
January 15, 1843 John H. Taylor, J.P.

Andrew M. Wilson to Nancy A. Dobbins, January 17, 1843
July 18, 1843 By H. B. Warren, M.G.

Henry Robison to Mildred Crowder, January 18, 1843
January 19, 1843 David Smith, J.P.

Andrew Duke to Nancy Hazelwood, January 23, 1843
January 24, 1843 J. H. Taylor, J.P. (Seal)

Wilson Smith to Elizabeth Cruse, January 23, 1843
January 26, 1843 W. C. Jennings, J.P.

Newton McGuiddy to Nancy A. Shofner, January 26, 1843
January 26, 1843 By W. Jenkins, V.D.M.

(p 78)

Joseph Montgomery to Mary A. Mansfield, January 26, 1843
                          January 26, 1843 By James B. Hudson, J.P.

George King to Susannah Lathain, January 28, 1843

John Reed to Elizabeth Cashin, February 6, 1843

Samuel Roan to Elizabeth D. Jannett, February 6, 1843
                          February 9, 1843 By James R. Chitwood, J.P.

Claborn Ishom to Parthena Parkes, February 6, 1843
                          February 9, 1843 By Woodroof Parks, Esqr.

Jacob Siler to Louisa Hunt, February 7, 1843
                          February 7, 1843 W. C. Jennings, J.P.

Matthew Allbright to Hester Ann Smith, February 8, 1843
                          February 9, 1843 By Robert Drennan, J.P. L.C.

Mattheas Waggoner to Catharine Waggoner, February 10, 1843
                          February 16, 1843 By W. Jenkins, V.D.M.

David B. Walker to Larey Erwin, February 13, 1843

Charles Mitchell to Mary J. Cooper, February 14, 1843
                          February --, 1843 By Bradley Kimbrough, M.G.

George Gant to Eliza Ann Garner, February 14, 1843

(p 79)

Massey Copeland to Mahalla Eslick, February 18, 1843

Peter A. Dale to Mary G. Phagan, February 20, 1843

William M. Lenard to Elizabeth C. Cole, February 20, 1843
                          February --, 1843 By Bradley Kimbrough, M.G.

Benjamin Warren to Emily Parks, February 22, 1843
                          February 22, 1843 By Woodroof Parks, Esqr.

John W. Nichol to Minerva S. Kimes, February 22, 1843
                          February 23, 1843 Henry Turney, J.P.

William R. Warren to Mary J. McFarland, February 23, 1843
                          February 23, 1843 By John Weaver, G. M.

Manly M. Hairston to Martha P. Koonce, February 23, 1843

Patrick H. Wanslow to Elizabeth A. Rhoten, February 24, 1843
                          March 2, 1843 By John H. Taylor, J.P.

William Sorrells to Eleaner M. King, March 1, 1843
                          March 2, 1843 By E. B. King, J.P.

William Malone to Louisa Suttrell, March 1, 1843
                          March 2, 1843 W. C. Jennings, J.P.

Eureron W. Kyser to Maronda Stone, March 3, 1843
                    March 5, 1843 By Joel Rees, J.P. (Seal)

(p 80)
John Roach to Martha D. Parkes, March 6, 1843
                    March 7, 1843 W. B. Rhea, J.P.

Jacob D. Drake to Martha Jane Stamphill, March 10, 1843
                    March 11, 1843 By Wm. Pryor, J.P.

John Blue to Clementine J. Roberts, March 11, 1843
                    March 12, 1843 By J. Bland, J.P.

William W. Cobble to Elizabeth Brown, March 11, 1843
                    March 16, 1843 J. H. Taylor, J.P.

Benjamin K. Daniel to Sarah J. Baxter, March 13, 1843
                    March 16, 1843 By S. S. Woodard, J.P. (Seal)

John Chastine to Sarah White, March 13, 1843
                    March 15, 1843 S. Leatherwood, J.P.

Thophilus Harris to Sinai A. Buchanan, March 14, 1843
                    March 16, 1843 Joseph Smith

Joseph Taylor to Caroline George, March 21, 1843

Spartin G. Crane to Jane Steelman, March 21, 1843
                    March 23, 1843 John Weaver, G.M.

George Bowers to Winney West, March 21, 1843
                    March 23, 1843 By W. R. Jones, J.P. L.C.

K. H. Burford to Elizabeth K. Baxter, March 22, 1843

(p 81)
David M. McCleur to Sarah Collier, March 16, 1843
                    March 16, 1843 By Lewis Newsom, J.P.

Alexander Allbright to Harriet Hamblin, March 16, 1843
                    March 16, 1843 By Robert Drennan, J.P. L.C.

William G. Mackey to Martha Rivers March 28, 1843
                    April 11, 1843 J. H. Leftwitch, M.G.

William Moffett Jr. to Rebecca K. Buchanan, April 2, 1843
                    April 3, 1843 W. B. Rhea, J.P.

James W. Walker to Lavina Flack, April 3, 1843
                    April 6, 1843 By John H. Taylor, J.P.

Jesse Warrin to Rebecca Bedwell, April 3, 1843
                    April 4, 1843 James P. Brown

George Broadway to Frankey West, April 4, 1843
                    April 5, 1843 By John McDaniel, J.P.

Thomas J. Stockton to Margaret Moffitt, April 6, 1843
                     April 6, 1843 C. H. Edmindson, J.P.

Puffin C. Steunett to Sarah A. Flannagan, April 8, 1843
                     April 8, 1843 Wm Neold, J.P. for L.C.

Pleasant Mullens to Milley Locke, April 8, 1843
                     April 8, 1843 By David J. Powell, J.P.

Edwin T. Thomas to Jane Moore, April 8, 1843
                     April 9, 1843 A. W. Pickins, M.G.

(p 82)
George Bates to Susan J. Roach, April 11, 1843
                     April --, 1843 John Weaver, G.M.

George F. Renegar to Sarah Cashion, April 12, 1843
                     --   By J. Copeland

John K. Moore to Elizabeth Gray, April 13, 1843
                     April 13, 1843 By W. F. Jones, J.P.

Anderson Cashion to Polly Taylor, April 13, 1843
                     April 14, 1843 T. S. Williams, J.P.

Samuel H. Hall to Mary A. Famey, April 13, 1843
                     April 13, 1843 Joseph Smith

Thomas P. Summons to Eliza S. Drinkard, April 17, 1843
                     April 20, 1843 Davis Smith, J.P. for L.C.

Isaac Parks to Mary F. Collins, April 18, 1843
                     April 19, 1843 By S. S. Woodard, J.P.

Alexander Forester to Minirva Eaton, April 22, 1843
                     May 2, 1843 Samuel Boon, J.P. (Seal)

Thomas J. Cotten to Lucinda Nelson, April 22, 1843

Henry A. Lazenby to Sarah Seagraves, April 23, 1843

(p 83
Milton A. Edmondson to Mary A. Williams, April 29, 1843
                     May 11, 1843 T. Kimes, J.P.

John S. McCarven to Eliza A. Clark, May 2, 1843
                     May 4, 1843 By Benjamin Butler, J.P.

William Upton to Eliza Watson, May 5, 1843
                     May 7, 1843 Wm B. McLaughlin, J.P.

Mathew Price to Jemma G. Gore, May 15, 1843
                     May 18, 1843 By A. W. Parks, J.P.

William C. White to Elizar Wilkerson, May 17, 1843
                     May 20, 1843 By John King, J.P.

Isaac Kelso to Cynthia Jones, May 24, 1843
                May 25, 1843 By W. R. Jones, J.P. L.C. (S)

John Sathure to Sarah Surmy, May 30, 1843

William J. Thompson to Ellender J. Ezell, June 1, 1843
                June 4, 1843 S. Leatherwood, J.P.

Madison Beatie to Martha A. Cunningham, June 1, 1843
                June 1, 1843 A. M. Pickins, M.G.

Constanline A. Ball to Martha I. Painey, June 24, 1843
                July 4, 1843 Rev. Jos. Smith

Preslley Rocker to Lavina Jones, July 3, 1843
                July 4, 1843 By Benjamin Butler, J.P. for L.C.
                House of Casey Jones.

(p 84)
Jonas L. Keith to Margarit B. Clarke, July 3, 1843
                July 6, 1843 By N. B. Warren, M.G.

Moses McWhorter to Matilda Watson, July 4, 1843
                July 4, 1843 Wm B. McLaughlin, J.P.

Henderson Harris (Colored) to Martha Harris (Colored), March 1, 1843
                March 2, 1843 Wm Neeld, J.P. for L.C.

John Whitworth to Frances W. Baily, March 4, 1843
               March 5, 1843 By John H. Taylor, J.P.

Thomas Kelso (Colored) to Eliza Dean (Colored), July 14, 1843
                July 18, 1843 By W. R. Jones, J.P.

Jessee M. Roland to Mary Cole, July 18, 1843
                July 18, 1843 By Benjamin Butler, J.P. for L.C.
                House of Bennett Deal
Joseph Boyd to Lucretia Webb, July 19, 1843

John Burns to Nancy McNatt, July 19, 1843
                July 20, 1843 By M. M. Bedwell, M.G.

Mortimon Hurst to Sarah A. Jarred, July 25, 1843
                July 27, 1843 By Joel Reese, J.P.

C. W. Montgomery to O. F. Moon, July 25, 1843
              --   By Bradley Kembro, M.G.

V. Tolly to G. E. Landess, July 25, 1843

(p 85)
William Sanders to Sarah Wheeler, July 25, 1843
                July 27, 1843 By Wm R. Jones, J.P.

Sam'l Crabtree to Nancy Bradford, August 3, 1843
                August 6, 1843 By E. B. King, J.P. L.C.

Edward Gabble to Emelene Clay, August 4, 1843
                    August 6, 1843 By L. S. Woodard, J.P.

J. A. Laws to Cyntha Steed, August 5, 1843
                    August 13, 1843 By A. W. Parks, J.P.

Robert P. Garman to Lulira Sanders, August 7, 1843
                    August 10, 1843 By William Pryor, J.P. for L.C.

Austin Morgan to Adiliza Isaacs, August 7, 1843

James M. Moore to Sarah Harper, August 7, 1843

Isham Sorrels to Penena Pylant, August 8, 1843
                    August 8, 1843 By I. A. Simmons, J.P.

Joel M. Dollins to Margaret Summerford, August 9, 1843
                    August 10, 1843 By A. G. Gibson, Minister

Jessie P. McGeehee to Susan Waggoner, August 9, 1843
                    August 10, 1843 By Sam'l Boon, J.P.

Peter C. Webster to Narcissa Wickson, August 12, 1843
                    August 17, 1843 By Wm Pryor, J.P.

(p 86)
Marian Dodd to Emily West, August 12, 1843
                    August 13, 1843 By Wm R. Jones, J.P.

William Huffman to Narcissa Braden, August 12, 1843

Joseph Holman to Irena L. Quarles, August 16, 1843
                    August 17, 1843 By Woodruff Parks, Esqr.

George W. Clements to Luvina Wright, August 16, 1843
                    August 16, 1843 By E. R. King, J.P.

David B. Dollins to Elizabeth Tucker, August 23, 1843
                    August 24, 1843 Amos Small, J.P. for L.C.

Willis Gattis to Mary J. White, August 28, 1843
                    August 28, 1843 By Wm. Gattis, J.P.

Ephraim Weaver to Sarah C. Sullivan, August 28, 1843
                    August 31, 1843 By Sam'l Boone, J.P.

Thomas Hampton to Martha Smith, August 31, 1843
                    August 31, 1843 D. Smith, J.P. for L.C.

Charles Bethany to Margaret Williams, August 31, 1843
                    September 5, 1843 By David Snoddy, J.P.

John Armstrong to Mariel McCollum, September 5, 1843
                    September 7, 1843 By A. G. Gibson, M.

John Brown to Lucretia Shuffield, September 5, 1843
                    September 6, 1843 By D. J. Rowell, J.P.

(p 87)

Solomon Blades to Rachel Moody, September 6, 1843
                    September 6, 1843   T. W. Ledbetter, J.P.

Hardy Sanders to Susan Crabtree, September 12, 1843
                    September 13, 1843   T. W. Ledbetter, J.P.

John C. Troup to Martha A. Cumners, September 12, 1843
                    September 14, 1843   Davis Smith, J.P. for L.C.

William Kidd to Margaret Nowlan, September 13, 1843

William O. Barns to Martha A. Beasley, September 14, 1843
                    September 14, 1843   D. Smith, J.P. for L.C.

Jonathan N. Davis to Elizabeth F. Tatum, September 14, 1843
                    September 14, 1843   Jno. McDaniel, J.P.

David McClusky to Elizabeth Dowmen, September 15, 1843
                    September 19, 1843   By William Pryor, J.P.

Joseph Gray to Susan Mullins, September 19, 1843

Joseph Hitchcock to Nancy Inman, September 22, 1843
                    September 27th, 1843   W. B. McLaughlin, J.P.

John L. Martin to Louise J. Bailey, September 25, 1843
                    September 25, 1843   By E. B. King, J.P.

Berry Norman to Betty McVay, September 28, 1843
                    September 28, 1843   By T. S. Williams, J.P.

(p 88)

L. L. Cole to Elizabeth F. Small, September 30, 1843
                    October 5, 1843   S. Wood

T. M. Ledbetter to Frances N. Moores, October 2, 1843
                    October 3, 1843   By A. G. Gibson

Ludy C. Byram to Susan King, October 2, 1843
                    October 4, 1843   By W. R. Brice, J.P.

Samuel S. Morrow to Jane E. Moore, September 3, 1843
                    September 3, 1843   M. E. Rhea, J.P.

Kisor Mullins to Mary Harrison, September 5, 1843
                    October 3, 1843   By M. R. Bruce, J.P.

James M. Buchanan to Elzina Ramey, September 7, 1843
                    October 3, 1843   By Jos. Smith

Elijah Normon to Malinda Broyles, September 10, 1843

Charles Dellender to Brunetta Wilson, September 11, 1843

James Andrews to Nancy Griffis. October 8, 1843
October 8, 1843 By David J. Rowell, J.P.

Lewis F. Aoney to Catharan W. Butts, October 9, 1843
October 12, 1843 By John McDaniel, J.P.

James Simmons to Martha A. Mullins, October 13, 1843
October 15, 1843 By M. P. Bruch, J.P.

(p 89)
William Crawford to Nancy P. Gibson. October 16, 1843
October 16, 1843 By A. G. Gibson

Jessee M. Cole to Jane B. Kolly, October 17, 1843
October 17, 1843 By S. J. Bland, J.P.

Benj. M. Land to Elizabeth A. Wells, October 17, 1843
October 17, 1843 By Lee Walker, J.P.

Levi Smith to Elizabeth Malone, October 21, 1843
October 22, 1843 By William Pryor, J.P.

Spencer Williams to Rebecca Jones, October 24, 1843
October 24, 1843 By E. B. King, J.P.

Randolph Houge to Eliza Wanslow, October 25, 1843
October 27, 1843 J. C. Taylor. J.P.

Peter Ashby to Mary Jane George, October 26, 1843
October 26, 1843 John Weaver, G.M.

William Langston to Lydia McClure, November 1, 1843
November 3, 1843 By H. Buchanan, J.P.

James A. Walker to Catharin J. Chambers, November 4, 1843
November 6, 1843 D. Jacks

John M. Hill to Burchet F. Campbell, November 6, 1843
November 7, 1843 By A. G. Gibson

George Small to Naomi Steed, November 14, 1843
November 16, 1843 T. M. Ledbetter, J.P. for L.C.

(p 90)
James Parrish to Catharine Priwitt, November 8, 1843
November 8, 1843 By M. R. Jones, J.P.

Emaziah Dinison to Martha Wilkins, November 8, 1843
November 8, 1843 By David J. Rowell, J.P. for L.C.

F. M. Bearden to Lucinda Burrow, November 15, 1843
November 18, 1843 By Lewis Newson, J.P.

John L. Brown to Susan Williams, November 21, 1843
November 23, 1843 Lemuel Brondon, J.P.

W. C. Brown to Elizabeth McClure, November 22, 1843
                        November 23, 1843 William Fryer, J.P.

James Bates to Caroline Wallace, October 31, 1843
                        November 5, 1843 By Wm F. Jones, J.P.

James G. Woods to Susan J. Boyce, November 23, 1843
                        November 30, 1343 By Matt Marshall, V.D.M.

Lorenza D. Jones to Polly Sandland, November 23, 1843
                        November 23, 1843 By --

James Cattis to Sarah McCollum, November 25, 1843
                        November 28, 1343 By John Moorehead, J.P. L.C.

John A. Bruce to Clarinda J. Vanhooser, November 28, 1843
                        November 28, 1343 S. Leatherwood, J.P.

Zebulon Vickers to Mary Mullins, November 28, 1843
(p 91)
David M. Beaty to Mary Motlow, November 30, 1843

Jos. M. McFarlin to Riney Ann Deal, November 30, 1843
                        November 30, 1843 M. B. Rhea, J.P.

Newell Ingle to Martha Ann Chadwell, November 30, 1843
                        December 3, 1843 By H. A. Simmons, J.P.

Pennel Ramsey to Eleanor Eveline Rosebrough, December 6, 1843

James M. West to Elizabeth Sullivan, December 7, 1843
                        December 7, 1843 A. M. Pickens, M.G.

William Jiffers to Eliza Pamplen, December 8, 1843
                        December 13, 1843 By Woodroof Parks

Barney Albright to Susannah Ivans, December 13, 1843
                        December 13, 1843 By Robert Drennon, J.P.

Wm C. Woods to Sarah A. Boyce, December 14, 1843
                        December 14, 1843 By M. Marshall, V.D.M.

Zachariah Kelsoo to Gilina Forbus, December 18, 1843
                        December 21, 1843 By David J. Rowell, J.P.

John Rogers to Julia Smith, December 19, 1843
                        December 19, 1843 John Weaver, C.M.

Richard A. Fitch to Nancy Fuller, December 20, 1843
                        December 20, 1843 --

(p 92)
Enoch Hamilton to Anna D. Stewart, December 21, 1843
                        December 22, 1843 By James W. Holman, J.P.

Peter M. Morgan to Mary Smith, December 21, 1843
December 21, 1843 By C. H. Edmondson, J.P.

William Polk to Sarah Warren, December 26, 1843
December 28, 1843 By J. A. Simmons, J.P.

N. B. Early to Catharine Harris, December 31, 1843
December 31, 1843 Wm Neeld, J.P.

John Kines to Mary Ann Chapman, January 1, 1844
January 6, 1844 J. Kimes, J.P.

James H. Bray to Sarah Packentor, January 5, 1844

Harey Eslick to Lucinda McGehee, January 5, 1844

Eristus Lock to Louisa Mullins, January 9, 1844
January 11, 1844 By D. J. Powell, J.P.

Geo. Sanders to Minirva Claunch, January 16, 1844
January 16, 1844 By Lee Walker, J.P.

John M. Cobble to Sophia R. Tinsley, January 16, 1844
January 25, 1844 By John N. Taylor, J.P.

(p 93)
John H. Heflin to Mary Eliza Hester, January 18, 1844
January 18, 1844 J. Smith, J.P.

John H. Meetman to Emily Hardin, January 23, 1844
January 25, 1844 John Weaver, G.M.

Joshua Yates to Sarah J. Pibus, January 25, 1844

Isaac W. McCown to Isabilla Jackson, January 29, 1844

Wilson B. Shofner to Mary Snoddy, January 31, 1844
February 1, 1844 W. C. Jennings, J.P.

William C. Gray to Catharine L. Hague, January 31, 1844
February 1, 1844 By B. Kimbrough, M.G.

Charles L. Goodrum to Mary Ann Clark, February 1, 1844

Joseph G. Smith to Frances M. Dooley, February 5, 1844
February 6, 1844 William Harris, J.P.

Alfred Nichols to Martha Waters, February 6, 1844
February 8, 1844 By William Harris, J.P.

Josiah Hamilton to Eliza Stone, February 10, 1844
February 12, 1844 D. Jack, M.G.

Daniel Westerman to Sarah Freeman, February 12, 1844

(p 94)

James H. Taylor to Martha Simmons, February 13, 1844

John M. Winstead to Matilda Carin, February 13, 1844
                        February 15, 1844 By Lewis Newsom, J.P.

W. R. Williams to Amand Tanksley, February 19, 1844
                        February 20, 1844 Joseph P. Williams, J.P.

John M. Pead to Eliza C. Summers, February 21, 1844
                        February 21, 1844 Davis Smith, J.P.

Daniel Marsh to Elizabeth A. Leach, February 26, 1844
                        February 28, 1844 John Weaver, G.M.

William Staton to Letetia Beasley, February 26, 1844

Joseph Buchanan to Cyntha Bryant, March 2, 1844
                        January 21, 1844 By David J. Rowell, J.P.

Montgomery Carter to Ann Cunnigham, March 12, 1844
                        March 12, 1844 Henry Turrey, J.P.

Robt. Martin to Mary A. C. Smith, March 12, 1844
                        --   By Bradly Kembro, G.M.

Thomas Warren to Ann Bedford, March 20, 1844
                        March 20, 1844 Lewis Newsom

James Henderson to Ruthe Hazzard, March 21, 1844

(p 95)

Elihu McGeehee to Polly A. Leach, March 23, 1844
                        March 26, 1844 John Woodruff

John Hancok to Elizabeth Hamilton, March 25, 1844
                        March 28, 1844 Henry Turney, J.P.

Martin Harbin to Louisa J. Couch, March 27, 1844
                        March 28, 1844 T. S. Williams, J.P.

John B. Milam to Mary Spray, March 27, 1844
                        April 3, 1844 By W. R. Jones, J.P.

John D. Stwart to Eliza E. Wells, April 1, 1844

William W. Gavin to Jane Merril, April 3, 1844
                        April 3, 1844 By Woodruff Parkes, J.P.

Thomas Moore to Annia M. Bell, April 1, 1844
                        April 4, 1844 A. G. Gibson, G.M.

Isaac Nelson to Elizabeth Beard, April 6, 1844

George Carter to Cintha Hill, April 8, 1844
                        April 8, 1844 By W. Bridges, J.P.

Washington Rogers to Mary Martin, April 8, 1844
April 8, 1844 by Lewis Howsom

Thomas Botcher to Mary C. Hague, April 10, 1844
April 11, 1844 A. Bradshaw, G.M.

(p 96)
T. W. Stephenson to Margaret Crofford, April 11, 1844
April 11, 1844 A. G. Gibson, G.M.

Lemul N. Sikes to Catharine Fose, --

William H. Muse to Martha A. Echols, April 18, 1844
April 19, 1844 Wm Nield, J.P. of L.C.

David Counts to Sarah Yarbrough, April 21, 1844
April 25, 1844 D. Jacks, M.G.

Robert Buchanan to Mary Cunningham, --
May 2, 1844 Henry Turney, J.P.

John Carter to Elizabeth Cunningham, May 3, 1844
May 3, 1844 Henry Turney, J.P.

Joseph Scott to Sarah E. Smith, May 5, 1844
May 5, 1844 By Philip Row., G.M.

Ronis Lealkerwood to Barbary A. Randolph, May 15, 1844
May 16, 1844 By G. W. Puckett, M.G.

William H. Cimmons to Easter C. Harkins, May 17, 1844
May 16, 1844 James D. Cole, G.M.

Wm Hardin to Liza J. Woodbay, May 24, 1844
March --, 1845 By S. Leatherman, J.P.

(p 97)
John M Beaty to Catharine Edmondson, June 4, 1844
June 4, 1844 A. G. Gibson, G.M.

Wm H. Marshall to Delina Childres, June 4, 1844

Edward A. Brown to Elizabeth D. Soloman, June 6, 1844
June 6, 1844 Thomas Williams, J.P.

Andrew J. Hallam to Harriett Soloman, June 6, 1844
June 6, 1844 By Thomas Williams, J.P.

William Murphy to Tullilon Mitchell, June 6, 1844

Littlebuy Strowd to Samantha Hiptin, June 11, 1844
June 13, 1844 by David J. Rowell, J.P.

Mathew Mussengale to Mahaly Reed, June 12, 1844
June 12, 1844 By David J. Rowell, J.P.

John Joins to Christiana Nip, June 24, 1844
                June 24, 1844 By R. T. Clark, J.P.

David M. Cordal to Nancy J. Sewel, June 27, 1844
                June 27, 1844 Wm Nield, J.P.

John Fitch to Malinda Yerbo, June 29, 1844
                June 30, 1844 By T. S. Williams, J.P.

(p 98)
William Rully to Mary Holt, July 2, 1844
                July 3, 1844 By Wm R. Jones, J.P.

George W. Millikin to Mary Clark, July 5, 1844
                July 11, 1844 Henry Turney, J.P.

Thomas A. Owing to Sonronia M. Russel, July 17, 1844
                July 17, 1844 A. G. Gibson, G.M.

Green Feril to Minerva Qualls, July 18, 1844
                July 18, 1844 By Benj. F. Clark, J.P.

Robert W. Burton to Octavo Whitlock, July 25, 1844
              --   By   John H. Taylor, J.P.

John Roun to Rainy Deshasen, July 25, 1844
                July 26, 1844 By W. R. Jones, J.P.

Abraham Vinson to Nancy Hall, July 25, 1844
                July 26, 1844 W. R. Jones, J.P.

Wiley Worly to Louisa H. Trimble, --
                August 6, 1844 Davis Smith, J.P.
                Tucker
Gabriel Pylant to Nancy Bucker, July 29, 1844
                July 29, 1844 By John Kimes, J.P.

Bazel Muse to Sarah Foster, July 30, 1844
                August 1, 1844 By Richard Anderson, M.G.

(p 99)
Smith lee to Partheny Dunson, August 1, 1844
                August 2, 1844 By David J. Rowell, J.P.

Hardy F. M. Ramey to Martha Ticker, August 1, 1844
                August 1, 1844 By John McDaniel, J.P.

Lorenzo D. Aikin to Elizabeth J. Foster, August 1, 1844
                August 1, 1844 J. P. Campbell

Thos. Gray to Martha Night, August 5, 1844
                August 6, 1844 By James W. Holman, J.P.

Andrew Davidson to Elmyra A. E. Farrow, August 6, 1844
                August 8, 1844 By J. H. Leftwich, M.G.

Samuel Rutledge to Louisa Dariel, August 8, 1844
                        August 8, 1844   James W. Holman, J.P.

Samuel Caddy to May A. Butler, August 12, 1844
                        August 12, 1844   By W. R. Bryce, J.P. for L.C.

James M. Crofford to Cintha A. Phelps August 13, 1844
                        August 13, 1844   Benjamin Butler, J.P.

Alexander Lewis to James Lewis, August 15, 1844

James Stevenson to Elizabeth Griffin, August 21, 1844

John Turher to Lydia A. Parish, August 21, 1844
                        August 21, 1844   By Lee Walker, J.P.
(p 100)
William S. Curtis to Margaret J. Russel, August 28, 1844
                        August 29, 1844   A. M. Pickens, M.C.

Harrison S. Wilson to Ann Shuford, August 29, 1844
                        August 29, 1844   By A. M. Pickens, G.M.

Elius Neely to Emily Buchanan, September 2, 1844
                        September 3, 1844   By Samuel J. Bland, J.P.

William Davis to Nancy E. Hancock, September 10, 1844

John L. McCown to Elizabeth A. Jackson, September 12, 1844   Retured

Peter C. Taylor to Lucinda Taylor, September 12, 1844
                        September 12, 1844   By T. S. Williams, J.P.

Zachriah Little to Lydia Swinford, September 20, 1844

John L. Rosebrough to Sarah A. Smith, September 24, 1844
                        September 24, 1844   By Benj. F. Clark, J.P.

Christopher Boyd to Mary Fincher, September 27, 1844
                        September 26, 1844   By H. Philips, J.P.

Stephen C. Butler to Elizabeth Y. Jacky, October 1, 1844
                        October 1, 1844   Benj. Butler, J.P.

(p 101)
Thompson Sullivan to Rachel Wila, October 2, 1844
                        October 3, 1844   By Jesse Neece, J.P.

Obediah Swanner to Rutha Barrs, October 2, 1844
                        October 9, 1844   Benj. Butler, J.P.

Hardin Wardin to Eliza P. Ruth, October 3, 1844
                        Executed at Asbery 1844   John Weaver, J.P.

Albert G. King to Minetta Whitaker, October 3, 1844
                        October 3, 1844   W. R. Rhea, J.P.

George W. Davidson to Margret S. Norwood, October 5, 1844

David O. Lingo to Abeth Semmong, October 8, 1844
December 13, 1844 By W. R. Bruice, J.P.

Soloman Womack to Lucinda Evrin, October 11, 1844

William R. Hurley to Elizabeth Johnson, October 11, 1844
October 15, 1844 A. M. Pickens, M.G.

Henry Spary to Mary Ann Abbott, October 17, 1844
October 17, 1844 By Robert Drennon, J.P.

John S. Sneed to Ann Eliza Webster, October 23, 1844
November 7, 1845 By J. F. Buckner, J.P.

(p 102)
Slanford M. McElroy to Louisa A. Smith, October 29, 1844
October 29, 1844 A. G. Gibson, G.M.

Eli George to Mary Brown, October 29, 1844
October 29, 1844 By Lee Walker, J.P.

James L. Peaves to Lucinda J. Carrithers, October 30, 1844
October 31, 1844 Bej. Butler, J.P.
Home of Matthew Carrithers
John W. Micheel to Martha A. Philips, October 30, 1844
October 31, 1844 Amos Small, J.P.

John H. B. Walker to Martha Moore, November 5, 1844
November 4, 1844 By John F. Buckner, J.P.

Jonathan E. Prosser to Epsey Johnson, November 5, 1844
December 5, 1844 By Jesse Nees, J.P.

Samuel Kenedy to Mary A. Smith, November 7, 1844
November 7, 1844 H. Philips, J.P.

William W. Carpenter to Sarah W. Maddox, November 11, 1844
November 14, 1844 By C. W. McGuire, J.P.

Joseph Clark to Encline E. Brown, November 13, 1844
November 14, 1844 By Jesse Graham, G. P.

George W. Brown to Cisa Ann Small, November 14, 1844
November 14, 1844 John Weaver, J.P.

Jacob Looke to Manda S. Mullins, November 21, 1844
November 21, 1844 By David J. Rowel, J.P.

(p 103)
John C. Saint to Mary H. Fiser, November 19, 1844
November 21, 1844 By Jesse Nees, J.P.

Alexander Sevier to Martha Ward, November 20, 1844
November 30, 1844 H. Philips, J.P.

James M. Brown to Mary Myrick, November 28, 1844
                    November 28, 1844 Charles H. Edmundson, J.P.

Edward Blades to Mary Ann Bevil, December 2, 1844

Thomas Hammons to Elizabeth T. Wilson, December 9, 1844

Filex Douthit to Nancy Ellis, December 9, 1844
                    December 9, 1845 By Thomas Childs, M.G.

William W. Reese to Nancy T. Calhoun, December 10, 1844
                    December 12, 1844 By J. H. Leftwitch, C.M.

John Dale to Elizabeth A. Phagan, December 11, 1844

Young T. Taylor to Catharine Spencer, December 11, 1844
                    December 12, 1844 J. Copeland, G.M.

Thomas Franklin to Elizabeth Forbes, December 13, 1844
                    December 19, 1844 C. W. Puckett, G.M.

(p 104)
Hiram Franklin to Louisa J. Ship, December 13, 1844
                    December 13, 1845 By Samuel J. Blank, J.P.

Willis Vanhoosier to Nancy C. Webb, December 14, 1844
                    December 19, 1844 C. W. Puckett, G.M.

James D. Neeld to Sarah J. Wallace, December 14, 1844
                    December 15, 1844 Joseph Smith, J.P.

William H. Hall to Awiller Smith, December 16, 1844
                    December 16, 1844 A. S. Randolph, J.P.

Hugh B. McGuerter to Eliza Ledderdale, December 17, 1844

Samuel Fife to Margaret Jane Towery, December 18, 1844
                    December 19, 1844 By Robert Drennon, J.P.

John Ashby to Lucy C. Waggoner, December 18, 1844
                    December 26, 1846 John Weaver, G.M.

David S. Patterson to Elizabeth R. Cheatam, December 21, 1844
                    December 23, 1844 By C. W. McGuire, J.P.

Bennet Soloman to Elizabeth A. Love, December 23, 1844

Levin G. Ready to May Baker, December 24, 1844
                    December 25, 1844 Amos Small, J.P.

(p 105)
Richard C. Barns to Rosina Holbert, December 25, 1844
                    December 23, 1844 By Thomas Childs

William H. Hazzlewood to Margret Thea, December 26, 1844
                    December 26, 1844 By John Kines, J.P.

thew Mullins to Susan Simmons, December 27, 1844
                    December 29, 1844 By W. R. Bruice, J.P.

orge W. Wood to Anoma Caroline Harden, December 29, 1844

. R. Kilpatrick to Sopha R. Brown, December 30, 1844

njamin E. Spencer to Mary T. Waggoner, January 1, 1845

illiam Howard to Sarah Stiles, January 5, 1845
                    January 5, 1845 By John Moorehead, J.P. for L.C.

ul A. Shans to Mary S. Turner, January 5, 1845
                    January 7, 1845 By Robert Drennon, J.P.

oloman Gily to Euticia Witt, January 8, 1845
                    January 9, 1845 By John F. Buckner, J.P.

amuel H. Ventress to Mary E. Parker, January 9, 1845
                    January 9, 1845 Woodruff Parkes, J.P.

106)
ohn Vance to Elizabeth Walker, January 11, 1845
                    January 13, 1845 By Sammie J. Bland, J.P.

orge Thompson to Leapfy Puly, January 15, 1845
                    February 13, 1845 By Wm Gattis, J.P.

lizah T. Williams to Nancy M. Steteer, January 16, 1845
                    January 19, 1845 By John H. Taylor, J.P.

ander Locke to Catharine Mullins, January 22, 1845

ohn Acles to Martha King, January 18, 1845

obert Franc to Nancy Ervin, January 23, 1845

ter W. Walton to Musouri A. Collins, January 25, 1845
                    January 30, 1845 By John McDaniel, J.P.

illiam Hail to Louisa F. Taylor, January 29, 1845
                    January 29, 1845 By David Snoddy, J.P.

gustus M. B. Alley to Elizabeth E. Taylor, January 31, 1845

roy Edwards to Louisa Grant, February 3, 1845
                    February 3, 1845 Wm Pryer, J.P.

107)
ohn H. Gamblen to Cintha M. Johnson, February 4, 1845
                    February 4, 1845 By Ricd. Anderson, M.G.

nson Picket to Mary Shelton, February 6, 1845
                    May 6, 1845 Geo. Arnold, J.P.

Thomas M. Hudson to Sarah Boone, February 16, 1845
February 19, 1845 By Joseph Smith, M.G.

William B. Smith to Issabella J. Wyatt, February 18, 1845
February 18, 1845 By Thomas Childs, M.G.

Ellis Renegar to Susan McGee, February 24, 1845
February 25, 1845 By Wm. Gattis, J.P.

Isam Kent to Elizabeth Goff, February 26, 1845
February 27, 1845 By Travis Ashby, J.P.

George W. Brown to Elizabeth Wilkins, February 26, 1845
February 20, 1845 By Isaac Lingo, G.P.
Certified February 26, 1843 Isaac Lingo, G.P. (Seal)

James E. Brown to Dilila Brown, March 3, 1845
March 6, 1845 By Isaac Conger, G.M.

Berry Duke to Enoline Beasley, March 3, 1845
March 4, 1845 By Wm Gattis, J.P.

John M. Lewis to Josephine Hickman, March 8, 1845
March 8, 1845 By Jesse Nees, J.P.

(p 108)
James W. Davis to Hannah J. Danvel, March 10, 1845
March 13, 1845 By A. Alexander, J.P.

James Fanning to Sarah Honey, March 13, 1845
March 13, 1845 By William Gattis, J.P.

John B. Bedwell to Pheban Rhea, March 17, 1845
March 19, 1845 J. H. Leftwitch, M.G.

Sandy Henderson to Nancy Land, March 19, 1845
March 20, 1845 William Pryer, J.P.

Robert A. Taylor to Sarah Easlick, March 26, 1845
--   By J. Copeland, J.M.G.

William Smith to Eliza Gunter, March 26, 1845
March 26, 1845 By Thomas Childs, G.M.

Absalom G. Bunnel to Kissiah A. M. Gusbay, March 31, 1845
April 6, 1845 A. W. Parkes, J.P.

George W. Reese to Harriett P. Garner, April 1, 1845

George G. Woodruff to Elizabeth Summerford, April 2, 1845
April 3, 1845 Amos Small, J.P.

William P. Smith to Martha Jane Wilson, April 5, 1845
April 8, 1845 A. M. Perkins, M.G.

(p 109)

Charles Bright to Frances D. Robinson, April 7, 1845
     April 8, 1845 By A. G. Gibson, M.G.

Cornelius Thomas to Sarah A. H. Withers, April 7, 1845
     April 7, 1845 A. G. Gibson, M.G.

John Surler to Cyntha Rees, April 10, 1845
     April 10, 1845 By A. G. Gibson, M.G.

Westley Smith to Rachael E. Lemmonds, April 15, 1845
     April 16, 1845 By Davis Smith, J.P.

Simpson Buchanan to Sarah Commons, April 15, 1845

James Woodall to Sarah Ann Stephenson, April 21, 1845
     April 22, 1845 By John Moore, J.P.

Francis W. Little to Florida M. Rourot, April 22, 1845

William Harbin to Elizabeth Norman, April 22, 1845
     April 24, 1845 By D. S. Gray, J.P.

George Mills to Sarah Griffin, April 23, 1845
     April 23, 1845 By W. R. Bruice, L.C.

James L. Danron to Terry L. Hamilton, May 5, 1845
     May 8, 1845 By Aaren Alexander, G.M.

(p 110)

John Chapman to Eliza J. Baker, May 5, 1845
     May 15, 1845 By Lemuel Branden, J.P.

Henry Moore to Dicy King, May 10, 1845

William C. Frewett to Elizabeth R. Prewet, May 24, 1845
     June 2, 1845 S. W. Parkes, J.P.

Alexander Mccolloch to Barthena Bell, June 11, 1845

Thomas J. Shelton to Mary Wilson, June 12, 1845
     June 12, 1845 Mathew Wilson, J.P.

James M. Eaton to Tabitha Forrester, June 13, 1845
     June 15, 1845 John Weaver, G.M.

David S. Hobbs to Nancy Keath, June 13, 1845
     June 18, 1845 By Willis Bridgess, M.G.

Cornelius Hughs to Ragnell Nipp, June 16, 1845

Leroy W. Woodall to Elizabeth Ann Pitts, June 18, 1845
     June 18, 1845 John Moore, J.P.

George W. Moyers to Susanah Tranthan, June 21, 1845
     June 24, 1845 D. Smith, J.P.

63

(p 111)
James Campbell to Martha Gowell, June 24, 1845
                    June 26, 1845 By Jesse Nees, J.P.

Thomas Gattis to Eliza Waggoner, June 24, 1845

William Olliver to Mary Radican, June 25, 1845
                    June 26, 1845 By S. W. Arnold, J.P.

Samuel M. Cooper to Louisa Waggoner, June 25, 1845
                    June 25, 1845 W. B. Rhea, J.P.
                    House of Hugh Shaw.
Franklin Gunter to Elizabeth Jane Crowder, June 30, 1845
                    June 30, 1845 By Thomas Childs, J.P.

Joab Heflin to Mary Walker, July 2, 1845
                    July 17, 1845 By G. W. Pucket, G.M.

Hardin H. Landrith to Elizabeth Pully, July 5, 1845
                    July 6, 1845 By W. Gattis, J.P.

Edward Summerford to Martha Allen, July 10, 1845
                    July 16, 1845 By Jesse Nees, J.P.

Wiley M. Neenan to Elizabeth A. Parker, July 10, 1845
                    July 10, 1845 W. C. Jennings, J.P.

John G. Gledwell to Francis Freeman, July 12, 1845

(p 112)
Wilson L. Westerman to Malinda M. Robertson, July 16, 1845
                    July 17, 1845 By Jesse Nees, J.P.

Alexander G. Noah to Rebecca Gunter, July 21, 1845
                    July 24, 1845 By John McDaniel, J.P.

Silas Michael to Martha P. Hobbs, July 23, 1845
                    July 23, 1845 W. C. Jennings, J.P.

Thomas R. Wind to Martha A. Beatey, July 26, 1845

Samuel R. Farris to Menica Tate, July 29, 1845

Carrol Evans to Milley Pearce, August 1, 1845
                    August 5, 1845 By J. W. Hamilton, J.P.

Samuel L. English to Hannah Hall, August 3, 1845

William W. Parkes to Sophia A. Koonce, August 5, 1845
                    August 5, 1845 W. B. Rhea, chr.

Henry Brown to Nancy Ann Smith, August 5, 1845
                    August 5, 1845 By C. H. Edmondson, J.P.

Jacob C. Gobble to Tabitha Thompson, August 6, 1845
                    August 6, 1845 By L. S. Woodward, J.P.

(p 113)

David G. Davis to Amanda Harris, August 6, 1845
August 7, 1845 D. Smith, J.P.

William Thompson to Louisa Moore, August 6, 1845
August 7, 1845 By Woodruff Parkes, J.P.

Benjamin Hill to Clarrisa Dorsey, August 9, 1845
August 10, 1845 W. C. Jennings, J.P.

James T. S. Dance to Susan F. B. Landees, August 9, 1845
August 14, 1845 By John H. Taylor, J.P.

Samuel H. Sloan to Martha J. McColla, August 9, 1845

Jesse L. Bryant to Finetta B. Loftwioth, August 18, 1845
August 21, 1845 By Jesse Nees, J.P.

William Hawk to Frankey McCleese, August 20, 1845
August 20, 1845 W. C. Jennings, J.P.

Wilkersen W. Rees to Mary J. Smith, August 25, 1845
August 26, 1845 By Jesse Nees, J.P.

Stephen D. Loyd to Sarah C. Watson, August 26, 1845
August 26, 1845 By W. Gattis, J.P.

Thomas H. Holland to Narcissa J. Bridges, August 28, 1845
August 28, 1845 Wm Dyer, J.P.
(p 114)
Obidiah C. Echols to Milly Mullins, August 29, 1845
August 9, 1845 Absalom Forbes, J.P.

William A. Hicks to Nancy Blair, September 2, 1845
September 9, 1845 By Absalon Forbes, J.P.

William Jones to Mary L. Bland, September 6, 1845
September 7, 1845 By Wm. P. Jones, J.P.

John H. Huckabee to Mary Cobb, September 10, 1845
September 11, 1845 Davis Smith, J.P.

John Warren to Margaret Gibson, September 13, 1845
September 14, 1845 H. C. Cowan, J.P.

Green B. Duke to Eliza Ledford, September 18, 1845
September 18, 1845 By Wm Gattis

Samuel McDonald Woodward to Sarah Caroline Franc, September 20, 1845
September 23, 1845 By Rev. John Scivally

Nevos Ledford to Cyntha White, September 24, 1845
October 14, 1845 By William Gattis, J.P.

Joseph Petty to Emeline Keller, September 27, 1845
October 3, 1845 By John L. Buckner, J.P.

John Allen to Sarah Ann Foster, October 7, 1845
                    October 9, 1845   Josse Nees. J.P.

Stephen M. Farmer to Sarah A. B. Clift, October 8, 1845
                    --   By Davis Smith, J.P.

(p 115)
Robert Daniel to Rebecca Logan, October 8, 1845

Henry Heathcoat to Martha Michael, October 9, 1845
                    October 9, 1845   By Lee Walker, J.P.

James M. Davis to Nancy Rainey, October 11, 1845
                    October 14, 1845 By B. T. Clark, J.P.

Ezekiah L. Parms to Susanah Reeves, October 11, 1845
                    October 13, 1845 By C. W. McGuire, J.P.

Calvin L. Hodge to Manerva Templeton, October 13, 1845
                    October 16, 1845 By S. J. Bland, J.P.

David L. Riggery to Caroline Street, October 13, 1845
                    October 23, 1845 By Saml. J. Bland, J.P.

John P. Moore to Priscellar Beavers, October 13, 1845
                    October 14, 1845 H. C. Cleeman, J.P.

Jefferson D. Ling to Eliza J. Young, October 14, 1845
                    October 14, 1845 J. W. Arnold, J.P.

Anthony Hensley to Rebecca Ward, October 14, 1845
                    October 14, 1845 Herman Philips, J.P.

Fenton Hill to Mary Ann Sewel, October 20, 1845
                    October 30, 1845 L. V. Griffin, G.M.

John O. Tucker to Ruth Honey, October 20, 1845
                    October 20, 1845 By Wm Gattis, G.M.

(p 116)
Ansel W. Irvin to Narcisa N. Davis, October 21, 1845
                    October 24, 1845 C. W. McGuire, J.P.

John H. Hamlet to Calva Goforth, October 23, 1845
                    October 26, 1845 By W. R. Jones, J.P.

Henry H. Rivers to Nancy Buchanan, October 18, 1845
                    October 20, 1845 By D. L. Michael, J.M.

John Evans to Malinda Hamilton, October 29, 1845
                    October 30, 1845 By Rev. John Scivally

William G. Commons to Mary M. Boone, November 3, 1845
                    November 5, 1845 By J. H. Lettwict, G.M.

Henry Hawkins to Caroline Marshall, November 3, 1845
                November 3, 1846 By W. R. Jones, J.P.

Ewing Grayham to Sarah C. Niear, November 4, 1845
                November 5, 1845 By Henry Parkes. M.G.

James W. Perry to Sally Ann Gattis, November 5, 1845
                November 6, 1845 By D. S. Gray, J.P.

William N. Collins to Mary J. Clift, November 3, 1845
                November 5, 1845 By Davis Smith, J.P.

William Holt to Anne S. Sandlin, November 10, 1845
                November 11, 1846 By W. R. Jones, J.P.

(p 117)
Samuel Merrell to Marena Whitaker, November 10, 1845

John King to Rhoda Eslick, November 12, 1845
                December 2, 1845 By W. O. Tucker, J.P.

William C. Sikes to Sarah S. Enochs, November 13, 1845

Isaac W. King to Hetty S. Scott, November 18, 1845
              --   By G. B. Kunbrough, M.G.

Nicholas Renegar to Selina Stone, November 18, 1845
                November 18, 1845 By T. S. Williams. J.P.

Isaac Weeks to Mary Shinalt, November 18, 1845
                November 18, 1846 Hiram Philips, J.P.

Thomas Baily to Amanda Shofner, November 21, 1845
                November 23, 1845 Jesse Nees, J.P.

William J. Pool to Larina McCown, November 22, 1845

Daniel McCollum to Sarah B. Tatum, November 24, 1845

Joseph Bunch to Mary J. McCollum, November 24, 1845

John F. Ervin to Narcissa Wanslow, November 22, 1845
                November 30, 1845 Lewis Ashby, J.P.

(p 118)
John B. Wright to Nancy Castleman, November 25, 1845
                November 26, 1845 Amos Small, J.P.

David C. Finney to Elephia Critchet, November 26, 1845

Jesse Scroggins to Louisa J. Epps, November 26, 1845
                November 28, 1845 By Benjamin F. Clark, J.P.

Joseph T. Landess to Amerrilda M. Howel, November 27, 1845
                November 27, 1845 By C. H. Edmondson, J.P.

William P. Baxter to Martha Snoddy, December 1, 1845

John N. Morse to Mary E. Malier, December 3, 1845
December 4, 1845 By A. G. Gibson, M.G.

Currin D. Benson to Narcissa E. Hayes, December 5, 1845
December 11, 1845 By C. W. McGuire, J.P.

William W. Mayyers to Mary Paysinger, December 5, 1845
December 7, 1845 John McDaniel, J.P.

Thomas W. Meese to Jane Nichols, December 6, 1845
December 9, 1845 By Richard Anderson, M.G.

James Siellinger to Caroline Eslicke, December 8, 1845
December 18, 1845 By Wm Gattis, J.P.

(p 119)
William T. Staten to Margaret E. Wersham, December 9, 1845
Tuesday Eving the 9th, 1845 C. A. French, J.P.

John W. Brundrige to Sarah Young, December 9, 1845
December 9, 1845 By S. S. Yarbrough, G.M.

William S. Cooper to Caroline A. P. Enochs, December 11, 1845

George W. Campbell to Keziah Williams, December 13, 1845
December 17, 1845 By John F. Buckner, J.P.

Farmer Franklin to Phebe Fannen, December 13, 1845

William Posey to Rachael Durham, December 15, 1845
December 15, 1845 By John Moore, J.P.

Abraham Setliff to Margret E. Morris, December 15, 1845
December 18, 1845 By John F. McCutchen, G.M.

Augustus T. Echols to Mary Anderson, December 16, 1845

Alexander M. Endsley to Margret J. Peyton, December 16, 1845
December 17, 1845 By Thos. Childs, G.M.

James W. Broadaway to Nancy A. Motlow, December 16, 1845
December 18, 1845 Samuel Boone, J.P.

George W. Swinebrand to Charlotte Keith, December 17, 1845
December 18, 1845 By William Burgeson

(p 120)
Willis H. Holman to Ann Rebecca Ruthedge, December 16th, 1845

Thomas Taylor to Mary W. Hill, December 17, 1845
December 18, 1845 By Wm Thomison, J.P.

Hiram H. Cooper to Mary Louisan Landrith, December 20, 1845
December 23, 1845 By Wm Gattis, J.P.

Peter F. Walker to Rebecca J. Walker, December 22, 1845
                    December 24, 1845   G. W. Pockett, G. M.

Charles W. Timmons to Eliza Jane Gragg, December 24, 1845
                    December 24, 1845 By D. R. Hooker, J.P.

James Harris to Elizabeth Yarbrough, December 25, 1845
                    December 26, 1845 By John T. Buckner, J.P.

Eppe Sullivan to Elizabeth Wisham, December 27, 1845
                    December 28, 1845 John Weaver, G.M.

Felix G. Parkes to Margaret Ann Hagen, December 29, 1845
                    --   By B. Kunbrough, M.G.

John Stephens to Caroline Wheeler, December 29, 1845
                    January 5, 1846 By W. R. Jones, J.P.

Josiah L. Webb to Margaret J. Gelleland, December 30, 1845

(p 121)
John C. Rogers to Eliza Jane Fulton, December 31, 1845
                    December 31, 1845 By A. G. Gibson, M.G.

John M. Edens to Mary Blythe, January 1, 1846

Thomas P. Ramsey to Jane R. Smith, January 1, 1846
                    January 1, 1846 By S. S. Yarborough, M.G.

James George to Jane Walker, January 3, 1846
                    January 11, 1846 By W. R. Jones, J.P.

Anderson C. Martin to Louisa Buchanan, January 6, 1846
                    January 6, 1846 By A. G. Gibson, M.G.

John Shapard to Nancy E. Street, January 7, 1846
                    January 8, 1846 By W. R. J. Husband, M.G.

Joel Higgins to Mary S. Smith, January 8, 1846
                    January 10, 1846 G. W. Puckett, G.M.

Ashey J. Hampton to Aeder Collins, January 13, 1846
                    January 14, 1846 By W. F. Bruice, J.P.

Lossen J. Whitaker to Eliza J. King, January 13, 1846
                    January 15, 1846 By W. B. Rhea, J.P.

(p 122)
Isaac W. Holman to Mary H. Higgins, January 13, 1846
                    January 14, 1846 By Hiram Philips, J.P.

Jacob C. Beard to Sarah Birmingham, January 14, 1846

Lewis C. Blair to Martha C. Hosch, January 16, 1846
                    January 18, 1846 By S. J. Bland, J.P.

Samuel M. White to Mary Crenshaw, January 19, 1846

Cyrus Eastland to Mary Trantham, January 21, 1846
                January 22, 1846 By B. F. Clark, J.P.

Samuel P. White to Emeline Sanders, January 22, 1846
                January 22, 1846 By Wm Gattis, J.P.

Nathaniel R. Hill to Amenda Pack, January 24, 1846
                --   1. 1846 W. R. Rhea, J.P.

John W. Gunter to Sarah Holt, February 2, 1846
                 February 2, 1846 By W. R. Jones, J.P.

John Hicklin to Malissa Evans, February 9, 1846
                February 9, 1846 By Robert Drennon, J.P.

William R. Smith to Prudence C. Johnson, February 18, 1846
                February 19, 1846 Woodruff Parkes, J.P.
(p 123)
John Collins to Susan A. Edmondson, February 19, 1846
                --   By A. W. Parkes, J.P.

Joel L. Cole to Nancy Woodruff, February 19, 1846
                February 19, 1846 Amos Small, J.P.

William Heraldson to Matilda Poole, February 21, 1846
                February 22, 1846 By Samuel J. Bland, J.P.

Washington Foster to Amilda J. Allen, February 23, 1846
                February 25, 1846 By Jesse Neere, J.P.

William L. McMilican to Matilda Clark, February 24, 1846

Doct Carley Huff to Mary F. Huchison, February 24, 1846
                February 24, 1846 By W. D. Chadick, G.M.

John O. Cole to Nancy Templeton, February 25, 1846
                February 25, 1846 By S. J. Bland, J.P.

John Vickers to Fanny M. Martin, February 26, 1846
                February 26, 1846 By Robert Drennon, J.P.

Otho N. Moores to Sarah F. Grizard, February 28, 1846
                March 5, 1848 A. M. Pickens, M.G.

Joseph Broyles to Keziah M. Hague, March 4, 1846
                --   By S. S. Yarbrough, of the
                                M. E. Church

(p 124)
William Webb to Anny L. Calhoon, March 5, 1846
                March 8, 1846 By Lewis Newsom, J.P.

Henry Beck to Louisa C. Barns, March 9, 1846
                March 10, 1846 Mathew Wilson, J.P.

George W. Smith to Martha Ann Teems, March 12, 1846
March 12, 1846 H. Phillips, J.P.

John C. Summers to Mary Cunningham, March 12, 1846

J. Charles N. Woody to Nancy Ann Dawes, March 12, 1846
March 12, 1846 C. Smith, J.P.

William V. Foster to Cinith J. Anderson, March 18, 1846

Alvis Flack to Susan A. Harkins, March 18, 1846
March 19, 1846 By D. F. Mitchel, Min.

William D. Hunter to Adaliza T. Smith, March 26, 1846
March 26, 1846 By H. C. Cowan, J.P.

Elliot Moffette to Nancy A. Jones, March 19, 1846
March 19, 1846 W. B. Rhea, J.P.

Willis N. Milum to Margaret Beard, March 27, 1846
April 10, 1846 G. W. Puckett, G.M.

(p 125)
Joseph T. Land to Margaret A. Williams, March 30, 1846
March 30, 1846 By A. S. Randolph, J.P.

Albin P. Davis to Hellen M. Drinkard, April 2, 1846
April 2, 1846 By Jno. McDaniel, J.P.

William B. McLaughlin to Sinia S. Hart, April 4, 1846
-- By S. S. Yarbrough, of the M.E. Church

George W. Crunk to Margret Buchanan, March 6, 1846
April 9, 1846 A. G. Gibson, M.G.

Jesse Leatherwood to Malinda C. Milam, April 6, 1846
April 11, 1846 G. W. Puckett, G.M.

Daniel Bradley to Margaret Cunningham, April 7, 1846
April 7, 1846 By Davis Smith, J.P.

John Scott to Elleny Manley, April 15, 1846
April 15, 1846 M. R. J. Husbands, M.G.

Samuel Cunningham to Mary Ellis, April 17, 1846
April 23, 1846 W. B. Rhea, J.P.

Zechariah Walker to Polly Ann Lesley, April 18, 1846
April 25, 1846 D. S. Gray, J.P.

John Davis to Nancy F. Owen, April 28, 1846
April 30, 1846 John McDaniel, J.P.

(p 126)
Thomas J. Whitaker to Elizabeth N. Moores, May 2, 1846
May 27, 1846 A. M. Pickens, M.G.

Isaac S. Graves to Mary Catlen, May 11, 1846
                    May 12, 1846   H. C. Cowan, J.P.

Alexander P. Smith to Mary Allen, May 13, 1846
                    May 14, 1846   A. C. Gibson, M.G.

Asal. Sanford to Sarah Gean, May 19, 1846
                    May 20, 1846   T. S. Williams, J.P.

Willis C. Rivers to Eliza J. Hall, May 25, 1846
                    May 28, 1846   By David L. Michael, M.G.

Thomas McQuiston to Ann Garnon, May 26, 1846
                    May 26, 1846   G. W. N. Moore, J.P.

Washington Davis to Ann Lauderdale, May 28, 1846
                    June 31, 1846   H. C. Cowan, J.P.

Francis M. Wright to Lucinda V. Whittington, May 28, 1846
                    May 8, 1846   Thomas Childs, G.M.

James H. Shaw to Elizabeth V. Motten, June 8, 1846

John Forrester to Nancy Mansfield, June 11, 1846
                    June 14, 1846   By Travis Ashby, J.P.

(p 127)
Jonas L. Wilson to Dotia Ann Davis, June 23. 1846
                    June 25, 1846   By Willis Burgess, M.G.

Lewis Morgan to Samantha Hoppins, June 24, 1846
                    June 25, 1846   By Lewis Newsom, J.P.

Edward Harding to Nancy Whittington, June 29, 1846
                    June 30, 1846   Henry Turney, J.P.

David C. Mitchell to Martha A. Blake, June 30, 1846
                    July 2, 1846   A. C. Gibson, M.G.

Macon Franklin to Louisa Carless, July 1, 1846
                    July 1, 1846   A. C. Gibson, M.G.

James Olliver to Barberry Hamilton, July 1, 1846
                    July 2, 1847   Jno. W. Hamilton, J.P.

Charles F. Moore to Sarah Freeman, July 5, 1846
                    July 9, 1846   By G. W. R. Moore, J.P.

George W. Phillips to Mahola Hamilton, July 4, 1846

William P. Toole to Elizabeth Gray, July 8, 1846
                    July 9, 1846   By W. C. Dunlap, M.G.

Eli L. Hodge to Martha C. Griffis, July 13, 1846
                    July 16, 1846   Samuel J. Bland, J.P.

(p 128)

Morgan H. Higgins to Bethlhena Butler, July 17, 1846
               July 22, 1846 W. B. Bruce, J.P.

William C. Smith to Docia Millard, July 18, 1846
               July 18, 1846 Jno. Kimes, J.P.

Henry Clinton to Ann Jane Sloan, July 20, 1846
               July 23, 1846 C. W. McGuire, J.P.

Andrew J. Vann to Martha E. Hunt, July 22, 1846
               July 21, 1846 W. R. Jones, J.P.

Willis C. Higgins to Nancy A. Williams, July 22, 1846
               July 22, 1846 G. W. Puckett, G.M.

William N. Waggoner to Nancy A. Moorehead, July 23, 1846
               July 23, 1846 Wm Gattis, J.P.

Lemuel G. Mead to Martha Ann Isham, July 23, 1846
               July 23, 1846 W. B. Rhea, J.P.

Newton R. Westerman to Frances M. Santclair, July 27, 1846
               July 30, 1846 By Jesse Noes, J.P.

Robert T. Easton to Martha A. E. Childs, July 28, 1846
               August 2, 1846 D. Smith, J.P.

William Cashion to Elizabeth Shelton, July 29, 1846
               July 30, 1846 T. S. Williams, J.P.

(p 129)

Jesse L. Bryant to Nancy M. A. Buchanan, August 1, 1846
               August 6, 1846 G. W. Puckett, G.M.

Burrel W. Cooper to Ann Chamberlan, August 1, 1846
               --   By A. W. Parkes, J.P.

John Birmingham to Nancy A. Moore, August 3, 1846
               August 4, 1846 S. Leatherwood

Thomas Roe to Amy M Brown, August 3, 1846
               August 6, 1847 John Weaver, G.M.

Joseph W. C. Gray to Martha J. Hazzard, August 3, 1846
               August 3, 1846 Lee Walker, J.P.

Thomas Hazzard to Pelelope W. Allen, August 4, 1846
               August 4, 1846 Lee Walker, J.P.

John Crawford to Sarah F. Blake, August 5, 1846
               August 6, 1846 Albert G. Gibson, M.G.

George W. Timmons to Candess C. Edde, August 5, 1846
               August 6, 1846 Jeremiah Dean, G.M.

William Orrick to Martha Jones, August 6, 1846
August 6, 1847   John Weaver. G.M.

Stephen Freeman to Ellen King, August 8, 1846
August 23, 1846   G. W. R. Moore, J.P.

(p 130)
Philip J. Hall to Martha L. Hicks, August 10, 1846
August 10, 1846   By Hugh P. Penny

Henry L. Deavers to Nancy Finney, August 11, 1846
August 13, 1846   John Daniel, J.P.

John W. Buchanan to Cyntha J. Kimes, August 12, 1846
August 13, 1846   By D. L. Mitchel, M.G.

Pinkney J. Bolin to Elizabeth Redengfield, August 15, 1846
August 15, 1846   By C. W. McGuire, J.P.

Samuel Y. McCalla to Catharine B. Parkersen, August 18, 1846

William Simmons to Nancy A. Laird, August 21, 1846
August 21, 1846   William Pryer, J.P.

Hiram Tucker to Elizabeth Tingsley, August 21, 1846
August 25, 1846   D. S. Gray, J.P.

Leanbros Stafford to Emoline Breme, August 21, 1845
--   By A. W. Parkes, J.P.

Green Medkins to Harret Garman, August 31, 1846
August 31, 1846   William Pryor, J.P.

George Craig to Felda J. Brown, August 31, 1846
September 1, 1846   S. W. Arnold, J.P.

William Damron to Susan Parkes, September 2, 1846
--   By A. W. Parkes, J.P.

(p 131)
Thomas V. Greer to Elizabeth A. McMillin, September 5, 1846
September 3, 1846   W. C. Dunlap, G.M.

Benjamin Branren to Phireba J. Moore, September 7, 1846

Jesse M. C. Burke to Susan Tucker, September 8, 1846
September 13, 1846   D. S. Gray, J.P.

Shady D. Hopper to Elizabeth P. Lemonds, September 8, 1846
September 13, 1846   John McDaniel, J.P.

Joseph H. Lemonds to Emely R. McKee, September 8, 1846
September 13, 1846   John McDaniel, J.P.

Caleb Smith to Lydia Lock, September 9, 1846
September 10, 1848 By Hugh P. Penney, J.P.

Thomas Boaz to Manerva Germley, September 12, 1846
                    September 15, 1846 By J. H. Taylor

Jefferson Mullins to Martha Jane Gray, September 14, 1846
                    September 14, 1846 By H. Penrey. Esqr.

Hardy C. Holman to Sarah T. McConnel, September 15, 1846
                    September 15, 1846 J. W. Holman, G.M.

William Billion to Nancy McCollister, September 18, 1846
                    September 18, 1846 Wm. R. Jones. J.P.

(p 132)
Carroll McFee to Barshaby Paysinger, September 21, 1846
                    December 24, 1846 Henry Turner, J.P. for L.C.

John M. Alexander to Sarah V. McCollum, September 22, 1846

William H. Lay to Judith L. Conaway, September 24, 1846
                    September 24, 1846 By W. R. J. Pusbands, G.M.

Samuel D. Durham to Permelia Ray, September 28, 1846
                    September 29, 1846 N. L. Brown, J.P.

William E. Carter to Amanda Dyer, October 1, 1846

Solomah S. Yarbrough to Martha B. Hines, October 2, 1846
                    October 1, 1846 By John Sherrill, G.M.

Jonathan Frazier to Sarah Cole, October 3, 1846
                    October 7, 1846 By Hugh Parkeser, Esqr.

Nicholas H. McFee to Sarah A. Davis, October 5, 1846
                    October 6, 1846 Jno. McDaniel, J.P.

Miles H. McCown to Sophira C. Lee, October 5, 1846

Joseph Fritts to Emely Gattis, October 6, 1846
                    --   By A. W. Parkes, J.P.

Daniel R. Shull to Mary W. Clarke, October 7, 1846
                    October 8, 1846 Albert G. Gibson, M.G.
(p 133)
John F. Michael to Adeline Thompson, October 10, 1846
                    October 10, 1846 L. S. Woodward. J.P.

James C. Beeler to Sarah L. McGuire, October 14, 1846
                    October 15, 1846 Daniel Farrer, J.P.

Spencer N. Laws to Siotha Westerman, October 17, 1846
                    --   By A. W. Parks. J.P.

William Brown to Sarah Taylor, October 21, 1846
                    October 21, 1846 Wm Thominson, J.P.

Alexander A. Greer to Elmira R. Todd, October 20, 1846
October 20, 1846 W. C. Dunlap, G.M.

John W. Watt to Narcissa Givin, October 22, 1846
October 27, 1846 Daniel Farrer, J.P.

George A. Crawford to Martha J. Wilson, October 22, 1846

Thornton Letterall to Sophia E. Heath, October 22, 1846
October 29, 1846 S. W. Arnold, J.P.

James Bates to Cyntha Bostic, October 22, 1846
November 3, 1846 By Martin Towery

Needam Sorrels to Mary Morton, October 23, 1846

(p 134)
Willis Neeres to Lerony Jette, October 31, 1846
November 1, 1846 Samuel J. Bland, J.P.

John J. Bryan to Mary E. Seamoore, November 2, 1846
November 3, 1846 James C. Stevenson

Laben A. Webb to Rebecca J. Fox November 2, 1846
November 5, 1846 J. W. Holman, G.M.

Wormley Bance to Martha Mosley, November 2, 1846
November 5, 1846 By C. W. McGuire, J.P.

Ruel Lothrop to Mary Broadaway, November 6, 1846
November 8, 1847 H. Phillips, J.P.

Baker Luttrell to Elizabeth Brady, November 9, 1846

Burrel Bobo to Margaret M. Wilson, November 9, 1846
November 12, 1846 Daniel Farrer, J.P.

John Sanders to Sarah Sanders, November 15, 1846
November 15, 1846 By Lee Walker, J.P.

Spencer M. Laws to Leotha Westerman, November 17, 1846
--   By A. W. Parks, J.P.

Thomas Lock to Margaret Goode, November 21, 1846
November 23, 1846 By Samuel J. Bland, J.P.

Rodderick Barns to Amanda F. Keith. --, 1846
November 24, 1846 Willis Burgess, M.G.

(p 135)
Robert Moore to Margret Jane Strong, November 25, 1846
November 26, 1846 By Hugh Parkinson, Esqr.

James H. Pamplin to Mary M. Mulder, November 26, 1846
November 20, 1846 Berry F. Clarke, J.P.

James McClure to Sarah McBey November 28, 1846
                    November 29, 1846 D. S. Gray, J.P.

William S. Lackey to Nancy Moseley, November 28, 1846
                    December 1, 1846 James C. Stevenson

William P. Land to Eddey Henderson, November 30, 1846
                    December 1, 1846 William Pryor, J.P.

William D. Grigory to Amanda Harrison, December 1, 1846
                    December 2, 1846 W. P. Bruice, J.P.

Joseph Shaw to Mary L. Harper, December 2, 1846
                    December 2, 1846 By Thos. Childs

Owen Forester to Elizabeth Guin, December 4, 1846
                    December 6, 1846 Amos Small, J.P.

Larkin Johnson to Harret Walker, December 5, 1846
                    December 8, 1846 J. W. Holman, G.M.

Thomas J. Jones to Lucy M. Graves, December 7, 1846
                    December 8, 1846 By A. J. Stewart, M.G.

(p 136)
Thomas Wershburn to Mary Jane Dollins, December 14, 1846
                    December 22, 1846 Amos Small, J.P.

John Parkerson to Mary Ann McColla, December 16, 1846

Isaac J. Holman to Letha B. Fuller, December 16, 1846

Thomas Tucker to Margret A. Pitale December 18, 1846
                    December 22, 1846 Amos Small, J.P.

Thomas F. Mitchel to Sarah H. Mosely, December 21, 1846
                    December 24, 1846 C. W. McGuire, J.P.

Jacob L. Waggoner to Mary Ann Brown, December 21, 1846
                    --   By A. W. Parkes, J.P.

John Jean to Martha Taylor, December 21, 1846
                    December 24, 1847 S. W. Arnold, J.P.

Arabram Graves to Elizabeth V. Soloman, December 22, 1846
                    December 22, 1846 W. J. H. Martin, G.M.

William T. Grigery to Rebecca L. Hores, December 23, 1846
                    January 5, 1846 By D. N. Osburn, E.C.C.

Daniel Brazelton to Elmer N. Alexander, December 24, 1846

(p 137)
Henry Smith to Alvessa Gunter, December 25, 1846

Soloman Brown to Catharine Daniel, December 26, 1846
                    December 30, 1846 Wm Nield, J.P.

William W. Woodward to Susanah Hobbs, December 28, 1846
                    December 31, 1846 C. W. McGuire, J.P.

Alfred Heathcock to Rebecca B. Watson, December 28, 1846
                    December 30, 1846 S. J. Bland, J.P.

John C. Stephenson to Parthana E. Parker, December 30, 1846

Thomas C. Harper to Morgan A. Withoot, December 30, 1846
                    --   By A. W. Parkes, J.P.

Hugh T. Keneday to Jane West, December 31, 1846

James Spray to Lucinda Abbot, December 31, 1846

Joseph Wanslew to Mary Medkin, December 31, 1846

Watson Floyd to Ann R. Price, December 31, 1846

(p 138)
Absolem Beard to Malinda E. Echols, December 31, 1846
                    December 31, 1846 H. Phillips, J.P.

William Cole to Mary Ann Rawles, January 5, 1847 -

William J. A. Tapley to Mary N. Freeman, January 8, 1847
                    January 8, 1847 S. J. Bland, J.P.

Turner B. Watson to Margret Ann Moores, January 9, 1847
                    January 25, 1847 Henry Turney, J.P. for L.C.

Epomtas Sumoore to Elizabeth Temples, January 12, 1847
                    January 14, 1847 James C. Stevenson

Lorenzie Harrison to Lucinda Smith, January 12, 1847
                    January 15, 1847 D. Jacks, M.G.

George Dempsey to Cyntha Roach, January 13, 1847
                    January 15, 1847 Robt. Drennen, J.P.

James J. Gault to Mary Leonard, January 14, 1847
                    January 14, 1847 Wm. C. Joammy, J.P.

John T. Leonard to Harriet Drinkard, January 14, 1847

(p 139)
David W. Beck to Sarah Trantham, January 14, 1847

Richard Colvit to Sarah Brown, January 14, 1847
                    January 14, 1847 C. N. Edmondson, J.P.

John Bradford to Martha C. Roach, January 15, 1847
                    January 21, 1847

Linley Couch to Silina Norman, January 15, 1847
January 16, 1847. S. W. Arnold, J.P.

Hugh C. Gault to Jane Lottrell, January 16, 1847
January 16, 1847 W. C. Jenning, J.P.

Robert B. George to Manerva Cole, January 18, 1847
January 19, 1847 Daniel Farrer, J.P.

Andrew Loyd to Mary Ann Duke, January 20, 1847

Soloman D. Sisk to Elviry Jane Hedgepeth, January 20, 1847
January 21. 1847 Daniel Farrer, J.P.

Thomas W. Clark to Mary C. Swinebroad, January 21, 1847
January 27, 1847 By W. Burgess, M.G.

Andy Carin to Nancy Chapmen, January 21, 1847

(p 140)
Charles B. Hays to Sarah C. Blake, January 25, 1847
January 27, 1847 A. G. Gibson, M.G.

Alfred M. Spencer to Nancy A. Call, January 25, 1847
-- By J. Copeland, M.G.

Robert L. Templeton to Elizabeth Snoddy, January 26, 1847

James E. Burton to Nancy F. S. Whitlock, January 26, 1847
-- By A. W. Parkes, J.P.

Joshua D. Brown to Sarah Anderson, January 26, 1847

Samuel R. Brown to Francis S. Ashby, January 27, 1847
January 28, 1847 John Weaver, C.M.

William Eslick to Rosanah Shelton, January 28, 1847

Stephen M. Bedford to Mariah C. Clay, February 5, 1847

Wiley J. Heathcock to Emily Parrish, February 5, 1847
February 5, 1847 By Samuel J. Bland, J.P.

William Austin to Nancy C. Martin, February 6, 1847

(p 141)
Bennet Soloman to Clarinda Williams, February 6, 1847
February 7, 1847 Wm. Neeld, J.P.

Jesse W. Martin to Sarah Millard, February 8, 1847

Martin Shipman to Cincanatto Sikes, February 8, 1847
February 8, 1847 By John Byrum, M.G.

George W. Street to Mary Ann Brown, February 10, 1847
February 28, 1847 S. W. Arnold, J.P.

James A. Yerger to Mary L. Beggerly, February 16, 1847
　　　　　February 18, 1847　W. R. Jones, J.P.

John Burgess to Manerva Gess, February 17, 1847

Chesley Hambey to Eliza Carter, February 19, 1847
　　　　　February 19, 1847　W. D. Rhea, J.P.

William A. Walker to Mary A. M. Robertson, February 18, 1847
　　　　　February 18, 1847　Martin Turney, C.M.

Richard Smith to Margaret C. Fackener, February 22, 1847
　　　　　February 25, 1847　S. W. Arnold, J.P.

Thomas Lawood to Harriet McAfee, February 25, 1847
　　　　　February 26, 1847　Jno. McDaniel, J.P.

(p 142)
George W. Puckett to Martha E. James, March 1, 1847

James C. McClelland to Sarah Beares, March 1, 1847
　　　　　March 2, 1847　Benjamin F. Clarke, J.P.

William N. Moore to Martha Johnson, March 2, 1847
　　　　　March 4, 1847　W. C. Dunlap

Thomas J. Wells to Elizabeth J. Wells, March 3, 1847
　　　　　March 3, 1847　John Weaver, C.M.

Benjamin Buchanan to Elizabeth Smith, March 3, 1847
　　　　　March 4, 1847　W. R. Bruice, J.P.

Mathew T. Wilson to Elviry Jane Hughey, March 4, 1847
　　　　　March 4, 1847　A. M. Pickens, M.G.

Francis T. Drinkard to Josephine P. McMullin, March 8, 1847
　　　　　March 11, 1847　Jno. McDaniel, J.P.

George W. Glasscock to Lucy C. Hanes, March 10, 1847
　　　　　March 15, 1847　J. May, M.G.

John Carenon to Amanda J. Swinford, March 12, 1847
　　　　　March 12, 1847　J. D. Brown, J.P.

Elijah Merrell to Lucinda Cook, March 13, 1847
　　　　　March 14, 1847　Jeremiah Dean, M.G.

(p 143)
George R. Cowan to Julia A. Thomison, March 15, 1847
　　　　　March 14, 1847　H. C. Cowan, J.P.

William Cole to Junina Reddeck, March 16, 1847
　　　　　March 16, 1847　Daniel Farrer, J.P.

Joseph D. Dickson to Nancy M. Wear, March 16, 1847
　　　　　--　　　　　By William D. Chadick, M.G.

William Harris to Mary C. Yerger, March 19, 1847
     April 19, 1847 W. R. Jones, J.P.

George W. Wright to Elizabeth Bridges, March 20, 1847
     March 23, 1847 Amos Small, J.P.

James Martin to Lucinda Coffee, March 29, 1847
     March 30, 1847 Jeremiah Dean, M.G.

John McNatt to Mary S. Winstead, March 30, 1847
     April 1, 1847 Jesse Neese, J.P.

Robert Montgomery to Sarah Broadaway, April 5, 1847
     March 8, 1847 By H. P. Penney, J.P.

Joseph Stubblefield to Jrena Scott, April 14, 1847
     April 15, 1847 D. S. Gray, J.P.

Green A. Pylant to Sarah Tucker, April 14, 1847
     April 20, 1847 Amos Small, J.P.

(p 144)
William Good to Rachael Findley, April 15, 1847
     April 15, 1847 W. R. Jones, J.P.

Francis M. Ventress to Susan C. Parker, April 15, 1847
     April 15, 1847 By Woodroof Parkes, J.P.

Charles N. P. King to Eliza Smith, April 17, 1847
     April 17, 1847 By Jeremiah Denis, M.G.

William McCallister to Verlenia McWhorten, April 21, 1847
     April 21, 1847 A. S. Randolph, J.P.

Zangy McCartney to Elizabeth Grigory, May 1, 1847
     April 4, 1847 A. G. Smith, G.M.

William George to Nancy Perry, May 6, 1847
     May 6, 1847 Wm Cattis, J.P.

Samuel Fanning to Sarah A. Ally, May 8, 1847
     May 9, 1847 T. S. Williams, J.P.

Fielding L. Butler to Louisa Grigory, May 11, 1847
     May 12, 1847 W. R. Bruice, J.P.

William Olliver to Caroline Jewel, May 13, 1847
     May 13, 1847 William Neeld, J.P.

John Luttrell to Almyra Couch, May 15, 1847
     May 15, 1847 W. C. Jennings, J.P.

(p 145)
George W. Wilkins to Lucinda Veshshawn, May 20, 1847
     May 20, 1847 John Weaver, G.M.

Daniel J. Martin to Charlotte Black, May 21, 1847
                    May 21, 1847 William Neeld, J.P.

Fanson Ables to Sarah Sinktom, May 24, 1847
                    May 24, 1847 William Neeld, J.P.

Cullen C. Blades to Mary J. Moore, May 27, 1847
                    May 27, 1847 Benj. F. Clarke, J.P.

Robert H. Wheeler to Elizabeth L. Pinkerton, May 31, 1847
                    May 31, 1847 W. R. Jones, J.P.

A. C. Ross to Nancy A. Elum, June 2, 1847

William R. Staten to Martha J. Smith, June 4, 1847
                    June 5, 1847 B. F. Clarke, J.P.

Henry Easley to Martha Davis, June 7, 1847
                    June 16, 1847 L. S. Woodward, J.P.

Joel Bruice to E. A. Moores, June 7, 1847

Thomas H. King to Nancy A. Allison, June 10, 1847
                    June 11, 1847 Travis Ashby, G.M.
(p 146)
James C. Story to Sarah Story, June 12, 1847
                    June 12, 1847 Wm. Gattis, J.P.

William Bristen to Mary Heraldson, June 14, 1847
                    June 14, 1847 By Daniel Farrar, J.P.

Francis W. Thompson to Susan J. Mead, June 17, 1847
                    July 1, 1847 By Woodroof Parkes, J.P.

John Hunt to Rachael Edens, June 22, 1847
                    June 22, 1847 Jas. R. McClure, M.G.

James M. Crostwait to Jane Enochs, June 26, 1847
                    June 27, 1847 L. S. Woodward

Jesse Freeley to Elizabeth Crofferd, June 26, 1847
                    June 27, 1847 S. J. Blunn, J.P.

Albert Bennet to Elizabeth Abbot, June 29, 1847
                    June 29, 1847 By Jeremiah Dean, M.G.

Garner M. McConnico to Jane S. Weaver, June 29, 1847
                    --   By W. D. Chaddick, M.G.

Ahiagy B. Carter to Eliza B. White, June 30, 1847
                    July 1, 1847 T. S. Williams, J.P.

James Sikes to Nancy Parkes, July 5, 1847
                    July 7, 1847 By A. W. Parkes, J.P.

(p 147)
William G. Roundtree to Mary E. Mayfield, July 5, 1847
                July 8, 1847 By A. W. Parkes, J.P.

William B. Allisen to Susan C. Swinford, July 26, 1847
                July 29, 1847 By R. S. Brown, J.P.

William S. Murphy to Elizabeth L. A. McCoy, July 29, 1847
                July 29, 1847 W. R. Bruice, J.P.

Bennet Whitaker to Margret Ann Ellis, August 9, 1847
                August 10, 1847 W. H. Moores, J.P.

Joseph V. Cowan to Nancy B. Webb, August 10, 1847

James Cunningham to Elizabeth Vaughn, August 10, 1847
                August 10, 1847 A. S. Randolph, J.P.

Francis M. Wade to Rosanah Wiles, August 9, 1847
                August 12, 1847 By Jesse Neese, J.P.

Parker Campbell to Sarah Ann Womack, August 12, 1847
                August 12, 1847 Alphus Mesill, M.G.

Abner S. Woodward to Caroline Clarke, August 14, 1847

John Hamilten to Sarah Ann Melcalf, August 20, 1847
                September 26, 1847 J. W. Hamilton, J.P.

(p 148)
Claiborne Harris to Aloslena Moore, August 21, 1847
                August 8, 1847 Alphus Misell, G.M.

John W. M. Tham to Elizabeth M. Wilson, August 24, 1847

Jenial P. Robinson to Catharine Emmens, August 25, 1847
                August 26, 1848 Davis Smith, J.P.

Henry Sanders to Nancy M. Kellar, August 26, 1847
                --   By Lee Walker, J.P.

Stephen A. Walker to Rebecca Jane Harris, August 26, 1847
                August 26, 1847 W. R. Jones, J.P.

John W. Jean to Elizabeth Little, August 30, 1847
                September 1, 1847 By Woodroof Packs, J.P.

Benjamin A. Peach to Mary Echols, August 30, 1847
                September 2, 1847 By G. W. R. Moore, J.P.

George Whitaker to Ann Jane Higgins, September 1, 1847
                September 2, 1847 Nat Hillman, M.G.

Hardy D. Turner to Della C. Good, September 2, 1847
                September 2, 1847 Wm. R. Jones, J.P. L.C.

Quntin Marshall to Eliza Hill, September 2, 1847
September 2, 1847 A. G. Smith, G.M.

(p 149)
Neill McCollum to Rebecca Dobbins, September 4, 1847

Jesse Pearce to Elizabeth Rogers, September 8, 1847
September 9, 1847 John W. Hamilton, G.M.

Michael Garrett to Martha Gibson, September 8, 1847
September 9, 1847 A. G. Gibson, M.G.

John Clarke Jr. to Eliza C. Robertson, September 9, 1847
September 9, 1847 W. C. Dunlap, M.G.

John L. Pitts to Rachael J. Womack, September 11, 1847
September 12, 1847 W. B. Rhea, J.P.

Jas. Arendale to Mahaley Heathcock, September 13, 1847
September 14, 1847 A. S. Randolph, M.G.

John R. Heathcock to Adeline Heathcock, September 13, 1847
September 14, 1847 A. S. Randolph, M.G.

John Turner to Spicy Colvit, September 14, 1847
September 14, 1847 Lee Walker, J.P.

Thomas J. Cummins to Margret Jane Rhea, September 14, 1847
September 14, 1847 By G. W. F. Moore, J.P.

George W. Sawyers to Eliza Smith, September 14, 1847
September 14, 1847 B. F. Clarke, J.P.

(p 150)
Thomas W. Parkersen to Grissilda B. Sloan, September 14, 1847

William G. Hancock to Elizabeth Hudson, September 16, 1847

Coloman B. Smith to Martha J. McElroy, September 16, 1847
September 17, 1847 By Samuel J. Bland, J.P.

Elliot F. Moffett to Cathrine Stewart, September 16, 1847
September 16, 1847 W. B. Rhea, J.P.

William Crownover to Rebecca Ann Hamilton, September 17, 1847
September 23, 1847 J. W. Hamilton, J.P.

Union A. Wilson to Rebecca Price, September 18, 1847
September 19, 1847 J. A. Zirley, J.P.

Thomas Clark to Elizabeth Myers, September 25, 1847
September 23, 1847 Lee Walker, J.P.

Jasper N. Turner to Elizabeth McCan, September 27, 1847
September 27, 1847 By W. P. Penney

Joseph M. Greer to Mary M. Edmondson , September 25, 1847
                    September 26, 1847 By W. C. Dunlap

Benj. Olliver to Elizabeth Each, September 28, 1847
                    September 28, 1847 Wm R. Jones, J.P. L.C.

(p 151)
Andrew H. Armstrong to Mary Thomas, September 28, 1847
                    September 30, 1847 By W. C. Dunlap, G.M.

Joseph A. Blakemore to Elizabeth T. Blakemore, September 28, 1847
                    September 28, 1847 D. L. Mitchell

John Warden to Rachael Ashby, October 2, 1847
                    October 3, 1847 John Weaver, G.M.

Volentine C. Isom to Mary Camel, October 4, 1847
                    October 5, 1847 By Woodruff Parkes, J.P.

John Vining to Ann S. Carty, October 4, 1847
                    October 4, 1847 W. D. Chadick, M.G.

Charles B. Oliver to Eathen E. McWhorter, October 12, 1847
                    October 12, 1847 Alpheus Mizell, G.M.

Edward A. Jser to Eliza McAfee, October 14, 1847
                    October 14, 1847 Woodroof Parkes, J.P.

Sanferd Renegar to Ruhana McCollum, October 14, 1847
                    October 14, 1847 Wm Gattis, J.P.

James Hair to Nancy Sullivan, October 15, 1847
                    October 17, 1847 John Weaver, G.M.

William S. Waggoner to Nancy C. Scivelly, October 18, 1847
                    October 21, 1847 Wefon Rivers M.D.M.

(p 152)
William Wilson to Elizabeth Moores, October 19, 1847
                    October 24, 1847 G. W. McGuire, J.P.

William H. Roseborough to Francis N. Slack, October 25, 1847
                    October 27, 1847 By Lemuel Brandon, M.G.

William Cobble to Mary Brazier, October 27, 1347
                    --   By J. W. Holman

John T. Withoit to Caroline Morris, October 28, 1847
                    October 28, 1847 William Weeld, J.P.

John D. Gillam to Mary R. Holman, October 28, 1847
                    October 28, 1847 By Woodroof Parkes, J.P.

William Beavers to Charlotte Davis, October 29, 1847
                    October 29, 1847 John Kimes, J.P.

Arther B. Chuffield to Sarah J. Sloan, November 2, 1847

James A. Warren to Nancy McCarley, November 4, 1847
                    November 4, 1847 Wm Neeld, J.P.

James Coughran to Fanny Campbell, November 5, 1847
                    November 4, 1847 Daniel Farrar J.P. for L.C.

Francis M. Tucker to Nancy McClieve, November 6, 1847
                    November 16, 1847 Wm Gattis, J.P.

(p 153)
William Ashworth to Penolope Hardin, November 6, 1847
                    November 7, 1847 John Moores, J.P.

Green P. Rice to Sarah Ann Baptist, November 12, 1847
                    November 12, 1847 J. Azerley, J.P.

Micajah Ezell to Emely Green, November 13, 1847
                    November 14, 1847 Spencer Leatherwood, J.P.

James J. Allbright to Martha Hamlin, November 16, 1847
                    November 16, 1847 Robert Drennen, J.P.

Jackson Luttrell to Julia Ann Webb, November 17, 1847
                    November 18, 1847 John Weaver, G.M.

Henry Green to Caroline Myrick, November 20, 1847
                    November 25, 1847 T. L. Williams, J.P.

Thomas Webb to Julia A. Howel, November 22, 1847
                    November 22, 1847 J. J. Brown, J.P.

John Pelps to Malinda Wright, November 23, 1847
                    November 25, 1847 By G. W. B. Moore, J.P.

James Morn to Martha Richardson, November 23, 1847
                    November 24, 1847 John Weaver, G.M

Thomas P. Tucker to Roda Easlick, November 25, 1847

(p 154)
William C. Jackson to Samantha E. Franklen, November 27, 1847

James J. Owen to Mary Ann Moore, December 6, 1847
                    December 22, 1847 Jno. McDaniel, J.P.

James D. Dollins to Sarah E. Harbin, December 8, 1847
                    December 9, 1847 Amos Small, J.P.

Newton Luttrell to Julianna Howard, December 8, 1847
                    December 9, 1847 By T. L. Williams, J.P.

Jesse Graves to Ellen Heat, December 15, 1847
                    December 14, 1847 Wm Gale, M.G.

William J. Mattox to Martha Lee, December 15, 1847
                    December 16, 1847 B. U. G. Alsup, J.P.

Montgomery C. Forbes to Jane McDaniel, December 16, 1847

Robert Templeton to Nancy Meeks, December 18, 1847
                    December 23, 1847 A. S. Randolph, J.P.

William Goldsby to Nancy C. Adkins, December 20, 1847

James G. Harrison to Jane F. Hudson, December 21, 1847
                    December 2, 1847 Amos Small

(p 155)
William Richardson to Nancy Paney, December 22, 1847
                    December 28, 1847 John Weaver, G.M.

Robert Boyd to Rachel Holman, December 24, 1847
                    December 24, 1847 Wm Weeld, J.P.

James W. Troup to Sinah Louisa Blades, December 24, 1847
                    December 28, 1847 C. Smith, J.P.

William C. Sanders to Mary Ann Porch, December 27, 1847
                    December 27, 1847 W. Dyer, J.P.

Samuel Bates to Mary Jane Bostick, December 27, 1847
                    January 4, 1848 By Martin Towery

Robert Jacobs to Mary Jane Morris, December 30, 1847
                    December 30, 1847 B. F. Clarke, J.P.

Elsworth P. Fenner to Nancy C. Murdock, December 31, 1847
                    January 2, 1848 W. J. H. Martin, G.M.

George W. N. Moore to Martha King, January 3, 1848

Hugh Parkersen to Lucinda E. Sloan, January 4, 1848

Levin Benson to Susan Howell, January 5, 1848
                    October 5, 1848 Lee Walker, J.P.

(p 156)
Starlin A. Warren to Celia Pulley, January 5, 1848
                    January 7, 1848 Wm Gattis, J.P.

James R. English to Margaret Coughran, January 6, 1848

Abraham James to Susannah M. Walker, January 6, 1848
                    January 9, 1848 By Martin Towery

Albert S. Anderson to Rebecca R. Enochs, January 7, 1848
                    January 9, 1848 L. S. Woodward, J.P.

Joshua McDonal to Mary C. Anderson, January 8, 1848
                    January 8, 1848 G. W. Puckett, G.M.

C. W. Westmoreland to Margaret E. Davis, January 10, 1848

George W. Scott to Elizabeth Stone, January 10, 1848
January 19, 1848 D. Jacks, M.G.

James F. Reece to Elizabeth Reece, January 11, 1848
January 13, 1848 John Weaver, G.M.

Henry Jones to Margaret Johnson, January 12, 1848
January 13, 1848 Jno. F. Buckner, J.P.

James Henderson to Mary Monks, January 12, 1848
January 13, 1848 By Martin Towery

(p 157)
John L. Cochran to Mary T. Wiley, January 13, 1848

Bartin W. Heathcook to Jinoy P. Cannon, January 14, 1848
January 17, 1848 A. S. Randolph, J.P.

John Foster to Mary E. Nichols, January 15, 1848
January 20, 1848 By G. W. P. Moore, G.M.

John H. Jobe to Nancy P. Cleyhorn, January 17, 1848

Henry Peasley to Rachel M. Corder, January 19, 1848
January 20, 1848 By T. L. Williams, J.P.

Thomas C. Loyd to Emeline Wanew, January 24, 1848
January 25, 1848 Wm Gattis, J.P.

William T. Smith to Catharine E. Brown, January 24, 1848
January 27, 1848 Ira E. Douthet, M.G.

David C. Hall to Jane Russell, January 24, 1848

Theopelus Harris to Eliza E. Stewart, January 24, 1848
January 25, 1848 D. L. Mitchel, G.M.

James L. Hogan to Lemmanda T. Wright, January 25, 1848
January 27, 1848 Davis Smith, J.P.

(p 158)
William Allen to Elizabeth Ann Rhea, January 26, 1848
January 27, 1848 By Stephen M. Dance, M.G.

Noah Gold to Sarah E. C. Ellis, January 26, 1848
January 27, 1848 By G. W. P. Moore, J.P.

Henry J. Barnes to Nancy S. Gillom, January 27, 1848
January 27, 1848 Thos. Childs

Eli K. McCollough to Catharine Holt, January 27, 1848
January 27, 1848 Wm. R. Jones, J.P. L.C.

Massey Copeland to Eade E. Tucker, January 29, 1848
--   By J. W. Holman, J.P.

James H. Vidd to Manica Tate, February 1, 1848

Francis M. Hamilton to Elizabeth Ramsey, February 1, 1848
                    February 2, 1848 S. Leatherwood, J.P.

Andrew J. Cox to Mary Stone, February 1, 1848
                    February 4, 1848 D. Jacks, M.G.

Isaac L. Magers to Larina Vanhoozer, February 1, 1848
                    February 3, 1848 G. W. Puckett, G.M.

George L/Cunningham to Elizabeth Dudley, February 1, 1848
                    February 5, 1848 L. S. Woodward, J.P.

(p 159)
James Dennis to Elizabeth McColough, February 4, 1848
                    February 4, 1848 By W. C. Jennings, J.P.

Nathan F. Gibson to Elizabeth A. Sorrells, February 5, 1848
                    February 12, 1848 By G. W. R. Moore, J.P.

James Rutledge to Sarah Bandy, February 5, 1848
                    February 10, 1848 By John Weaver, J.P.

Robert L. Proctor to Margret L. Thomas, February 7, 1848
                    February 10, 1848 W. C. Dunlap, G.M.

William H. Howard to Sarah Jane Stegall, February 8, 1848
                    February 10, 1848 McHenry Summers G.M.

William T. Moore to Margret Buchanan, February 8, 1848
                    February 8, 1848 A. G. Gibson, M.G.

Thos. L. D. Parkes Jr. to Rebecca Gray, February 8, 1848

Henry C. Judy to Nancy E. Clarke, February 9, 1848
                    February 19, 1848 B. V. G. Phillips, J.P.

William Smith to Huldy W. Lunsford, February 10, 1848
                    February 10, 1848 Wm. Gattis, J.P.

Winfield S. Honeycut to Lucinda Smith, February 12, 1848
                    February 17, 1848 By William Levesgul, M.E. Church

(p 160)
Gidien Prince to Mary Russel, February 14, 1848
                    February 4, 1848 Wm. Neeld, J.P. for L.C.

Martin Massey to Nancy Abbot, February 14, 1848
                    --   By Jeremiah Dean, M.G.

David Wagoner to Jane Felps, February 21, 1848
                    February 24, 1848 By Saml. Boone, J.P.

William Nievls to Phebe Massey, February 23, 1848
                    February 24, 1848 By G. W. R. Moore, J.P.

Philip T. Phagan to Martha Ann Taylor, February 24, 1848

George Kirklin to Susan Patterson, February 24, 1848
      February 24, 1848 L. S. Woodward, J.P.

John Edmaston to Mary E. Fullerton, February 24, 1848
      February 26, 1848 W. J. H. Martin, G.M.

W. J. Gallaway to Mary Ann Lindsley, February 28, 1848

Ezekiah H. Ervin to Sarah Rainey, March 4, 1848
      March 8, 1848 L. S. Woodward, J.P.

Samuel Martin to Martha Marena, March 8, 1848
      March 9, 1848 A. S. Randolph, J.P.

(p 161)
James H. Pope to Elsira J. Stephensen, March 8, 1848
      March 8, 1848 G. W. Puckett, G.M.

James Rutledge to Martha Jane Hulsey, March 8, 1848
      March 9, 1848 By Woodroof Parkes, J.P.

William H. Petty to Ann Roberta Ricks, March 10, 1848

Austin A. Shipp to Sarah Ann McElroy, March 11, 1848

Aaron Alexander to Elizabeth M. Shook, March 13, 1848
      March 14, 1848 A. G. Gibson, M.G.

William T. Punnels to Elizabeth Gamble, March 17, 1848

William L. Alexander to Elizabeth Steelman, March 21, 1848
      March 21, 1848 By Woodroof Parkes

Andrew Flemings to Louisa Hoots, March 21, 1848
      March 21, 1848 Woodroof Parkes, J.P.

John H. Stewart to Mary A. O. McNiel, March 22, 1848

Calvin Lee to Clarrisa H. Hanks, April 1, 1848
      April 13, 1848 By B. M. G. Alsup

(p 162)
Newton F. Neil to Virginia Marshall, April 13, 1848
      April 13, 1848 By W. C. Dunlap, M.G.

Ambros James to Jane McBride, April 14, 1848
      April 14, 1848 Spencer Leatherwood, J.P.

Washington Wilson to Mary Hughey, April 17, 1848

John Sims to Martha A. Weeks, April 17, 1848
      April 20, 1848 John Moore, J.P.

Nicholas Burns to Elizabeth Wilson, April 22, 1848
      April 23, 1848 Jno. Weaver, G.M.

Wm. M. Phillips to Mary Walker, April 24, 1848
     April 26, 1848 Martin Towery, G.M.

James J. Finney to Martha J. Cole, April 25, 1848
     April 27, 1848 Daniel Farrer, J.P.

William A. Hopper to Julian Pasinger, May 1, 1848

John C. Ennis to Parthena Hughey, May 15, 1848

John V. Crossland to Mary Potter, May 16, 1848

(p 163)
Temple Tayler to Jane Shelton, May 18, 1848
     May 21, 1848 By T. S. Williams, J.P.

Hardin Hampton to Delia E. Pigg, May 25, 1848

Ephraim D. Bryan to Susan Shipp, May 27, 1848

James A. Prosser to Rebecca W. Bagley, May 29, 1848
     May 31, 1848 By Lewis Newson, J.P.

John Sherrell to Martha A. L. Morse, June 6, 1848
     June 6, 1848 By A. G. Gilmore, M.G.

T. S. Corder to Julia Ann Corder, June 17, 1848
     June 20, 1848 T. S. Williams, J.P.

Josiah Ellis to Sarah Bradford, June 24, 1848
     June 28, 1848 G. W. R. Moore, J.P. L.C.

F. A. Dickerson to Amanda J. Smith, July 5, 1848
     July 6, 1848 W. C. Dunlap, G.M.

John Coleman to Elizabeth Kensley, July 6, 1848

John G. Glidwell to Sarah Durham, July 8, 1848
     July 9, 1848 G. W. R. Moore, J.P. L.C.
(p 164)
John P. Austin to Nancy E. Burns, July 10, 1848
     July 11, 1848 By G. W. R. Moore, J.P. for L.C.

William C. Fanning to Martha Luttrell, July 12, 1848
     July 13, 1848 T. S. Williams, J.P.

Newten Eslick to Caroline Wilkerson, July 13, 1848
     July 13, 1848 Young T. Taylor, J.P.

Hugh W. Thompson to Sarah A. E. Newles, July 14, 1848
     July 14, 1848 Young T. Taylor, J.P.

Joab Moore to Martha Webster, July 18, 1848
     July 19, 1848 Jno. F. Buckner

James Miller to Elizabeth Scrimpshear, July 18, 1848
                    July 18, 1848 Wm. Heeld, J.P.

Pearson Milton to Nancy Huckabee, July 18, 1848
                    July 18, 1848 By B. M. G. Allsup, J.P.

Robert K. Pitts to Elizabeth A. Looker, July 18, 1848
                    July 18, 1848 W. W. Parkes, J.P.

Samuel L. Wilson to Lucretia H. Randolph, July 19, 1848
                    July 19, 1848 A. C. Sloan, M.G.

William Broadaway to Lucinda Polley, July 19, 1848
                    July 20, 1848 By Martin Towery, G.M.
(p 165)
Soloman George to Mary Gray, July 22, 1848
                    July 27, 1848 Al Downing, J.P.

Charles T. Neese to Eliza Delana, July 25, 1848

James C. Simmons to Martha Jane Davidson, July 25, 1848
                    July 27, 1848 G. W. R. Moore, J.P. L.C.

William H. Bagley to Martha A. Leftwich, July 26, 1848
                    July 27, 1848 Robert M. Whitman, Minister

Thomas Chasteen to Sarah Brimage, July 26, 1848
                    July 26, 1848 D. S. Gray, J.P.

Nicholas M. Evans to Martha Pierce, August 1, 1848
                    August 2, 1848 D. S. Gray, J.P.

Robert B. Nelson to Mary Nelson, August 1, 1848
                    --   By Wm. D. Chaddock, G.M.

James B. Armstrong to Manerva Jane Donner, August 2, 1848
                    August 3, 1848 By G. W. R. Moore, J.P.

Mathew M. Cowley to Caroline Warren, August 3, 1848

William W. Mullins to Emily Looke, August 9, 1848

(p 166)
William A. January to Emeline Gibson, August 10, 1848
                    August 14, 1848 D. S. Gray, J.P.

John B. Bandy to Elizabeth Adcock, August 12, 1848
                    August 15, 1848 By Woodroof Parkes, J.P.

Andrew Burns to Eveline Perry, August 12, 1848
                    August 13, 1848 G. W. R. Moore, J.P.

William son/Alch to Mary F. Brown, August 12, 1848
                    August 13, 1848 Joseph Dameron, J.P.

Jasper N. Felps to Caroline Anthony, August 15, 1848
                    August 15, 1848   Robert M. Whitman

Wilson P. Sawyers to Elizabeth Whitaker, August 16, 1848

Jacob T. Wright to Judith Buchanan, August 17, 1848
                    August 17, 1848   By A. J. Gilmore, M.G.

George P. Hunter to Crithanatta Howard, August 19, 1848
                    August 20, 1848   T. S. Williams, J.P.

Neil McCollum to Eliza Niell, August 21, 1848

Josiah Wells to Elnyra Trail, August 21, 1848
                    August 25, 1848   Samuel Boone, J.P.
(p 167)
Thomas M. Story to Lucy Cunningham, August 22, 1848

William J. Brown to Elizabeth Sullivan, August 22, 1848
                    August 24, 1848   By Woodroof Parkes, J.P.

Jeremiah L. Daughtrey to Minney Hardin, August 25, 1848

William J. W. Dollisen to Elizabeth E. Gibson, August 29, 1848
                    August 29, 1848   By G. W. F. Moore

Anthony Bates to Harriet C. Rutledge, August 30, 1848
                    August 31, 1848   Jno. Weaver, G.M.

Jas. R. Smith to Malinda Coasling, August 31, 1848
                    August 7, 1848   By John Reaves, Esqr.

John M. Brown to Eliza Soloman, September 3, 1848
                    September 7, 1848   W. W. Parkes, J.P.

William McGowen to Lucinda Clarke, September 5, 1848
                    September 5, 1848   Wm A. Gill, G.M.

John F. Jenkins to Mariah Waley, September 5, 1848
                    September 5, 1858   By Martin Towery

Thomas H. McGaugh to Mary V. Houston, September 6, 1848
                    September 7, 1848   A. G. Smith, J.P.

Norman H. Whittenberg to Malvina C. Cunningham, September 6, 1848
                    September 7, 1848   By McKinney Surreen, G.M.
(p 168)
John Holly to Susan K. King, September 7, 1848

Henry A. McLin to Katharine Toole, September 7, 1848
                    September 7, 1848   By A. G. Gibson, M.G.

Charles Miller to Mary Ann Hamby, September 7, 1848

David Tripp to Nancy A. Braden, September 9, 1848
                    September 19, 1848   By Rev. J. Scivally

Robert M. Shelten to Mary A. Hughs, September 10, 1848
September 13, 1848 By A. J. Gilmore, M.G.

Robert M. Uagen to Cordelia J. Alexander, September 13, 1848
September 14, 1848 Matt Marshall

Thos. J. Carter to Margret M. Neeld, September 20, 1848
September 20, 1848 By A. J. Gilmore, M.G.

Zachariah Arnold to Sarah C. Hunt, September 21, 1848
J. W. Holman, M.G.

William M. Spencer to Elizabeth Jane Frane, September 25, 1848
--   J. W. Holman, M.G.

Ezra Cole to Elizabeth Cole, September 27, 1848
September 25, 1848 Daniel Farrer, J.P.

Jno. Clinto to Arletia Joiner, September 30, 1848
November 13, 1848 John Weaver, C.M.
(p 169)
J. C. McElroy to Sinthry S. A. Smith, October 2, 1848

John Baker to Mary Jane Brim, October 3, 1848
October 5, 1848 By Lewis Newsen, J.P.

William Rearden to Nancy Clediwell, October 3, 1848
October 10, 1848 By G. W. P. Moore, J.P. L.C.

J. W. M. Dance to Mary C. Barter, October 4, 1848
October 5, 1848 By S. C. Dickson, M.G.

William W. Wilson to Manerva Ann Whiteside, October 5, 1848
October 5, 1848 D. Farrer, J.P. for L.C.

David Budd to Emily Stone, October 7, 1848
October 12, 1848 By Dempsey Sullivan, J.P.

Alexander P. Grace to Nancy Spence, October 10, 1848

Alfred J. Partin to Mary Alsup, October 12, 1848
October 12, 1848 T. P. Summers, J.P.

Felix M. Cook to Virginia Chamberlain, October 13, 1848
October 15, 1848 J. Saintclair, J.P.

William J. Hughs to Margret A. Cowan, October 15, 1848
October 15, 1848 Jno. Davis, M.G.

(p 170)
Robert Norvell to Martha M. Morris, October 22, 1848
October 25, 1848 Ira E. Douthet, M.G.

Jacob W. Moore to Frances G. Hardy, October 24, 1848
October 24, 1848 Jno. W. Ogden, M.G.

Logan Carpenter to Mary McDaniel, October 24, 1848

Thomas Gold to Mary Bradshun, October 25, 1848
                    October 26, 1848 G. W. E. Moore, M. for L.C.

Edward Snow to Mahaly Mattox, October 26, 1848

Anderson Davis to Martha Ann Warren, October 28, 1848
                    October 30, 1848 Lewis Newsom, J.P.

Anthony Crawford to Elizabeth Cashion, October 28, 1848
                    --   J. W. Holman, J.P.

William M. Scirally to Malindy Gray, October 30, 1848
                    November 2, 1848 J. A. Saintclair, J.P.

Drury Leatherwood to Elizabeth Leathwood, October 31, 1848

George Grant to Emeline Poseborough, November 2, 1848

Joseph Scott to Emily Price, November 2, 1848

(p 171)
William H. Bailey to Eliza Peese, January 3, 1849
                    January 4, 1849 By Samuel Boone, J.P.

William B. Cole to Mary Ann Armstrong, January 3, 1849
                    January 4, 1849 Amos Small, J.P.

Charles M. Collier to Elvira Borough, January 4, 1849
                    January 4, 1849 John Weaver, M.G.

John Clantin to Elizabeth Houston, January 4, 1849
                    January 4, 1849 A. G. Smith, G.M.

Young A. Taylor to Elizabeth B. Stiles, January 10, 1849
                    January 11, 1849 Young T. Taylor, J.P.

William B. Shum to Louisa B. Parkes, January 10, 1849

Felix Mc P. Crawford to Martha M. Malier, January 10, 1849
                    January 11, 1849 A. G. Gibson, M.G.

Elijah Warren to Elizabeth Painey, January 13, 1849
                    January 14, 1849 --

Hiram T. Hunnicut to Pharaba Yorke, January 13, 1849
                    January 11, 1849 By Wm. Leresger, Local M.E.
                                                      Church

George W. Madones to Sarah C. E. Blakemore, January 15, 1849
                    January 18, 1849 Wm. A. Gill, M.G.

(p 172)
Mathew Raiborn to Manerva Bevil, January 15, 1849
                    January 15, 1849 John Kimes, J.P.

Samuel Webb to Henretta Nicks, January 17, 1849

Andrew C. Gleyhem to Sarah C. White, January 23, 1849

Nathan Petty to Louisa Sanders, January 23, 1849
                    January 25, 1849 Wm Dyer, J.P.

George W. Reese to Manerva C. Hedgepeth, January 24, 1849

William H. Webb to Mary Brown, January 25, 1849

Edmond D. Lawood to Louisa Murdock, January 25, 1849
                    January 25, 1849 By P. W. Watten, J.P.

Joseph W. Trigg to Eliza Robertson, January 30, 1849
                    January 30, 1849 Wm. Gale, M.G.

Wilburn H. Wade to Margaret A. Mills, January 31, 1849
                    January 31, 1849 John Weaver, G.M.

John M. Renegar to Sarah Ann Franklin, February 3, 1849
                    February 4, 1849 T. S. Williams, J.P.
(p 173)
Anderson Fitch to Nancy Crabtree, February 3, 1849

James A. Silvertooth to Sarah A. Waggoner, February 5, 1849
                    February 7, 1849 By L. Brandon

Jno. A. Woodall to Delilah Langston, February 10, 1849
                    February 14, 1849 John Moore, J.P.

John Oldfield to Abegail Stone, February 12, 1849

Jesse L. Jeans to Mary Jane Jones, February 12, 1849
                    February 13, 1849 John Mathews, J.P.

Stephen L. Wiles to Elizabeth A. Mills, February 13, 1849
                    February 22, 1849 John Weaver, G.M.

William M. Hardin to Margaret M. Killpatrick, February 13, 1849
                    February 15, 1849 D. Jacks, M.G.

Aléxr. F. Collins to Sarah A. Sanders, February 14, 1849
                    February 15, 1849 P. W. Wallon, J.P.

Arch A. Johnsen to Mary A. McKinney, February 14, 1849

Rederick P. Taylor to Tempy Marshall, February 22, 1849
                    February 22, 1849 Woodroof Parks, J.P.

(p 174)
Joseph George to Elizabeth Mullins, February 25, 1849

Henry S. Blakemore to Martha M. Pratt, February 27, 1849
                    March 1, 1849 Wm. A. Gill, G.M.

George P. Mooney to Lucy Wofford, February 27, 1849
                    February 28, 1849 Daniel Farrer, J.P.

George Gant to Catharine Withers, March 1, 1849
                    --   By M. Marshall

John A. Porch to Calledona Caudle, March 3, 1849
                    May 4, 1849 Wm. Dyer, J.P.

Archibald S. Sloan to Elizabeth J. Sloan, March 14, 1849
                    March 14, 1849 By H. Bryson, M.G.

Thomas G. Bracken to Martha A. Crawford, March 17, 1849
                    March 17, 1849 John Kimes, J.P.

Caswell Birmingham to Nancy E. Weaver, February 17, 1849

Lewis C. Williamson to Martha J. Bends, February 26, 1849
                    March 27, 1849 James C. Stevenson

Martin L. Forehand to Manerva A. Ezell, February 27, 1849
                    March 27, 1849 James C. Stevenson
(p 175)
Andrew S. Montgomery to Lavina G. Tate, March 28, 1849

Williamson Colier to Jane Rainey, March 28, 1849
                    March 28, 1849 By Lewis Newsom, J.P.

James McNatte to Louisa Prosser, April 3, 1849
                    April 3, 1849 John Weaver, G.M.

Andrew J. Soloman to Elizabeth Ann Young, April 10, 1849
                    April 10, 1849 A. S. Randolph, J.P.

Jno. H. Price to Chaney S. Blakemore, April 19, 1849
                    April 20, 1849 Wm. A. Gill, G.M.

James W. Bruce to Mary Ann Saintclair, April 23, 1849

A. J. Beaver to Martha Hampton, May 2, 1849

Willis D. Cole to Nancy J. Phillips, May 5, 1849
                    May 9, 1849 A. G. Downing, J.P.

Jno. B. Copeland to Elizabeth Michael, May 12, 1849
                    May 27, 1849 John Feed, J.P.

Elihu Gleghem to Mary Ann Smith, May 14, 1849

(p 176)
William Philpot to Mariah R. Webb, May 15, 1849

John H. Daman to Maria E. Yeager, May 15, 1849
                    May 16, 1849 By A. S. Sloan

Franklin A. George to Elizabeth J. Allison, May 16, 1849
                    May 18, 1849 Jas. N. George

John R. Ransom to Susannah J. Wiley, May 24, 1849
                    May 24, 1849 By A. S. Slocon

Lilburn L. Clark to Margaret Buchanan, May 31, 1849
                    May 31, 1849 A. G. Smith

Morgan Reavis to Mary Moore, June 1, 1849
                    June 3, 1849 G. W. R. Moore

Joseph Scott to Rebecca Brim, June 2, 1849
                    June 3, 1849 John Mathews

Eldrege C. Williams to Elizabeth J. Lee, June 4, 1849
                    June 5, 1849 Jas. N. George, J.P.

Alexander M. Bedford to Elizabeth Warren, June 4, 1849
                    June 4, 1849 By Lewis Newsom, J.P.

Jasper R. Bates to Eliza J. Williams, June 6, 1849
                    June 9, 1849 Wm. Dyer, J.P.
(p 177)
George V. Webb to Jane Yell, June 12, 1849
                    June 13, 1849 John Mathews

George W. Moyers to Susan McClain, June 14, 1849

Thos R. Robinson to Sarah B. Hamilton, June 18, 1849
                    June 21, 1849 By H. Larkin

Eli Trip to Mary June Young, June 22, 1849
                    June 24, 1849 By Wm. Calo, M. Gospel

Joe Jefferson Farrel to Sarah Forrester, June 23, 1849
                    June 24, 1849 John Weaver, J.P.

Robert N. Whitaker to Cornelia S. Grantland, June 26, 1849
                    --   J. W. Holman, J.P.

Thos. B. Pitts to Sarah Ann E. Coulter, July 4, 1849
                    July 4, 1849 W. B. Shea, J.P.

Jacob R. Corder to Sarah McClure, July 6, 1849
                    July 10, 1849 T. S. Williams, J.P.

Joseph H. Ponegar to Nancy E. Tayler, July 10, 1849
                    --   By Young T. Tayler, J.P.

Jno. Brown to Sarah Price, July 12, 1849
                    July 14, 1849 John Weaver, M.G.
(p 178)
Allen McElroy to Luticia Mayfield, July 14, 1849
                    July 15, 1849 A. J. Saintclair, J.P.

Jacob Wagoner to Louisa Logan, July 16, 1849
                July 19, 1849 Dempsey Sullivan, J.P.

Nathaniel Hobbs to Margret Hampton, July 17, 1849
                July 17, 1849 Jas. N. George

James Bradley to Elizabeth Cunningham, July 18, 1849
                July 19, 1849 Robt. Drennen, J.P.

Stephen Chinnault to Sarah C. Cox, July 18, 1849
                July 19, 1849 Spencer Leatherwood, J.P.

Ruben Stuman to Leah Jane Scirally, July 18, 1849
                July 19, 1849 Wm. Gale, M.G.

James McCollisster to Eliza Ann McWhorter, July 19, 1849
                July 19, 1849 By A. S. Randolph, J.P.

Joseph P. Allisen to Margret E. McKenzie, July 21, 1849
                July 25, 1849 D. L. Mitchell

David Jones to Sarah Colbert, July 31, 1849
                July 31, 1849 Wm. R. Jones, J.P.

Samuel Stafford to Elizabeth Chapman, August 3, 1849
                August 6, 1849 D. S. Gray, J.P.
(p 179)
Joel J. Jones to Sarah F. Hall, August 6, 1849
                Instant 6th, 1849 W. A. Gill, G.M.

Robert A. Irwin to Nancy H. Brown, August 9, 1849

Bryant Hinkle to Jamimce Pritchett, August 9, 1849
                --   J. W. Holman, M.G.

William A. McClelland to Martha S. Randolph, August 9, 1849
                August 9, 1849 Robt. Drennen, J.P.

James S. Moore to Sarah J. Simpson, August 13, 1849
                14th Instant -- By Samuel Brandon, M.G.

James P. Morris, to Emily Pruitt, August 14, 1849
                August 19, 1849 W. C. Jennings, J.P.

Calvin Street to Sarah C. Bland, August 16, 1849
                August 19, 1849 Wm. R. Jones, J.P. for L.C.

Thos Franklin to Nancy Stufflefield, August 18, 1849

Woodroof Parker to Dorey Cashien, August 20, 1849
                --   J. Copeland, G.M.

Jno. C. Walton to Thatetha J. Davis, August 20, 1849
                October 1, 1849 John C. Reeves, J.P. for L.C.

(p 180)

Martin L. Parkes to Malindy M. Simmons, August 21, 1849
                    August 30, 1849 Ira E. Douthet, M.G.

Ambrose L. Parkes to Nancy M. Walker, August 21, 1849

William S. Pess to Eliza M. J. Edwards, August 23, 1849
                    August 23, 1849 John Mathews

Benj. F. Hutson to Rebecca Dobbins, August 25, 1849
                    August 26, 1849 Jno. McDaniel, J.P.

Zachariah J. Arnold to Martha C. Smith, August 25, 1849
                    August 26, 1849 W. C. Jennings, J.P.

John March to Nancy E. Price, August 26, 1849
                    August 26, 1849 A. G. Smith

Crofford Carter to Elizabeth Noblin, August 27, 1849
                    August 28, 1849 By Martin Towery, G.M.

A. E. Moore to N. J. Motlow, August 28, 1849

Geo. F. Smith to Judith A. Metcalfe, August 30, 1849
                    August 30, 1849 S. R. Chaddick, M.G.

Jno. W. Pool to Mary Williams, August 31, 1849
                    August 31, 1849 Robert Drennen, J.P.
(p 181)
Jno. E. Gore to June M. Cunningham, August 31, 1849
                    September 4, 1849 Ira E. Douthit

Benjamin M. Eddens to Pauline D. Blythe, August 31, 1849

Benjamin F. Soloman to Nancy H. Whittaker, September 3, 1849
                    September 5, 1849 W. B. Phea, J.P.

General S. Marcom to Minerva Hodgpeth, September 3, 1849
                    September 5, 1849 Matthew Wilson, J.P.   L.C.

Jas. N. George to Nancy H. McCuire, September 7, 1849
                    September 7, 1849 Daniel Farrer, J.P.

Spencer G. Rogers to Lucy A. Hill, September 10, 1849
                    13th instant,--   Rev. J. Scivally

William Parks to Elizabeth Phillips, September 13, 1849
                    September 13, 1849 W. B. Rhea, J.P.

James M. Gold to Harriet E. Bradshaw, September 13, 1849
                    September 14, 1849 Jacob Gillispie, J.P.

Mitchell Edde to Eliza J. Jenkins, September 13, 1849
                    --   J. W. Holeman, M.G.

James Blythe to Candis C. Timmons, September 13, 1849
                    --   J. W. Holeman, M.G.

(p 182)
George W. Fluty to Nancy M. Trimble, September 15, 1849
                    September 30, 1849 T. P. Sumners, J.P.

Jas. Yates to Almeta Lopey, September 17, 1849
                    September 20, 1849 Martin Towery, G.M.

William P. Beck to Lucy J. hughs, September 19, 1849
                    September 20, 1849 John Mathews, G.M.

John P. Smith to Martha Poyers, September 20, 1849
                    September 20, 1849 A. S. Randolph

William M. Lemonds to Louisa Kincade, September 21, 1849
                    September 26, 1849 Mathew Trentham, M.G.

Nathaniel Hopper to Elainor F. Clark, September 22, 1849
                    September 27, 1849 Benj. F. Clark, J.P. for L.C.

William M. Browning to Rachael M. Simpson, September 22, 1849
                    September 27, 1849 By John W. Spearman, M.G.

Jno. P. Holman to Elizabeth O. Wilson, September 25, 1849
                    September 25, 1849 By Woodroof Parks, J.P.

Brice C. Martin to Frances F. Moores, September 27, 1849
                    --   V. C. Dunlap

Hugh Moore to Mary Ann Steed, September 27, 1849
                    --   V. C. Dunlap
(p 183)
Joseph C. Whitaker to Sarah Jane Moores, September 29, 1849

Calvin Jeans to Louisa McCown, October 3, 1849

William Cunningham to Emariah Brown, October 6, 1849

Daniel H. Bearden to Mary Ann Blake, October 8, 1849
                    October 9, 1849 A. G. Gibson, M.G.

Jas. S. Findley to Lucy J. Lemonds, October 8, 1849
                    October 11, 1849 P. W. Walton, J.P.

Daniel Maddox to Mary Jane Eddings, October 9, 1849

Allen Stewman to Nancy M. Sumners, October 9, 1849
                    --   J. W. Holman, M.G.

Benjamin Handcock to Elizabeth Hays, October 9, 1849
                    October 9, 1849 A. G. Smith

James S. Spence to Mary Ann McCormack, October 9, 1849

Jno. M. Hopper to Martha A. Ramsey, October 9, 1849
                    October 9, 1849 Thomas Childs

James F. Renfrow to Esther Moore, October 9, 1849
                        --   W. C. Dunlap

Sanders Taylor to Charlotte Simmons, October 10, 1849
                    October 16, 1849 W. C. Jennings, J.P.

Isaah Hancock to Martha E. Haley, October 11, 1849
                    October 16, 1849 A. F. Driskell

William F. Steed to Emeline Ward, October 12, 1849
                    October 14, 1849 A. J. Saintclair, J.P. for L.C.

Benj. Sullivan to Emeline Marrs, October 15, 1849
                    October 18, 1849 John Weaver, G.M.

R. J. Nelson to Mary F. McKennan, October 15, 1849

Smith Scroggins to Eleanor Holt, October 18, 1849
                    November 1, 1849 By Martin Towery, G.M.

Philip Bolick to Elizabeth McGown, October 18, 1849

Stephen C. Smith to Elizabeth Ellis, October 20, 1849
                    October 24, 1849 Jno. Kimes, J.P.

Ephraim C. King to Sarah Jane Bagley, October 22, 1849
                    October 25, 1849 H. H. Rivers J.P.
Stephen B. Wilson to Rebecca F. Womack, October 23, 1849
                    October 24, 1849 J. A. Saintclair, J.P. for L.C.

James M. Wicker to Mary Ann Hays, October 23, 1849
                    October 23, 1849 Wm. Dyer

Franklin Stevinson to Elizabeth A. Norwood, October 29, 1849
                    November 1, 1849 A. G. Gibson, M.G.

Faisting Roane to Eliza Deshazer, October 29, 1849
                    October 29, 1849 Wm. R. Jones, J.P.

William D. Brown to Mary C. Wordow, October 30, 1849
                    October 31, 1849 John Weaver, G.M.

Jesse Austin to Mahala Brim, October 31, 1849
                    October 31, 1849 G. W. R. Moore, J.P. for L.C.

Joseph M. Robertson to Nancy Ann E. Williams, October 31, 1849
                    November 1, 1849 T. S. Williams

George W. Brown to Catherine Maroney, October 31, 1849
                    October 31, 1849 A. S. Randolph, J.P. for L.C.

Wesley Bresten to Nancy Noblin, November 2, 1849
                    November 5, 1849 By Martin Towery

William Moffett Jr. to Susan E. Clift, November 4, 1849
        November 4, 1849 John Kimes, J.P. for L.C.

Mathew Wilson to Jane Gragg, November 5, 1849
        November 5, 1849 D. S. Hobbs, J.P.
(p 186)
James N. Blackwell to Elizabeth Scott, November 6, 1849

Jno. F. Floyd to Amemantha T. Cole, November 12, 1849
        November 14, 1849 By D. L. Mitchell, M.G.

Robert Crofford to Mary M. Phillips, November 13, 1849
        November 13, 1849 Jno. Kimes, J.P.

Joseph Baker to Martha Briner, November 14, 1849

Isaac M. Jones to Elizabeth S. Sane, November 14, 1849
        November 18, 1849 By J. D. Davis, M.G. of the
                        M. P. Church

John Wagoner to Nancy C. Wagoner, November 16, 1849
        November 18, 1849 D. B. Cooper, J.P.

Thomas B. Buffalo to Martha R. Turner, November 19, 1849

John H. Carter to Nancy A. Gipson, November 19, 1849
        November 19, 1849 A. G. Gibson, M.G.

Isaac N. Siler to Charlotta M. Jennings, November 22, 1849
        November 22, 1849 S. W. Arnold, J.P. L.C.

Henry M. Morris to Elizabeth Parkes, November 27, 1849

(p 187)
Alfred N. Mosely to May Franklin, November 27, 1849

Samuel A. Slaughter to Martha Claborn, November 28, 1849
        November 27, 1849 By S. P. Chaddick, G.M.

Jacob Look to Sarah Mullens, November 28, 1849
        November 29, 1849 A. G. Downing, J.P.

H. W. Shuffield to Elizabeth M. Bland, December 3, 1849
        November 4, 1849 Wm. R. Jones, J.P.

William A. Parker to Martha Sullivan, December 6, 1849
        December 6, 1849 John Weaver, G.M.

Wm. B. Griffin to Louisia J. Martin, December 7, 1849
        December 10, 1849 G. W. R. Moore, J.P. for L.C.

Jefferson L. Rhea to Francis E. Cox, December 10, 1849
        December 11, 1849 John Corder, J.P.

Robert A. Overby to Nancy M. Brown, December 11, 1849

James A. Cooper to Eliza M. Colman, December 11, 1849
                    December 11, 1849 Mathew Wilson, J.P.

John Ramsy to Elen P. Hopper, December 12, 1849
                    December 12, 1849 Benjamin L. Clarke, J.P.

(p 188)
Henry Trantham to Emmey E. Reed, December 15, 1849
                    December 13, 1849 John C. Reeves, J.P. for L.C.

John Weaver to Mary B. Swanner, December 13, 1849
                    December 13, 1849 John Weaver, G.M.

Pleasant Marberry to Sebina A. S. Hall, December 13, 1849
                    December 13, 1849 John Moore, J.P.

Richard Forbus to Elizabeth Montgomery, December 17, 1849
                    December 18, 1849 A. G. Downing, J.P.

Andrew A. Dollins to Sarah J. Armstrong, December 17, 1849
                    December 18, 1849 Amos Small, J.P.

Amon A. Williams to Mary T. George, December 19, 1849
                    December 20, 1849 Jas. N. George

John Mitchel to Margaret Smith, December 19, 1849
                    December 23, 1849 Jas. N. George

George Perry to Eliza Duke, December 19, 1849

William S. Raymon to Nancy J. McCalla, December 20, 1849
                    December 20, 1849 By A. S. Sloan

(p 189)
A. J. Gillmore to Louisa J. Franklin, December 20, 1849
                    December 20, 1849 George W. Winn, M.G.

William D. Baldin to Nancy C. McWhorter, December 21, 1849
                    December 23, 1849 A. S. Randolph, J.P. for L.C.

William C. West to Julia Ann Tayler, December 21, 1849

William R. Collins to Annice M. Parkes, December 22, 1849
                    December 24, 1849 Ira E. Douthet, M. Gospel

Samuel P. McCullough to Eliza Strong, December 22, 1849
                    December 25, 1849 A. S. Sloan

Michael Miller to Jane M. Jennings, December 22, 1849
                    December 22, 1849 By S. R. Chaddick, M.G.

Washington Aikins to Lucinda Scotte, December 24, 1849

Thomas J. Parham to Louisa B. Davis, December 25, 1849
                    December 28, 1849 Thos. Childs, M.G.

Willis A. Carter to Elizabeth M. Strong, December 26, 1849
                    December 27, 1849 D. B. Cooper, J.P.

Lewis A. Cannon to Susan C. McMillen, December 27, 1849
                    December 27, 1849 By A. S. Sloan
(p 190)
Green Bolin to Lurena Mars, December 28, 1849
                    December 28, 1849 John C. Reeves, J.P. for L.C.

George J. McCarver to Mary Ann Lee, December 29, 1849

Daniel Carmicle to Susan S. Dandridge, December 30, 1849
                    December 31, 1849 A. G. Downing, J.P.

William McArtney to Milley Parrish, December 31, 1849
                    January 1, 1850 Wm. R. Jones, J.P.

Elijah Pamplin to Sarah R. Hall, January 1, 1850
                    January 2, 1850 By D. S. Hobbs, J.P.

Asa Smith to Rhodica Perry, January 2, 1850

George W. Lewis to Ruthy Church, January 2, 1850

John H. Gullinger to Penny Ann Carter, January 2, 1850
                    January 2, 1850 D. B. Cooper, J.P.

Henry J. Rich to Celia B. Damnw, January 5, 1850
                    January 10, 1850 By William Gale, M.G.

Albert W. Cheatam to Sarah E. Kennon, January 7, 1850
                    January 7, 1850 A. W. Smith, E.
(p 191)
Henry A. Grigg to Mary Moore, January 9, 1850
                    January 10, 1850 John Weaver, G.M.

Samuel B. Grigg to Elizabeth Moore, January 9, 1850
                    January 10, 1850 John Weaver, G.M.

Westly Franklin to Eliza Jane McCarver, January 9, 1850

Jas. N. Pewet to Mary C. Davis, January 10, 1850
                    January 10, 1850 H. C. Cowan, J.P.

Kenneln T. Harrison to Sarah Jane Duke, January 16, 1850
                    January 17, 1850 Young T. Tayler, J.P.

R. M. Crawford to Mary J. McElroy, January 16, 1850
                    January 17, 1850 H. C. Cowan, J.P.

Robert Fullerton to Mary F. Lauderdale, January 17, 1850
                    January 17, 1850 A. W. Smith

Calvin Graham to Mary S. Wicks, January 21, 1850
                    January 22, 1850 H. Larkin

Willis H. Echols to Elizabeth D. Smith, January 24, 1850
January 24, 1850 W. F. Moores, J.P.

Doke Hoots to Manda J. McAfee, January 24, 1850
January 24, 1850 By Woodroof Parkes, J.P.

(p 192)
Jas. P. Curry to America Jane Walker, January 29, 1850
January 31, 1850 Ira F. Douthet, M.G.

Saml. C. Strong to Sarah E. Carter, January 30, 1850
January 31, 1850 D. B. Cooper, J.P.

Robt. M. McMullin to Matilda Woodroof, January 30, 1850
January 30, 1850 A. S. Sloan

Jesse Michael to Mary Warren, February 1, 1850
February 3, 1850 G. W. R. Moores, J.P. for L.C.

George Sanders to Elizabeth Clouch, February 2, 1850
February 4, 1850 Lee Walker, J.P.

William Duncan to Margaret F. Yeates, February 4, 1850
February 7, 1850 Wm. R. Jones, J.P.

Allen Parker to Emily E. Crawford, February 11, 1850
February 19, 1850 H. C. Cowen, J.P.

Robert C. Davis to Narcissa C. Wills, February 13, 1850
February 13, 1850 John Kimes, J.P.

Silvester McKinney to Margreat A. Roan, February 14, 1850
February 14, 1850 W. W. Parkes, J.P.

John M. Smith to Elizabeth Sneddy, February 16, 1850

(p 193)
Jno. W. Fanning to Elizabeth Sneddy, February 21, 1850
February 21, 1850 John Corder, J.P.

Samuel Beaver to Letty B. Swanner, February 21, 1850
February 21, 1850 John C. Reeves, J.P. for L.C.

David P. Tooley to Emily C. Wright, February 22, 1850
February 28, 1850 By Wm. Dyer, Esquire

Zebuda Mulder to Eliza J. McCown, March 4, 1850

Charles Royerster to Mary Jane Gibsen, March 9, 1850
March 10, 1850 A. G. Gibson, M.G.

Edmond G. Punnels to Liney Gamel, March 12, 1850
March 13, 1850 J. A. Saintclair, J.P.

Jas. C. King to Sarah Evans, March 13, 1850
March 12, 1850 G. W. R. Moore, J.P. L.C.

Henry Snow to Martha Ann Barton, March 14, 1850
                    March 14, 1850 By J. W. Holeman, G.M.

Baily Pains to Sarah Mallard, March 19, 1850

William D. Baits to Edatha Nicks, March 23, 1850
                    March 31, 1850 Amos Small, J.P.
(p 194)
John J. Gassaway to Elizabeth Landreth, April 1, 1850
                    April 1, 1850 By D. B. Cooper, J.P. for L.C.

A. J. Childres to Margaret George, April 1, 1850
                    April 7, 1850 A. G. Downing, J.P.

William M. Hester to Mary E. A. Wells, April 11, 1850
                    April 17, 1850 Wm. A. Gill, M.G.

S. G. McLeroy to Lucy Ann Woodard, April 16, 1850
                    April 16, 1850 A. G. Smith, M.G.

Jno. Clarke to Mary Ann Sullivan, April 17, 1850
                    April 17, 1850 Wm. H. Moores, J.P.

Lemuel P. M. Dennis to Alpha A. McGee, April 19, 1850
                    April 19, 1850 W. H. Moores, J.P.

William R. Hudlow to Elizabeth M. Gabner, April 22, 1850

Jas. D. Campbell to Mary Jane Faulkner, April 24, 1850
                    April 25, 1850 By Woodroof Parkes, J.P.

John Smith to Rebecca Rogers, April 24, 1850
                    April 24, 1850 Leroy Jones, M.G.

A. Sanford to Martha A. Jeanes, April 30, 1850
                    April 30, 1850 Wm. B. Rhea, J.P.
(p 195)
William Stone to Sarah Gore, May 3, 1850

James C. Lee to Penina E. Williams, May 4, 1850
                    May 4, 1850 Joe N. George, J.P. L.C.

Henry Nichols to Malinda Sorrels, May 9, 1850
                    May 9, 1850 Jno. Wagster, M.G.

Bryant Tayler to Nancy Hughs, May 18, 1850
                    May 18, 1850 Mathew Wilson, J.P.

William A. Brown to Margret A. Keith, May 23, 1850
                    May 23, 1850 John Weaver, G.M.

Jno. M. King to Caroline Johnson, May 31, 1850
                    May 2, 1850 By D. B. Cooper, J.P.

Mitchel Collins to Mary A. Thompson, June 3, 1850
                    June 4, 1850 J. A. Saintclair, J.P.

Jonathan Langston to Eliza Woodall, June 3, 1850
                  June 9, 1850 By John Corder, J.P.

Paschal White to Malissa Arnold, June 8, 1850
                  June 9, 1850 By John Corder, J.P.

James T. Clark to Sarah Webb, June 8, 1850

L. P. Johnson to Nancy Martin, June 10, 1850

(p 196)
James M. Stephenson to Juily Whitworth, June 19, 1850
                  June 19, 1850 Lee Walker, J.P.

Benjamin March to Sarah E. Wilson, June 19, 1850

James P. Holeman to Emily F. Price, June 23, 1850
                  June 23, 1850 A. W. Smith

James C. Reed to Louisa McAfee, June 27, 1850
                  July 1, 1850 John C. Reeves, J.P. for L.C.

Caleb Z./Webb to Eliza Jane Kilpatrick, July 3, 1850

John Nichols to Malinda Pearce, July 3, 1850
                  July 5, 1850 Young T. Taylor, J.P.

Jno. R. Smith to Margaret E. Endsley, July 4, 1850
                  July 4, 1850 Thos. Chiles, M.G.

George W. Higgins to Sarah L. Stone, July 11, 1850
                  July 11, 1850 W. H. Moores, J.P.

George O. McDaniel to Minerva Dillon, July 13, 1850
                  July 18, 1850 Martin Towery, G.M.

William A. Philips to Martha A. Burr, July 15, 1850
                  July 15, 1850 Lewis Newsom, J.P.
(p 197)
James E. Smith to Nancy Rancy, July 16, 1850
                  July 16, 1850 By D. Sullivan, J.P. for L.C.

William McClusky to Nancy A. Towery, July 17, 1850
                  July 18, 1850 William Pryor, J.P. for L.C.

Jesse L. Grammer to Phachel Price, July 22, 1850
                  July 22, 1850 By D. Sullivan, J.P. for L.C.

Jas. M. Barham to Mary Jane King, July 22, 1850
                  July 22, 1850 G. W. R. Moore, J.P.

Wesley Lock to Emily Miller, July 23, 1850
                  July 28, 1850 P. P. Riddle, Lincoln County, Tenn.

Benjamin Perve to Matilda Smith, July 25, 1850

Wm. Steelman to Ann Miles, July 30, 1850
                    August 1, 1850 By Woodroof Parks, J.P.

Samuel Shelton to Sarah Cooper, July 31, 1850
                    August 2, 1850 John Moore, J.P.

Cambell F. Edmondson to Margret E. Buicharan, July 31, 1850
                    August 1, 1850 Jacob Gillespie, J.P.

Abel R. Smith to Nancy V. Reese, August 6, 1850
                    August 7, 1850 John Weaver, C.M.
(p 198)
Jas. C. Robison to Martha Hopper, August 8, 1850

William M. Smith to Emeline Koonce, August 13, 1850
                    August 13, 1850 W. W. Parks, J.P. for L.C.

Amos Heirs to Denoah Myers, August 16, 1850
                    August 17, 1850 John Weaver, C.M.

James M. Smith to Nancy E. Michael, August 17, 1850
                    August 18, 1580 D. S. Gray, J.P.

Wm. E. Bradford to Mary Reece, August 22, 1850
                    August 22, 1850 D. F. Clark, J.P.

Samuel S. Smith to Cintha A. McElroy, August 22, 1850
                    August 22, 1851 A. C. Smith, M.

William H. Smith to Amanda S. Norris, August 24, 1850
                    September 11, 1850 W. J. Mitchell, J.P. L.C.

Wiley Cunningham to Jane Smith, August 28, 1850
                    September 1, 1850 Jas. N. George, J.P. L.C.

Milton N. Moore to Elizabeth L. Shaw, August 29, 1850
                    September 3, 1850 J. E. Douthet, M.G.

Jesse Eaton to Sarah Cox, September 2, 1850
                    September 22, 1850 John Bryson, M.G.
(p 199)
Silas Bryan to Tabitha Harris, September 6, 1850
                    September 6, 1850 Joseph Scott, J.P.

William A. Morrison to Mary Hardy, September 7, 1850

Stephen G. Tankersby to Manerva Graham, September 9, 1850
                    September 11, 1850 N. Larkin

Jas. A. Tankersby to Sarena Graham, September 9, 1850
                    September 11, 1850 N. Larkin

John F. Robertson to Margaret A. Dameron, September 10, 1850
                    September 12, 1850 N. Larkin

Thos. Roland to Permelia Smith, September 10, 1850
                    September 10, 1850 Y. T. Taylor, J.P. for L.C.

Jordin C. Holt to Jane Waggoner, September 11, 1850
                    September 12, 1850 By Saml. Boone, J.P.

Dolphus A. Stone to Dorthmany Strong, September 12, 1850

Reuben G. Bryant to Jane Logan, September 14, 1850
                    September 22, 1850 By L. Sullivan J.P. for L.C.

James Edens to Mary R. Landers, September 16, 1850

(p 200)
Horace L. Benedict to Nancy Hobbs, September 16, 1850

Andrew J. Davidson to Mary E. Abbit, September 20, 1850
                    September 22, 1850 J. McDaniel

William P. Duke to Mary Panther, September 24, 1850

Elisha Bobo to Oliva Wilson, September 24, 1850
                    September 24, 1850 Daniel Farrar, J.P.

James Sullivan to Jane Wishon, September 26, 1850
                    September 26, 1850 John Weaver, G.M.

William J. Hulsey to Sarah A. Waggoner, October 3, 1850

Irail P. Dennis to Sarah E. Patrick, October 3, 1850
                    October 3, 1850 W. W. Parks, J.P.

George Carter to Martha Warren, October 4, 1850

Wm. Stanley to Polly A. Chetwod, October 7, 1850
                    October 10, 1850 W. Dyer, J.P.

George W. Pilant to Barthena E. Sharp, October 7, 1850
                    October 10, 1850 By John Coder, J.P.
(p 201)
Jos. O. Dellmon to Eliza Jane Heard, October 8, 1850
                    October 8, 1850 Daniel Farrar, J.P. L.C.

Johnson J. Cleghorn to Margret Jones, October 8, 1850
                    October 8, 1850 W. Dyer, J.P.

John F. Wilkins to Jeffries E. Landess, October 10, 1850

Jas. F. Pool to Eliza Isom, October 12, 1840
                    October 13, 1850 W. R. Martin, J.P.

Moses Temple to Eliza Reeves, October 12, 1850
                    October 16, 1850 Jas. N. George, J.P. L.C.

Jas. C. Green to Lavins Smith, October 16, 1850
                    October 16, 1850 Jno. Weaver, M.G.

Geo. W. Reese to Cordilia A. Pratt, October 14, 1850
                    October 14, 1850 Wm. H. Moores, J.P.

Stephen A. White to Martha A. Jones, October 17, 1850
                    October 18, 1850 Wm. R. Moores, J.P.

Samuel Perry to Elizabeth Tennison, October 18, 1850
                    October 20, 1850 Y. T. Taylor, J.P.

Fedorick Price to Elizabeth Ann Busby, October 21, 1850
                    October 21, 1850 W. B. Rhea, J.P.
(p 202)
William H. Bryan to Julia A. J. E. Smith, October 22, 1850
                    October 22, 1950 Daniel Farrar, J.P.

George Fereman to Sophia E. Walker, October 19, 1850
                    October 20, 1850 Ira E. Douthet, M.G.

Eli A. Lacky to Elizabeth C. West, October 24, 1850
                    October 24, 1850 James C. Stevenson

Charles A. Robinson to Martha A. Bell, October 24, 1850
                    October 24, 1850 A. G. Smith

Mathew S. Gowan to Laoma Mullins, October 25, 1850
                    October 27, 1850 Leroy Jones, M.G.

Archibald V. McDaniel to Mary F. McKee

Charles Adkins to Mary Scorber, October 28, 1850
                    October 28, 1850 A. G. Smith

Wm. Petty to Cincinnatta F. Sullivan, October 29, 1850
                    October 31, 1850 F. W. Walton, J.P.

Nicholas J. House to Malinda Cook, October 29, 1850

Joseph L. Sherell to Martha E. Patterson, October 30, 1850
                    October 30, 1850 James Kirlland, M.G.
(p 203)
H. N. Mauldin to Mary L. Sullivan, November 5, 1850
                    November 5, 1850 W. Dyer, J.P.

Mark H. Cole to Lucinda L. Hedgepeth, November 7, 1850

Gabriel Davis to Dicy King, November 7, 1850
                    November 7, 1850 G. W. R. Moore, J.P. L.C.

Jonathan Smith to Febe Jane Rainey, November 8, 1850
                    November 10, 1850 By Saml. Boon, J.P.

James Rainey to Nancy Smith, November 8, 1850
                    November 10, 1850 By Saml. Boone, J.P.

A. M. Prosser to America Sullivan, November 12, 1850
                    November 14, 1850 By Saml. Boon, J.P.

Jas. M. Banks to Elizabeth J. Brady, November 12, 1850
                    November 14, 1850 B. M. G. Alsup, J.P.

Henry Jacobs to Tursey A. Tate, November 13, 1850
                    November 1?, 1850 M. Dyer, J.P.

James Bradley to Polly Roberson, November 12, 1850
                    November 12, 1850 W. R. Moores

William Smith to Amanda Fackenter, November 18, 1850
                    November 18, 1850 Wm. C. Jowingrs, J.P.
(p 204)
George Fanning to Martha Ann Smith, November 23, 1850
                    November 24, 1850 Y. T. Taylor, J.P.

James Bowling to Mary Moyers, November 25, 1850
                    November 25, 1850 Jas. N. George

John W. Bland to Martha E. Blain, November 27, 1850
                    November 28, 1850 Wm. J. Milchel, J.P.

William L. James to Persilla Anh Moore, December 2, 1850
                    December 2, 1850 A. G. Downing, J.P.

A. A. Bell to C. E. Biggar, December 10, 1850
                    December 10, 1850 By A. G. Gibson, M.G.

George Pingram to Mary Ann Stephens, December 10, 1850

James Daniel to Catharine Wagoner, December 10, 1850

Phillips Cooper to Lucinda McNeace, December 11, 1850
                    December 11, 1850 W. N. Moore, J.P.

John W. Clarke to Martha J. Buchanan, December 12, 1850
                    December 12, 1850 A. G. Smith
(p 205)
David R. Hamilton to Sarah F. Moore, December 12, 1850
                    December 12, 1850 A. G. Smith

Joseph George to Eldender M. Burten, December 13, 1850
                    December 13, 1850 Wm. J. Milchell, J.P.

William Montgomery to Nancy R. McNiel, December 16, 1850
                    December 17, 1850 A. G. Smith

Epp Hardin to Clarenda C. Webb, December 16, 1850

E. F. Berry to Elizabeth Caton, December 19, 1850
                    December 19, 1850 By Woodroof Parks, J.P.

William Upton to Ellen Crawford, December 19, 1850
                    December 24, 1850 John Kimes, J.P.

Josiah A. Norris to Mary E. Raymond, December 19, 1850
                    December 19, 1850 By A. S. Stone

Charles G. Crump to Lucinda Davidson, December 20, 1850
                    December 24, 1850 By A. G. Gibson, M.G.

John Mason to Elizabeth Smith, December 14, 1850
                    December 19, 1850 By Martin Towery

Manson Albright to Martha A. Jewell, December 21, 1850
                    December 23, 1850 Robt. Drennon, J.P.
(p 206)
William Vickers to Rebecca Vickers, December 21, 1850
                    December 24, 1850 R. Drennon, J.P.

Thomas Easlick to Sarah Taylor, December 21, 1850
                    December 22, 1850 T. S. Williams, J.P.

Davis M. Holloway to Amandia C. Randolph, December 23, 1850
                    December 24, 1850 A. G. Downing, J.P.

Wright H. Watson to Charlott M. Hedgepeth, December 23, 1850
                    December 24, 1850 Wm. Dyer, J.P.

James H. Jones to Francis E. Smith, December 24, 1850
                    December 24, 1850 A. G. Smith, M.G.

James H. Harrison to Margaret J. Moyers, December 24, 1850
                    December 24, 1850 S. Pecord, M.G.

William J. Rainey to Elizabeth Shipp, December 25, 1850

Robert Jacobs to Elizabeth McCree, December 26, 1850
                    December 26, 1850 Wm. Dyer, J.P.

Allen Smith to Arrena Owen, December 27, 1850
                    December 29, 1850 Wm. R. Martin, J.P.

Jno. A. Norwood to Elizabeth Inman, December 27, 1850
                    January 2, 1851 W. B. Rhea, J.P.
(p 207)
Edward Taylor to Eliza Fouster, December 28, 1850
                    December 29, 1850 By Woodroof Parkes, J.P.

John Armstrong to Margret S. McCollum, December 28, 1850
                    December 29, 1850 H. C. Cowan, J.P.

Thomas Holman to Mary Perry, December 29, 1850
                    December 29, 1850 Jno. Kimes, J.P. for L.C.(Seal)

Hardy H. Cotton to Margret J. Dollins, December 30, 1850
                    January 2, 1851 By A. G. Gibson, M.G.

Newton W. Howel to Nancy J. Wiles, December 31, 1850
                    January 31, 1851 Saml. Boon, J.P.

Arthur Washburn to Mary G. Hodges, December 31, 1850

Austin Eslick to Martha J. George, January 1, 1851

C. G. Tucker to Nancy W. Turney, January 1, 1851
                    --   R. W. Walton, J.P.

Mamous Flint to Sarah Ann Jennings, January 6, 1851

Lee Smith to Elizabeth A. McNimm, January 6, 1851
                    January 7, 1851   A. G. Smith
(p 208)
Henry Shelton to Leah Shellon, January 7, 1851
                    January 8, 1851   T. S. Williams, J.P.

Obadiah Clark to Louisa N. Canada, January 8, 1851
                    January 8, 1851   J. McDaniel, J.P.

Marshall Ceatty to Elizabeth Gragg, January 8, 1851
                    January 8, 1851   A. G. Smith, M.G.

Beriah Lackey to Martha Evans, January 11, 1851
                    January 14, 1851 By Rev. J. Scivally

Archibald L. Moyers to Margret M. Alsup, January 11, 1851
                    March 3, 1851   John C. Reeves, J.P.   L.C.

Henry Taylor to Mary Smith, January 11, 1851

Elihu Leatherwood to Mary F. Smith, January 13, 1851
                    January 16, 1851   John L. Henderson, J.P.

James Culbreath to Elizabeth A. Overby, January 14, 1851
                    December 12, 1852 By L. M. Dance, M.G.

Jno. W. Cole to Elizabeth Panter, January 15, 1851

Elisha Bryant to Phebe Taylor, January 16, 1851
                    January 16, 1851 Wm. C. Jennings, J.P.
(p 209)
William M. T. Cook to Adaline Trimble, January 22, 1851
                    March 5, 1851   T. P. Sumners, J.P.

F. C. A. Troop to Mahala Jane Cummins, January 27, 1851
                    January 28, 1851 Jacob Gillespie, J.P.

Eli Evans to Mary Ann Massey, January 27, 1851

Thos. B. McClure to Mary Smith, January 28, 1851
                    January 30, 1851 D. S. Gray, J.P.

Jas. A. J. Alexander to Sarah P. Jorden, February 1, 1851
                    February 4, 1851 Y. T. Taylor, J.P.

Thos. J. Reese to Perliria Ann Reese, February 1, 1851
                    --   By Demps Sullivan, J.P.

McDonald Tucker to Elizabeth Ann Duke, February 4, 1851

Joel Cunningham to Susan E. Wyrick, February 4, 1851
                    February 13, 1851 By John Moores, J.P.

Philip McBray to Harret A. Walker, February 4, 1851
                February 6, 1851 Wm. M. Newman, J.P.

Robert Hill to Mary E. McConnell, February 4, 1851
                February 4, 1851 By W. C. Dunlap, M.G.
(p 210)
William J. Stephens to Elizabeth E. Eddington, February 5, 1851

William S. Hill to Margret Pullam, February 8, 1851
                February 9, 1851 Wm. H. Moores, J.P.

Simon A. Pearce to Letty Cashein, February 11, 1851
                February 25, 1851 W.M. Newman, J.P.

Floodle Micheal to Drucillar Jane Bledsoe, February 12, 1851
                February 15, 1851 N. R. Bray, M.G.

Jno. Chapman to Elizabeth A. Graves, February 12, 1851
                February 12, 1851 Lemuel Brandon

Jas. W. Soloman to Mary Tayler, February 13, 1851
                February 13, 1851 Y. T. Taylor, J.P.

W. Y. Chesser to Martha Scott, February 17, 1851
                February 18, 1851 John Weaver, G.M.

John F. Baxter to Hannah A. E. Robertson, February 17, 1851
                February 20, 1851 J. A. Saintclair, J.P.

Joseph T. Hopper to Louisa Sawyers, February 18, 1851
                February 18, 1851 J. McDaniel. J.P.

David P. Cooper to Eliza J. Clarke, February 19, 1851
                February 20, 1851 Allison Akin, M.G.
(p 211)
William B. Martin to Levina Ann Soloman, February 19, 1851
                February 20, 1851 Wm. B. Rhea, J.P.

Enoch G. Baker to Sarah Fuller, February 22, 1851

Benjamin Nerrin to Elizabeth West, February 24, 1851
                February 29, 1851 By Rev. J. B. Warren

Mathew Bethum to Sarah Juhe Sanders, February 24, 1851
                February 25, 1851 A. G. Downing, J.P.

James M. Roughton to N. C. Womack, February 25, 1851
                February 27, 1851 J. A. Saintclair, J.P.

Jasper Rowe to Jane McGee, February 25, 1851
                February 26, 1852 By Demps Sullivan

Drury C. Wheeler to Mary C. Cole, March 6, 1851

Jno. R. McGee to Sarah Jane Putledge, March 12, 1851
                March 12, 1851 Wm. H. Moores, J.P.

James M. Sims to Jonuma D. Greer, March 17, 1851
                    April 10, 1851 Alison Dakin, M.G.

Bailey E. Lunn to Luvina J. Ashby, March 21, 1851
                    March 23, 1851 Jno. Weaver, G.M.
(p 212)
John M. Smith to Mary E. Berry, March 26, 1851
                    March 27, 1851 James A. Saintclair, J.P.

Robert B. Young to Elizabeth A. Owens, April 3, 1851

Francis M. Bryant to Susan D. Williams, April 4, 1851
                    April 10, 1851 Robert Drennon, J.P. L.C.

Wm. M. Woodward to Elizabeth McElroy, April 5, 1851

Wm. H. Stephenson to Frances Luna, April 7, 1851
                    April 7, 1851 Wm. Dyer, J.P.

Josiah S. Thompson to Dulsena Stephenson, April 9, 1851
                    April 10, 1851 A. G. Gibson, M.G.

Nathan McCalister to Catharine Scott, April 16, 1851

Halifax A. Steelman to Nancy Warden, April 21, 1851
                    April 24, 1851 By Woodroof Parks, J.P.

Richard Smith to Anna Faulkner, April 25, 1851
                    July 10, 1851 John Corder, J.P.

James Watson to Martha J. Edmiston, April 25, 1851

(p 213)
Neoplin Benson to Mary Doss, May 1, 1851
                    May 1, 1851 Wm. H. Moores, J.P.

John H. Scott to May Ann Cheser, May 1, 1851
                    May 1, 1851 Wm. Dyer, J.P.

Stephen Patterson to Gilliam Patterson, May 3, 1851
                    May 4, 1851 J. E. Douthet, M.G.

James A. Grills to Julia Ann Cunningham, May 13, 1851
                    October 5, 1851 Wm. M. Newman, J.P.

Robert Patterson to Elizabeth N. Shull, May 16, 1851
                    May 16, 1851 Wm. H. Moores, J.P.

Jno. B. Fairs to Nancy J. Forrester, May 16, 1851
                    May 18, 1851 By Saml. Boon, J.P.

Albert G. Wheeler to Elizabeth Philpot, May 17, 1851
                    May 18, 1851 J. N. George, J.P.

Simpson Abbot to Nancy F. Dickey, May 22, 1851
                    May 22, 1851 Robt. Drennon, J.P.

M. R. Cherill to Eliza A. Pemberton, June 12, 1851

William D. Prosser to Mary Wilson. --
                    June 12, 1851 John Wagster, M.G.
(p 214)
Alfred W. Williams to Nancy Stephens, June 12, 1851
                    June 13, 1851 D. Jacks, M.G.

Stephen Hart to Catharine V. Beaty, June 17, 1851
                    June 17, 1851 A. F. Dreskill

James S. Davis to Jane Davis, June 20, 1851
                    June 20, 1851 J. W. Holman, M.G.

Peter Hamilton to Sarah Cunningham, June 24, 1851

Peyton Foyester to Claskey Jane Guinn, June 28, 1851
                    June 29, 1851 By Saml. Boon, J.P.

Willis H. Foster to Mary Lambert, July 1, 1851
                    July 1, 1851 James D. Cole, M.G.

Thos. B. Hicks to Elizabeth W. Alexander, July 1, 1851
                    July 9, 1851 R. Drennon, J.P.

William H. Sparkes to Mary C. Matton, July 3, 1851
                    July 13, 1851 Jno. McDaniel, J.P.

Willis F. Cobbert to Mary Ann Saunders, July 3, 1851
                    July 3, 1851 A. A. Bell, M.G.

Jno. L. Pylant to Elizabeth W. Lord, July 4, 1851
                    July 6, 1851 D. L. Mitchell
(p 215)
Jas. Kirkpatrick to Josephine Beardin, July 9, 1851

Geo. Cumberland to Elizabeth Lindsey, July 14, 1851

William L. McCann to Mary Jane Rawls, July 16, 1851
                    July 16, 1851 Wm. R. Martin, J.P. (Seal)

Jno. H. Morrison to Martha Jane Davidson, July 17, 1851

Adolphis B. Holiday to Martha J. Fanning, July 19, 1851
                    July 20, 1851 Wm. H. Moores, J.P.

Tilman L. McGee to Margret S. Taylor, July 21, 1851
                    July 23, 1851 Saml. Boon, J.P.

James D. Paddie to Nancy Ann Brodaway, July 21, 1851

M. D. Carpenter to Sarah McNatt, July 23, 1851
                    July 27, 1851 By D. Sullivan, J.P.

E. W. Moore to Martha Jane Cross, July 26, 1851
                    July 29, 1851 By Woodroof Parkes, J.P.

Jos. A. Casey to Eliza Ann Parker, July 26, 1851
July 31, 1851 Wm. C. Jenninghs, J.P.
(p 216)
Wm. C. Luna to Sarah Jane Chitwood, July 28, 1851
Issd. July 30, 1851 Jno. Weaver, G.M.

Jno. W. Carmicle to Jane Bush, July 28, 1851

Thos. M. Benefield to Letty Reives, July 29, 1851
July 30, 1851 J. N. George, J.P.

Henry Luttrell to Sarah L. Templeton, August 2, 1851
August 7, 1851 By Wm. C. Jennings, J.P.

Enoch Warren to Malinda C. Carter, August 4, 1851

Samuel Warren to Martha Pamplin, August 4, 1851

William J. Grills to Sarah P. Heath, August 4, 1851
August 6, 1853 W. M. Newman, J.P.

William Kelly to Sarah McClure, August 5, 1851
August 5, 1851 By John Corder, J.P.

Decatur Barnes to Margret J. Holbert, August 6, 1851
August 7, 1851 Thomas Childs, G.M.

James Satterfield to Caroline Hankins, August 11, 1851

Henry C. Hamilton to Nancy Martin, August 11, 1851
August 11, 1851 J. E. Douthet, M.G.
(p 217)
Samuel C. Holman to Sarah Lindsey, August 12, 1851
August 12, 1851 Y. T. Taylor, J.P.

Samuel V. Commons to Sarah Isom, August 12, 1851

William Waterman to Sarah L. Commins, August 14, 1851
--   By W. C. Dunlap, M.G.

Elisha Shelton to Elizabeth Hooper, August 19, 1851

Martin Trantham to Mary F. Moyers, August 20, 1851
August 25, 1851 Jno. C. Reeves, J.P. L.C.

Elijah Parker to Martha L. Crawford, August 20, 1851
August 21, 1851 A. G. Smith, M.G.

Noah W. Cooper to Lucy H. Webster, August 21, 1851

Samuel J. Howell to Cynthia Ann Steelman, August 22, 1851
August 24, 1851 John Weaver, M.G.

A. T. Nicks to Jane M. Wright, August 23, 1851
August 24, 1851 A. G. Smith

James B. Slain to Elizabeth C. Medkiff, August 26, 1851
                    August 27, 1851, J. N. George, J.P.

(p 218)
Robt. A. Morrison to Racheal J. Scott, August 28, 1851
                    --
Peter Cunningham to Mary A. Grills, August 28, 1851
                    August 30, 1851 W. M. Newman, J.P.

August Hess to Priss Prosser, August 29, 1851
                    August 29, 1851   Lewis Newsom, J.P.

Wm. F. Jared to Mildred Davidson, August 30, 1851
                    August 31, 1851 D. Sullivan, J.P.

Alexander D. Ferguson to Margaret M. Baxter, September 2, 1851
                    --   By B. Kimbrough, M.G.

William Metcalf to Elizabeth F. Cole, September 4, 1851
                    September 4, 1851 Jas. N. George, J.P.

Barksdale Neece to Sarah Eaton. September 8, 1851
                    September 11, 1851 By D. Sullivan, J.P.

John A. Crew to Cyntha Eaton, September 8, 1851
                    September 16, 1851 Jno. Weaver, M.G.

Charles S. Rutledge to Sulthany Wade, September 9, 1851
                    September 10, 1851 By Saml. Boon, J.P.

Samuel P. Smith to Pelina Colman, September 9, 1851
                    September 11, 1851 By Wm. R. Martin, J.P. (Seal)

(p 219)
Charles McCartney to Lucy Coil, September 10, 1851
                    September 11, 1851, A. G. Downing, J.P.

Jerih. M. Fauttenbury to Mary Ann Caughran, September 10, 1851
                    September 22, 1851 A. J. Childres, J.P. L.C.

Benjamin L. Commons to Elizabeth King, September 10, 1851
                    September 11, 1851 By W. C. Dunlap, M.G.

Henry H. Winkler to Mary Ann Jones, September 11, 1851
                    September 15, 1851 By Wm. C. Jennings, J.P.

George M. Martin to Caroline Wilkins, September 11, 1851
                    September 11, 1851 Robt. Drennon, J.P.

John C. Maroney to Nancy Jane Jewell, September 11, 1851
                    September 11, 1851 Robt. Drennon, J.P.

John W. Walker to Nancy A. Hamilton. September 13, 1851
                    September 15, 1851 D. Jacks, M.G.

William McClure to Susan E. Cox, September 16, 1851

William P. Careveen to Manerva Gold, September 16, 1851

Jas. W. Erin to Eliza Sumners, September 17, 1851

(p 220)
Henderson Barnes to Pamelia A. Cumpton, September 18, 1851
          --   By Jno. McDaniel, J.P.

William M. Thompson to Louisa Jane Pedwell, September 18, 1851

Benjamin Boone to Sarah Jane Parker, September 20, 1851

Seneca Clarke to Mary M. Patton, September 22, 1851
          September 26, 1851 A. G. Gibson, M.G.

William H. Blue to Nancy Anderson, September 22, 1851
          February 7, 1852 By G. W. Puckett, M.G.

George Hains to Nancy M. Brown, September 23, 1851

Samuel G. Aurin to Martha C. Cray, September 23, 1851
          --   By J. W. Holman, M.G.

Madison Dozee to Sarah Jane Branson, September 23, 1851
          September 24, 1851 Wm. H. Moore

James R. Butler to Nancy A. Ables, September 24, 1851

R. M. Bryant to Francis C. McKenzie, September 24, 1851
          September 25, 1851 D. L. Mitchell, M.G.

(p 221)
John A. Gilham to Mary F. Dallas, September 25, 1851
          September 25, 1851 A. G. Smith

Enoch E. Harbin to Ann E. Sneed, September 26, 1851
          October 27, 1851 T. S. Williams, J.P.

Thomas B. Eastland to Sarah Pearson, September 27, 1851
          September 29, 1851 Jno. McDaniel, J.P.

Silas Stephenson to Charlotte Bradford, September 29, 1851

Hugh B. Wallace to Rebecca Van Hooser, October 2, 1851

David C. Myers to Sarah Trantham, October 4, 1851
          October 5, 1851 John C. Reeves, J.P.

James J. Emmons to Manlday C. Carithurs, October 8, 1851
          October 11, 1851 John C. Reeves, J.P. for L.C.

David M. Tafts to Nancy M. Smith, October 9, 1851
          October 9, 1851 Wm. R. Martin, J.P.

John Jock to Nancy Faney, October 14, 1851
                 October 14, 1851 By D. Sullivan, J.P.

Henry Austin to Mary Barrow, October 14, 1851
                 October 14, 1851 John Wagster, M.G.

(p 222)
Wilson Thompson to Sarah Sullinger, October 15, 1851

James J. Davis to Nancy Brimm, October 16, 1851
                 October 16, 1851 John Wagster, M.G.

Samuel D. Hope to Eliza M. Cummins, October 16, 1851
                 --   By A. G. Gibson, V.D.M.

Andrew J. Jones to Harriet E. Mitcheal, October 20, 1851
                 October 20, 1851 Joe E. Douthet, M.G.

William Lipscomb to Sarah A. Fulgham, October 21, 1851
                 October 21, 1851 S. E. Jones, M.G. in the
                                 Church of Christ

Tandy W. Ford to Mary R. Armstrong, October 23, 1851
                 October 26, 1851 Jno. W. Oxder, M.G.

Milton Parks to Emily A. Raines, October 23, 1851
                 October 23, 1851 Woodroof Parkes, J.P.

N. T. Pittelle to Martha Ann Koonce, October 25, 1851

Craven W. Nees to Rebecca Allen, October 28, 1851
                 October 29, 1851 By D. Sullivan, J.P.

A. J. Nichols to Susanah Parish, October 28, 1851
                 October 28, 1851 A. J. Childress

(p 223)
Jno. F. Turney to Louisa Beck, October 29, 1851
                 October 30, 1851 Thomas Childs, G.M.

Marshall Bruice to Matilda E. Campbell, October 29, 1851
                 October 30, 1851 J. A. Saintclair, J.P. L.C.

Doct. Jno. D. Whitaker to L. L. Todd, November 1, 1851
                 November 2, 1851 Wm. H. Moores, J.P. (Seal)

Wonnly F. Bruice to Mary F. E. McCoy, November 3, 1851
                 November 5, 1851 James C. Stevenson

Robert McGehey to Elizabeth Shelton, November 5, 1851
                 October 5, 1851 T. S. Williams, J.P.

William H. Peyton to Rosariah A. Jackson, November 6, 1851
                 November 6, 1851 Thomas Childs, G.M.

William J. Cole to Martha K. Cole, November 7, 1851

William F. Cole to Martha Reece, November 11, 1851

Isaac F. Cole to Mary Jane Farrer, November 12, 1851
                    November 13, 1851 Jas. N. George, J.P.

Joshua D. Gray to Elizabeth Moorehead, November 12, 1851
                    November 10, 1851, W. M. Newman, J.P.

(p 224)
B. F. Dennis to Samyra Andrews, November 13, 1851

Mark Colier to Virginia Reese, November 13, 1851
                    November 13, 1851 R. M. Whitman, J.P.

William C. Dunham to Frances E. Pullam, November 19, 1851
                    November 20, 1851 J. L. Thompson, J.P.

Josiah P. Wallace to Mary Ann Joins, November 20, 1851
                    November 20, 1851 A. J. Childress, J.P. L.C.

James Daves to Margret Holley, November 21, 1851

James N. Ford to Sally S. Green, November 22, 1851
                    November 23, 1851 By Jno. Weaver, G.M.

Joshua Phillips to Elizabeth Waggoner, November 25, 1851
                    November 27, 1851 By Samuel Boon, J.P. for L.C.
                                        (Seal)

D. P. C. Allen to Emeline McAfee, November 26, 1851

Samuel Heathcock to Caroline Isham, November 27, 1851
                    November 27, 1851 R. Drennon, J.P.

William T. Lauderdale to Margret A. E. Fullerton, November 27, 1851
                    November 27, 1851 A. G. Smith, M.G.

(p 225)
Samuel G. Beard to Julia Ann McKinney, November 27, 1851
                    November 29, 1851 Rev. W. W. Beard

John G. McClellen to Caroline E. Stonebraker, December 3, 1851
                    December 4, 1851 William Gayle

Jesse A. Shands to Mary Hathcock, December 5, 1851

Westley Lettrell to Lucillar Pruett, December 8, 1851

Allen C. Jones to Sebra Powers, December 8, 1851
                    December 9, 1851 Martin Towery, M.G.

Emanuel Punnels to Louisa J. Moon, December 9, 1851
                    December 9, 1851 By John Weaver, M.G.

Jesse W. Parkes to Mary A. Snoddy, December 11, 1851
                    December 11, 1851 By Woodroof Parkes, J.P.

G. W. Owen to Kanzetty Forbes, December 11, 1851

Joseph C. Wiley to Rachael Sloan, December 11, 1851
          December 11, 1851 John C. Record, J.P. L.C.
(p 226)
Alfred R. Smith to Mary E. Steadman, December 13, 1851
          December 17, 1851 By A. S. Randolph, J.P.

James A. Wilson to Sarah W. Caughran, December 16, 1851
          December 16, 1855, A. S. Sloan

Henry H. Dunn to Avorilah Cathrun, December 16, 1851
          December 18, 1851 By Saml. Boon, J.P. L.C.

Daniel Warren to Elizabeth Felps, December 17, 1851

Alfred W. Smith to Nancy Ann Clift, December 18, 1851
          December 18, 1851 Benjamin F. Clark, J.P.

Ira W. Beard to Racheal M. Martin, December 20, 1851
          December 22, 1851 By T. P. Sumners, J.P.

Aaron D. Trimble to Mary E. Whitman, December 22, 1851
          --   By Kimbrough, M.G.

Alfred O. Bivingham to Elvira Jane Ayres, December 22, 1851
          December 22, 1851 J. N. George, J.P.

Wm. B. Boughton to Eliza A. McGee, December 23, 1841
          December 25, 1851 J. A. Saintclair, J.P.

Elijah C. McLaughlin to Sarah A. Hart, December 24, 1851

(p 227)
Elisha S. Brown to Artimsey J. Brown, December 24, 1851
          December 25, 1851 By Saml. Boon J.P. for L.C.

John Warren to Sarah Prosser, December 27, 1851

Thos. C. Marks to Emmaranda J. Robinson, December 27, 1851
          December 30, 1851 D. D. Harwell

William W. Johnson to Mary Morris, December 29, 1851

Charles V. Fortune to Mary M. March, December 29, 1851
          December 31, 1851 Alexander Smith, M.G.

Benjamin Marshall to Hannah G. Ashby, December 31, 1851
          January 1, 1852 John Weaver, M.G.

William Moseley to Mary Keton. January 1, 1852
          January 1, 1852 Daniel Farrar, J.P.

William Buntley to Nancy Forester, January 3, 1852
          January 4, 1852 Amos Small, J.P.

Jackson C. Tinly to Mary Ann Murdock, January 5, 1852
                    January 5, 1852 Wm. Dyer, J.P.

David Smith to Elizabeth Creacy, January 10, 1852
                    January 11, 1852 James C. Stevenson

(p 228)
Jno. N. Moorehead to Mary E. Wagoner, January 12, 1852
                    January 12, 1852

John Cole to Nancy Reeves, January 12, 1852

Richard T. Marshall to Sarah C. Grills, January 12, 1852

P. L. Twitty to Evelen Templeton, January 15, 1852
                    January 15, 1852 A. G. Smith, M.G.

George W. Sanders to Mary C. Floyd, January 15, 1852
                    January 15, 1852 By A. S. Randolph, J.P.

William C. Bates to Margret E. Moyers, January 16, 1852

Silvester H. Wright to Amanda M. Swinebroad, January 24, 1852

William W. Fautner to Henretta Smith, January 24, 1852
                    January 25, 1852 By Jeremiah Dean, M.G.

Jesse Fraley to Sarah Ann Jackson, January 27, 1852

Alfred W. Dooley to Ana Hudson, January 27, 1852
                    January 28, 1852 A. G. Gibson, M.G.
(p 229)
Joe B. Smith to Leah C. Scroggins, February 2, 1852
                    February 5, 1852 B. F. Clark, J.P. L.C.

Wiley G. Burrow to Mary A. Crane, February 2, 1852

Flephaz Bearden to Cilea Cunningham, February 3, 1852

John Good to Elizabeth Mays, February 4, 1852
                    February 5, 1852 By A. S. Sloan

Joseph W. Winslow to Martha Warren, February 4, 1852

Shephard Rogers to Elizabeth Hester, February 6, 1852
                    February 6, 1852 John Wagster, M.G.

Joseph C. Hendrick to Martha A. Gill, February 9, 1852
                    February 9, 1852 By W. C. Dunlap

John D. White to Martha Gibson, February 5, 1852

Alexander Daves to Hannah Simmons, February 10, 1852
                    February 10, 1852 G. W. R. Moore, J.P.

(p 230)

Brice M. Abbott to Mary J. Dickey, February 11, 1852
                    February 11, 1852 R. Drennon, J.P.

Robt. J. Lively to Sarah Ann Good, February 14, 1852

Jacob Vanhoozer to M. A. J. Ballow, February 17, 1852
                    Febfuary 19, 1852 R. C. W. Puckett, M.G.

James Phillips to Martha Pinkerton, February 19, 1852
                    February 19, 1853 A. G. Downing, J.P.

Nicholas Copland to Phoda Easlick, February 21, 1852

William McGee to Mary Ann Photon, February 23, 1852
                    February 25, 1852 By Samuel Boon, J.P. (Seal)

James Sanders to Frances Vickers, February 23, 1852

William F. Taylor to Almeda E. Eaton, February 23, 1352
                    February 23, 1852 J. W. Holman, M.G.

John Spray to Nancy Canlin, February 24, 1852

Temple Lackey to Elizabeth Taylor, February 24, 1852

(p 231)

George W. Posey to Margaret Wiley, February 24, 1852

Jacob Cruise to Elizabeth C. Smith, February 28, 1852
                    February 29, 1852 W. C. Jennings, J.P.

Wm. Y. Taylor to Jinsey Scott, March 1, 1852
                    March 2, 1852 Tho. Williams, J.P.

Josiah Armstrong to Elizabeth Cook, March 3, 1852
                    March 4, 1852 A. G. Gibson, M.G.

Lewis L. W. Selleff to Malinda Morris, March 4, 1852
                    May 1, 1852 By J. P. Williams, M.G.

Charles W. Hodge to Susan F. Parkes, March 5, 1852

Thomas L. D. Midkiff to Mahaly Snow, March 10, 1852

John Montgomery to Melinda Jane Vickers, March 10, 1852
                    March 11, 1852 Wm. R. Morten, J.P.

Garrett Merrell to Ana Walker, March 11, 1852

Thomas H. Rawls to Alzny Moore, March 13, 1852
                    March 14, 1852 By John Moore, J.P.

Alfred L. Templeton to Mary Hobbs, March 18, 1852
                    March 18, 1852 By McHenry Sumners, M.G.

(p 232)

James Jewell to Martha Gilliland, March 18, 1852
                    March 18, 1852 Wm. R. Morten, J.P.

Muntford R. Townsen to Rilla Randolph, March 20, 1852
                    March 25, 1852 A. G. Downing, J.P.

Manson H. Caughran to Julia Buchanon, March 22, 1852
                    March 23, 1852 A. S. Sloan

Drury P. Land to Nancy R. Howell, March 23, 1852
                    March 25, 1852 By Wm. Pryor, J.P.

Saml. H. A. Roan to Lydia McDaniel, March 24, 1852
                    March 24, 1852 F. M. Ventress, J.P.

Robert McElvany to Emelen Cox, March 25, 1852

F. M. Dillon to Sarah C. Hancok, March 27, 1852
                    March 30, 1852 A. G. Gill, G. M.

W. W. Templeton to Lucy J. Bland, March 31, 1852
                    April 1, 1852 Robt. Drennon, J.P.

M. G. Williams to Sarah Ann Gunter, April 1, 1852
                    April 1, 1853 T. S. Williams, J.P.

(p 233)
George Cunningham Clerk County Court of Lincoln County, Sworn and entered
upon the duties of his office the 5th April 1852.

John T. Armstrong to Martha J. Hardy, April 6, 1852
                    April 7, 1853 A. Walker Morison

Pleasant Halbert to Emely Buchanan, April 8, 1852 (No. 2)
                    April 8, 1852 A. G. Smith, M.G.

Simon Hart to Vianna Bailey, April 17, 1852
                    April 18, 1852 By Rev. J. Scivally

Isham Wells to Nancy Ann Stanly, April 17, 1852
                    April 29, 1852 T. T. Sumners, J.P.

Charles W. Marshall to Martha Sanders, April 19, 1852
                    April 20, 1852 A. G. Downing, J.P.   L.C.(Seal)

Calvin Y. Douthit to Mary Jane Dunlap, April 20, 1852
                    April 20, 1852 Jas. N. George, J.P.

Saml. J. Wakefield to Nancy E. Payton, April 21, 1852

James R. Steelman to Mary Jane Whitaker, April 24, 1852
                    April 28, 1852 Amos Small, J.P.

John L. Jones to Mireah L. Wiley, April 27, 1852
                    April 27, 1852 W. H. Moores, J.P.

(p 234)

Thomas Howell to Rosena Shephard, April 28, 1852
                    April 28, 1852 William Land, M.G.

Bartlett Hindman to Sarah Pittman, April 30, 1852

Peter Warren to Eliza Wilkerson, April 30, 1852
                    April 30, 1852 Lewis Newson, J.P.

Jno. H. Roden to Mary M. Watson, May 1, 1852
                    May 3, 1852 T. T. Sumners, J.P.

F. G. Jandess to Natora Luck, May 1, 1852

Tillman Davis to Margaret Bailey, May 3, 1852
                    May 4, 1853 J. A. Saintclair, J.P.

William Claunch to Mary White, May 6, 1852
                    May 6, 1852 Wm. H. Moores, J.P.

David M. Gray to H. Caroline King, May 12, 1852
                    May 12, 1852 M. M. Marshall

John G. Enochs to Margaret F. Blackwell, May 15, 1852
                    May 20, 1852 By William G. Hensley, M.G.

James Claunch to Mary Jeans, May 18, 1852
                    May 20, 1852 By John Moores, J.P. for L.C.

(p 235)

William B. McKee to Bettie F. Gill, May 21, 1852
                    May 25, 1852 Allison Akin. M.G.

James S. Brown to Sarah Creck, May 27, 1852
                    May 27, 1852 Amos Small, J.P.

Wm. C. Coloman to Harriett Harrison, June 5, 1852

Joseph Surber to Rebecca K. Crawford, June 10, 1852

Henry F. Mills to Martha M. Pamplin, June 12, 1852
                    June 13, 1852 By Jno. L. Rosebrough, J.P.

James W. Mills to Sarah M. Wade, June 12, 1852
                    June 13, --   By Travis Ashby, J.P.

Walker Fox to Elizabeth Harper, June 17, 1852
                    June 17, 1852 By Lemuel Brandon

Francis M. Beard to Emily A. Cook, June 21, 1852

Adison H. Bishop to Louisa Clark, June 22, 1852

Riley W. Pitts to Susan F. C. George, June 22, 1852
                    June 22, 1852 John Wagster, M.G.

127

(p 236)

Robert Boyd to Elizabeth Pelcock, June 22, 1852
                    June 22, 1852 F. M. Ventress, J.P.

Wm. M. White to Margaret A. Buchanan, June 23, 1852
                    June 23, 1852 A. G. Smith, M.G.

Reuben Runnels to Elizabeth Sikes, June 28, 1852

A. W. Morrison to Julia Ann Hardy, July 3, 1852
                    July 6, 1852 By Rev. James Watson, M.G.

Wm. D. Gill to Jane Braden, July 5, 1852
                    July 8, 1852 John C. Reeves, J.P.

Bryant Mayers to Lempey Bates, July 6, 1852
                    July 6, 1852 By Travis Ashby, J.P.

A. V. Mills to Nancy Griffen, July 7, 1852
                    July 7, 1852 Jas. N. George, J.P.

Thomas Couch to Huldy Jane Taylor, July 8, 1852
                    July 8, 1852 Wm. C. Jennings. J.P.

America F. Stone to Nancy E. Bostick, July 8, 1852
                    July 9, 1852 D. Jacks, M.G.

Huston Hill to Rebecca A. Thurman, July 8, 1852
                    --   By W. B. Rhea, J.P.

Jas. A. Templeton to Mary Ann Dennis, July 8, 1852
                    July 8, 1852 F. M. V. Ventress, J.P. for L.C.
(p 237)
Wm. H. Reese to Hannah Dean, July 9, 1852
                    July 9, 1852 By Demcy Sullivan, J.P.

William Pearce to Mahala E. Coffee, July 10, 1852

Alfred Kiblecason to Mary Ann Adaline William, July 12, 1852
                    July 13, 1852 A. G. Downing, J.P.

Allen Davis to Elizabeth Phillips, July 12, 1852
                    July 12, 1852 John Cary, J.P. for L.C.

Jasper Ellis to Elizabeth A. McElroy, July 14, 1852
                    July 16, 1852 H. C. Cowen, J.P.

Matheas Rickets to Mary E. Harben, July 14, 1852
                    July 18, 1852 Wm. J. Grills, J.P.

William Faulkner to Elizabeth Smith, -- 1852

William G. Motlow to Sarah E. Gray, July 21, 1852
                    --   By J. W. Holman, M.G.

Asa Smith to Martha J. Perry, July 21, 1852

Edmond E. Hicks to Louisana Williams, July 22, 1852
                    July 22, 1852 Robert Drennon, J.P.

(p 238)
Thomas J. Scott to Elizabeth Jones Hester, July 27, 1852
                    July 27, 1852 G. W. R. Moor, J.P. L.C.

James E. Fulerton to Sarah A. Kennedy, July 29, 1852
                    July 29, 1852 T. W. Parkison

Francis M. McHaffy to Martha A. Smith, July 28, 1852
                    July 28, 1853 A. F. Driskill

William George to Mary A. E. D. Luttrell, July 31, 1852
                    August 1, 1852 T. S. Williams, J.P.

Joseph G. Pullin to Martha A. Dyer, July 31, 1852

William B. Fouville to Martha N. Blackwell, August 2, 1852
                    August 3, 1852 D. L. Mitchell, M.G.

Drury M. Perkins to Mariah H. Sherrell, August 3, 1852
                    August 24, 1852, Matt Marshall, M.G.

Logan Owen to Sina Franklin, August 4, 1852
                    August 5, 1852 By Amos Small, J.P.

Jehu Wadkins to Permela Burton, August 4, 1852

Isaac R. Pitts to Rebecca M. Ashby, August 5, 1852
                    August 5, 1852, A. S. Sloan

Robert P. Carman to Arrotter Bailey, August 5, 1852
                    August 8, 1852 John Wagster, M.G.

(p 239)
Wm. H. Gattis to Mary S. Brown, August 6, 1852
                    --   By J. W. Holmah, M.G.

Joseph Hopper to Milly Caton, August -- , 1852

James Roane to Jane M. King, August 7, 1852
                    August 8, 1852 James D. Cole, M.G.

James McBride to Rachael Roughton, August --, 1852
                    August 12, 1852 J. E. Douthitt, M.G.

Henry Holloway to Mary Marshall, August 14, 1852
                    August --, 1852 A. G. Downing, J.P.

Thos. J. Spence to Amanda West, August 18, 1852
                    August 19, 1852 Martin Towry, M.G.

Joseph George to Louvena Lackey, August 18, 1852
                    August 19, 1852 J. N. George, J.P.

Galen A. McKinney to Martha J. Wright, August 18, 1852
August 19, 1852 Wm. Dyer, J.P.

Daniel J. Watson to Mary Ann McAfee, August 23, 1852
August 23, 1852 By Woodruff Parks, J.P.

William C. Blackwell to Catherin B. Blake, August 24, 1852
August 25, 1852 D. L. Mitchell, M.G.

(p 240)
William A. Robertson to Sophia S. F. Emmons, August 24, 1852

William Smallman to Pounelia Williamson, August 30, 1852
August 30, 1852 B. M. G. Allsup, J.P.

James C. Pinkerton to Nancy J. Pinkerton, August 31, 1852

John M. Buchanan to Nancy B. Weaver, September 6, 1852
September 7, 1852 James N. George, J.P.

James Shelton to Syntha Story, September 6, 1852
September 6, 1852 Thomas Childs, M.G.

James H. Wright to Anna Trantham, September 9, 1852
September 9, 1852 S. M. Emmons, M.G.

Giles Davis to Elizabeth Warren, September 9, 1852

John S. Dusenberry to Susan J. James, September 11, 1852
September 13, 1852 J. W. Holman, M.G.

Byram L. R. Chem to Martha B. Gillun, September 13, 1852
September 15, 1852 D. Jacks, M.G.

P. G. Prosser to America Pruett, September 23, 1852
September 23, 1853 By Demcy Sullivan, J.P.

James H. Rhea to Elizabeth Jenkins, September 27, 1852

(p 241)
Samuel Hawkins to Minerva Williams, September 29, 1852
October 3, 1852 A. G. Downing, J.P.

Samuel Wakefield to Malinda James, September 30, 1852
September 30, 1852 By Wm. Dyer, J.P.

Robert Stevenson to Nancy Jeans, October 6, 1852
October 6, 1852 J. Moore, J.P.

A. S. Poone to Avarilla B. Shapard, October 4, 1853
October 4, 1853 A. F. Driskill

Giles Davis to Elizabeth Warren, September 9, 1852
September 9, 1852 Robert M. Whitman, M.G.

William Sumners to Sarah Camper, October 7, 1852

William Cramay to Frances L. Burton, October 7, 1852

William Snoddy to Clarenda Mason, October 8, 1852
                              October 8, 1852 Wm. Dyer, J.P.

Anderson Robertson to Mary Looney, October 8, 1852
                              November 14, 1852 John Weaver, M. G.

James Pearce to Mary Lindsey, October 11, 1852

Martin L. Parks to Elizabeth A. Edens, October 11, 1852

A. M. Galloway to Martha Spence, October 18, 1852

Jno. H. Timmins to Susan E. Whitaker, October 21, 1852
                              October 21, 1852 C. S. Knott, M.G.

John A. Bruce to Louisa Jane Coats, October 23, 1852
                              October 24, 1852 William R. Martin, J.P.

(p 242)
William J. Howard to Nancy O. Pruett, October 25, 1852

William H. Ashby to Mary E. Ramsay, November 2, 1852
                              November 2, 1852 By W. B. Rhea, J.P.

Alexander Bradey to Amanda M. Gattis, November 3, 1852
                  --   By J. W. Holman, M.G.

William M. Parr to Louisa Baily, November 10, 1852
                  --   By J. W. Holman, M.G.

John Mills to Nancy N. Reese, November 11, 1852

John Motlow to Elvena J. Green, November 15, 1852
                  --   J. W. Holman, M.G.

John L. Mitchell to Nancy J. Pardon, November 16, 1852
                              November 18, 1852 John Reed, J.P.

John A. Motlow to Eliza J. Womack, November 17, 1852

William H. Malden to Martha C. Tooley, November 17, 1852
                              November 18, 1852 William Dyer, J.P.

William Eakes to Jane George, November 20, 1852

(p 243)
Samuel Edmiston to Margaret F. Robinson, November 23, 1852
                              November 23, 1852 Thos. W. Randle, M.G.M.

J. H. Jobe to Sarah E. Scott, November 23, 1852

Daniel Farrar to Nancy Jane Owen, November 24, 1852
                              November 25, 1852 J. N. George, J.P.

Jefferson Phelps to Sarah Warren, November 23, 1852
                    November 25, 1852 By D. Sullivan, J.P.

James P. Williams to Rebecca J. Watson, November 25, 1852
                    November 25, 1852 Martin Towry, M.G.

Needham George to Emeline R. Coleman, November 25, 1852
                    November 28, 1852 James N. George, J.P.

Joseph Cashin to Catharin Parkes, November 25, 1852
                    --   J. W. Holman, M.G.

John R. McCombs to Susan C. Sorrells, November 26, 1852

Robert H. McMillen to Amanda J. Fulgham, November 29, 1852

George W. Blake to Henrietta Metcalf, November 30, 1852
                    December 1, 1852 D. L. Mitchell, M.G.
(p 244)
William C. Soloman to Susan McLaughlin, November 30, 1852
                    November 30, 1852 By W. B. Rhea, J.P.

James D. Cooper to Coralee Marr, December 1, 1852
                    December 2, 1852 By John Moore, J.P. for L.C.

William Crabtree to Nancy Foster, December 2, 1852
                    December 2, 1852 O. P. Hill, J.P. for L.C.

Alexander Timmons to Martha J. Parkes, December 6, 1852

Davidson Renegar to Sarah Buchanan, December 9, 1852
                    December 9, 1852 William R. Mart, J.P. L.C.

Wm. C. Ray to Matilda Stegall, --
                    December 9, 1852 Stephen M. Dance, M.G.

Leroy Carpenter to Evalen Mattox, December 11, 1852

William L. Easley to Eloza J. Abernathy, December 15, 1852
                    December 16, 1852 James C. Stevenson

Wiley J. Pitts to Mary Ann Allbright, --
                    December 16, 1852 A. S. Randolph, J.P. for L.C.

Abner S. McGee to Mary A. Marshall, December 20, 1852
                    December 23, 1852 By Samuel Boone, J.P. for L.C.
(p 245)
D. B. Sholl to Sarah L. Higgins, December 20, 1852
                    December 23, 1852 R. B. McGough, M.G.

James P. Forsythe to Margaret McBay, December 22, 1852
                    December 23, 1852 By John Reed, J.P.

George A. Craig to Jane Murphy, December 22, 1852
                    December 23, 1852 G. W. R. Moores, J.P.

homas Norman to Julia Lindsey, December 26, 1852
                    December 26, 1852 By John Corder, J.P.

. T. Cates to Jane Reeves, December 28, 1852

amuel D. Pruett to Catharine A. Dunphney, December 28, 1852
                    December 29, 1852 Jas. L. Thomson, J.P.

arol C. Harden to Phenas Ann Counts, December 28, 1852
                    --   By J. P. Williams

ames Cox to Sarah Rennegar, December 29, 1852
                    December 30, 1852 Samuel Boone, J.P.

avid S. Buchanan to Nancy Douthett, December 30, 1852
                    December 30, 1852 Thomas Childs, M.G.

obt. D. Harden to Eliza M. Ewing, December 31, 1852
                    January 6, 1853 By Rev. James Kirkland

illiam F. Lynch to Frances E. Woodward, January 1, 1853

. G. Sawyers to Eliza Whitaker, January 3, 1853
                    January 4, 1853 B. F. Clark, J.P.

tephen F. Spencer to Margaret J. Smith, January 6, 1853
                    January 7, 1853 John Copland, M.G.

p 246)
rancis M. Fannon to Elizabeth J. Echoles, January 5, 1853
                    January 6, 1853 Young T. Taylor, J.P.

arrison Hanks to Malinda Upton, January 6, 1853
                    January 6, 1853 R. Forguherson, J.P.

acob Buntley to Elizabeth Forester, January 8, 1853
                    January 9, 1853 John Vagster, M.G.

asper Tankesly to Harriett Raney, January 8, 1853

ames Price to Sarah E. Faulkenberry, January 11, 1853
                    January 11, 1853 A. S. Randolph, J.P. for L.C.

illiam D. Chick to Sarah D. Sumnerford, January 13, 1853
                    January 13, 1853 John Vagster, M.G.

athan J. Thompson to Charity J. Noles, January 18, 1853
                    January 24, 1853 Young T. Taylor, J.P.

. N. McClure to Martha J. Lesley, January 19, 1853
                    January 20, 1853 John Reed, J.P.

eter Ellis to Diana Rickets, January 21, 1853
                    January 23, 1853 By John Moore, J.P.

ohn H. Mills to Tempy Mansfield, January 25, 1853
                    January 26, 1853 By Dancy Sullivan, J.P.

(p 247)
John C. Hanks to Delena Buchanan, January 27, 1853
                    January 27, 1853 R. Farguharson, J.P.

Thomas M. Lane to Elizabeth E. Cannon, January 31, 1853
                    --   By J. W. Holman, M.G.

Errin M. McAdams to Elizabeth S. Sanders, January 31, 1853
                    February 3, 1853 By Jno. McDaniel. J.P.

William Smith to Cassena McFarin, February 1, 1853
                    March 24, 1853 By A. S. Sloan

William T. Caughran to Luvina E. Drennon, February 14, 1853
                    February 15, 1853 By A. S. Sloan

Willis L. Dodwell to Sisly Ann Davis, February 14, 1853
                    February 14, 1853 John Wagster, M.G.

Isaac Hays to Delenia A. McRee, February 16, 1853
                    February 16, 1853 P. W. Walton, J.P.

David L. Smith to Louisa Smith, February 17, 1853
                    February 17, 1853 A. S. Randolph, J.P. L.C.

Hardy Reavis to Elizabeth Brown, February 17, 1853
                    February 17, 1853 J. W. Tarant, M.G.

E. S. N. Bobo to E. G. Landess, February 19, 1853
                    --   J. W. Holman, G.M.

(p 248)
James Wilburn to Nancy C. Walker, February 21, 1853
                    February 23, 1853 Wm. A. Gill, M.G.

Wiley A. Hobbs to Amanda Eddins, February 21, 1853
                    --   J. W. Holman, G.M.

William Prosser to Elizabeth Creson, February 23, 1853
                    February 23, 1853 By Demcy Sullivan, J.P.

B. F. Smith to Nancy King, February 26, 1853
                    February 27, 1853 By Ths. P. Sumners, J.P.

James W. Luter to Martha Jane Irvin, February 26, 1853
                    February 27, 1853 H. R. Bray, M.G.

Nathan Curry to Sarah Chapman. March 3, 1853
                    March 3, 1853 By Lemuel Brandon

Elijah A. Bray to Mary I. J. Barker, March 3, 1853
                    March 3, 1853 W. C. Jennings. J.P.

George W. Sims to Martha Land, March 5, 1853
                    March 8, 1853 William Pryor, J.P.

John Merrell to Margaret R. Anderson, March 8, 1853

Daniel T. Wiliburn to Miry E. Tate, March 9, 1853
March 10, 1853 By Rev. Jas. Kirkland, G.M.

(p 249)
William M. Freeman to America Fannon, March 10, 1853
March 15, 1853 By Woodruff Parkes, J.P.

William F. Williams to Rebecca Nepp, March 12, 1853
March 13, 1853 P. W. Walton, J.P.

Sebron Evans to Jane Wilkins, March 16, 1853
March 16, 1853 Robert Drennon, J.P.

Asa S. Reddick to Martha A. Gledwell, March 24, 1853
March 24, 1853 Robert Whitman, M.G.

Rufus A. McGee to Eliza Locker, March 24, 1853
March 24, 1853 F. M. Ventress, J.P.

Joal B. Smith to Elizabeth Tell, April 5, 1853
April --, 1853 By S. M. Cowen, V.D.M.

David J. Revis to Clarasa Brown, April 7, 1853
--   J. W. Tarrant, M.G.

William M. Todd to Mary O. Bagley, April 12, 1853
April 12, 1853 W. C. Dunlap, M.G.

David Parker to Susan E. Grisard, April 18, 1853
April 19, 1853 C. H. Remington, M.G.

Daniel Warden to Mary Little, April 21, 1853
April 21, 1853 J. W. Tarrant, M.G.

(p 250)
S. H. Kimes to S. A. Sawyers, April 23, 1853
April 24, 1853 A. G. Gibson, M.G.

Brice Dillingham to Sarah M. Woodward, April 30, 1853

James M. Davis to Mary J. Pradford, May 10, 1853
May 1, 1853 A. G. Smith

William Wilson to Mary A. Freeman, May 7, 1853
May 8, 1853, John Wagster, M.G.

C. H. Remington to Mary F. Ellis, May 7, 1853
May 12, 1853 J. W. Holman, M.G.

Luther M. Pilant to Caladena Fowler, May 17, 1853

Alven Tucker to Susannah George, May 21, 1853
May 24, 1853 Jas. N. George, J.P.

Hiram Commons to Mary M. Woodward, May 21, 1853
May 22, 1853 John Carey, J.P. L.C.

Freeman Burrow to Louisa C. Nichols, May 28, 1853
                    May 28, 1853   G. W. R. Moore, J.P.   L.C.

John W. Webb to Margaret M. Philpot, June 6, 1853
                    June 7, 1853   Jas. N. George, J.P.   L.C.

(p 251)
A. S. Duval to Mary Ringo, June 7, 1853
                    --   M. Marshall, G.M.

William Thompson to Nancy Ann Fox, June 15, 1853
                    June 16, 1853   A. Walton, J.P.

James C. Pylant to Lydia B. Bonner, June 16, 1853
                    --   M. Marshall

John H. Brady to Elizabeth Shires, June 20, 1853
                    June 20, 1853   S. M. Emmons, M.G.

Druory Richardson to Mary J. Wade, June 22, 1853
                    June 23, 1853   By Demps Sullivan, J.P.

Patrick Thompson to Mary Pully, June 23, 1853
                    August 2, 1853   T. H. Freeman, J.P.

William S. Harris to Nancy Ann Pickle, June 25, 1853
                    June 26, 1853   O. T. Hill, J.P.   L.C.

F. Ennis to Mary E. Walace, June 26, 1853
                    June 26, 1856   S. M. Cowen, V.D.M.

William Steelman to Nancy B. Bearden, June 27, 1853
                    June 29, 1853   John Wagster, M.G.

Jacob P. Wright Jr. to Harriett Collins, June 28, 1853
                    June 30, 1853   B. M. G. Allsup, J.P.

(p 252)
Pleasant H. Tucker to Margaret J. George, June 30, 1853
                    June 30, 1853   By John W. Braden, J.P.

Thomas P. Roughton to Sarah T. Landers, June 30, 1853

Joseph S. Clark to Laura Ann Walker, June 30, 1853
                    June 30, 1853   William Pryor, J.P.

G. B. Keller to J. C. Blackburn, July 4, 1853
                    July 4, 1853   John Corder, J.P. for L.C.

Joseph T. Moore to Nancy Ann Ashby, July 4, 1853
                    July 5, 1853   Samuel Boone, J.P.   L.C.

James W. Smith to Marilla E. Fox, July 9, 1853
                    July 10, 1853   By Lemuel Brandon, M.G.

Jacob Blue to Sealy Abel, July 13, 1853
                    July 13, 1853   Robert Drennon, J.P.

John C. Stacy to Sarah Jane Sullivan, July 20, 1853
                    July 21, 1853 Lewis Newsom, J.P.

S. P. Vess to Frances Joiner, July 23, 1853
                    June 3, 1853 T. H. Freeman, J.P.

James Broadaway to Martha Caskey, July 24, 1853
                    July 26, 1853 W. Dyer, J.P.

(p 253)
Theodore G. Smith to Elizabeth McElroy, July 27, 1853
                    July 28, 1853 R. Farguharson, J.P.

T. M. McHuffey to Martha A. Smith, July 28, 1853

R. H. Mitchel to Eliza C. Hamilton, August 1, 1853
                    August 4, 1853 Jacob Nare, J.P. L.C.

Asa Oliver to Mary Eadens, August 3, 1853
                    August 4, 1853 By Demps Sullivan, J.P.

James Dooley to Mary Washburn, August 6, 1853
                    August 7, 1853 A. G. Gibson, M.G.

Daniel B. McAnn to Martha Ann Hunt, August 8, 1853
                    August 8, 1853 Wm. E. Martin, J.P. (Seal)

Archibald Johnson to Emily H. Pamplin, August 9, 1853
                    August 10, 1853 By Woodruff Parks, J.P.

Augus D. Johnson to Elizabeth J. Alexander, August 10, 1853
                    August 11, 1853 By Woodruff Parks, J.P.

Jerome B. Brady to Nancy E. Owen, August 11, 1853
                    August 11, 1853 By W. R. Hedgpeth

David J. Heflin to Maranda C. Hester, August 11, 1853
                    August 11, 1853 G. W. R. Moore, J.P.

(p 254)
 John S. Dickey to Elizabeth B. Gleghorn, August 11, 1853
                    August 11, 1853 T. W. Parkerson

Andrew Morgan to Polly Ann Raney, August 13, 1853
                    August 21, 1853 By Jeremiah Dean, M.G.

James Forester to Rebeca Taylor, August 8, 1853
                    August 11, 1853 By Demps Sullivan, J.P.

Samuel B. Galloway to Jane McCown, August 16, 1853

John Smith to Nancy M. Cunningham, August 22, 1853
                    August 24, 1853 O. P. Hill, J.P. for L.C.

William W. Butler to America J. Gibbs, August 22, 1853

Daniel Harrison to Eliza E. Cunningham, August 22, 1853
                    September 10, 1853   Jas. N. George, J.P.

Richard O. Hooper to Manerva Dexden, August 22, 1853
                    August 24, 1853   Jacob Gillespie, J.P.

Calvin W. Drenon to America Abbott, August 22, 1853
                    August 24, 1853   A. S. Randolph, J.P. for L.C.

Mark Purdom to Eglentine Neece, August 25, 1853
                    August 25, 1853   By Demps Sullivan, J.P.

(p 255)
William Edmiston to Mary M. Kilptrick, August 25, 1853
                    August 26, 1853   Young Taylor, J.P.

Thomas Look to Nancy Jane Stephens, September 6, 1853
                    September 6, 1853   A. G. Downing, J.P. for L.C.
                                        (Seal)

Marcus C. Taylor to Lettitia L. Raymond, September 7, 1853
                    September 7, 1853   By A. S. Sloan

A. J. McCollum to Mary A. Buchanan, September 7, 1853
                    September 8, 1853, A. G. Gipson, M.G.

Thomas A. Clark to Mary Ann Drown, September 7, 1853
                    September 8, 1853   Amos Small, J.P.

George W. Milliken to Caroline Reed, September 15, 1853
                    September 15, 1853   By T. F. Sumners, J.P.

Henry Jacobs to Martha E. Harper, September 12, 1853
                    September 12, 1854   Thos. Childs, M.G.

William H. Ellis to Jennett Rigg, September 15, 1853
                    September 15, 1853   By Wm. Dyer, J.P.

T. R. W. Crane to Susan C. Sorrells, September 15, 1853
                    September 15, 1853   G. W. R. Moore, J.P.

D. F. Smith to Mary M. J. Miller, September 17, 1853
                    September 18, 1853   F. Motlow, J.P.
(p 256)
Benjamin B. Ingle to Martha A. Dusenberry, September 19, 1853
                    September 20, 1853   By Samuel Boone, J.P.

Jasper S. Holman to Margaret A. E. Gibson, September 22, 1853
                    September 22, 1853   S. M. Cowen, V. D. M.

Isaac Vanhoozer to Nancy Ann Simpson, September 25, 1853
                    September 25, 1853   By Jacob Nare, J.P.

Nelson Yarborough to Sarah McWhorter, September 24, 1853
                    September 25, 1853   Thomas S. Williams, J.P.

John W. Allen to Tennessee W. Campbell, September 26, 1853

S. B. Fisk to Catharine E. Feld, September 26, 1853
                    September 26, 1853 S. M. Emors. M.C.

Thomas N. Ashby to E. Tennessee Conaway, September 27, 1853

Francis T. Fulton to Martha Edmiston, September 28, 1853
                    September 29, 1853 Matt Marshall, M.G.

Ansolem M. Brown to Nancy J. Hutson, September 29, 1853
                    September 29, 1853 B. B. McGough, M.G.

John Dillingham to Lucy E. Woodward, October 1, 1853
                    October 2, 1853 Lemuel Brandon, M.G.

(p 257)
John M. McFarin to Mary A. G. Spence, October 3, 1853

W. J. Womack to Elizabeth Ward, October 3, 1853
                    October 6, 1853 J. E. Douthit, M.G.

Robert Davis to Rutha Lee, October 4, 1853
                    October 4, 1853 B. M. G. Allsup, J.P.

A. S. Boone to Avarila E. Shapard, October 4, 1853
                    (See October 1852)

Alexander Smith to Mary Rone, October 4, 1853
                    October 6, 1853 F. M. Ventress, J.P.

Absolem Beard to Sarah Marshall, October 8, 1853
                    October 9, 1853 By John Moore, J.P.

David G. Butler to Mary J. Merrell, October 10, 1853
                    October 10, 1853 Jas. N. George, J.P.

John S. Deal to Eliza A. Marlow, October 12, 1853
                    October --, 1853 By John Copland

William Y. Nix to F. A. Pierce, October 12, 1853
                    October 13, 1853 Young T. Taylor

William E. McHaffey to Caroline Satterfield, October 13, 1853

Basdel C. Cathrine to Rebecca A. Duncan, October 18, 1853
                    October 18, 1853 By Travis Ashby, J.P.

(p 258)
Franklin D. Branson to Francis Vickers, October 22, 1853
                    October 22, 1853 A. S. Pandolph, J.P. for L.C.

William A. Walker to Mary E. Hamilton, October 24, 1853
                    October 27, 1853 A. J. Steel, M.G.

James H. Armstrong to Susan F. Hudson, October 27, 1853
                    October 27, 1853 Howell Harris, J.P.

William T. Moyers to Martha J. Rowe, October 27, 1853
          --   Matt Marshall, M.G.

Nathaniel Taylor to Marth Brown. October 29, 1853
                October 30, 1853 By Samuel Boone, J.P. for L.C.

Morgan E. Conaway to Martha A. Ashby, October 30, 1853

William Askins to E. A. Whitaker, October 31, 1853
                November 3, 1853 By A. S. Sloan

J. A. Burton to T. Cavet, October 31, 1853
                October 31, 1853 H. C. Holman, J.P.

Henry T. Fason to Martha A. Browning, November 2, 1853
                November 4, 1853 G. M. Pucket, M.G.

William J. Lively to Sally T. Floyd, November 2, 1853
                November 2, 1853 H. C. Cowen, J.P.

(p 259)
John M. Pigg to Mary Ramsey, November 3, 1853
                November 3, 1853 Orin P. Hill, J.P.

John E. Neece to Elizabeth Steelman, November 5, 1853
                November 6, 1853 Lewis Newsom, J.P.

Thomas Stovall to Moolda F. Smith, November 5, 1853
                November 10, 1853 By Jacob Nare, J.P.

E. A. Call to Susan A. Timmons, November 7, 1853

J. D. Reed to P. J. Williams, November 7, 1853
                November 9, 1853 A. H. Bishop, G.M.

John Felps to Luretha A. Winstead, November 9, 1853
                November 10, 1853 By Samuel Boone, J.P.

John Colman Boyles to Martha J. Leatherwood
                November 10, 1853 Jacob Nare, J.P.

Thos. A. Hazlewood to Mary J. Crenshaw, November 10, 1853

James B. Price to Mary C. Gore, November 12, 1853
                November 17, 1853 By Ira F. Douthitt, M.G.

Thomas H. Bledsoe to Elizabeth S. Hamilton, November 14, 1853
                November 14, 1853 A. G. Smith, M.G.

(p 260)
George W. Alexander to Mary J. Shores, November 14, 1853
                November 15, 1853 By S. M. Cowen, V.D.M.

A. D. Anderson to Sarah Ann Bledsoe, November 17, 1853

Hiram F. Freeman to Delia A. Wakefield, November 20, 1853
                November 20, 1853 By William Dyer, J.P.

Frances A. Thompson to Paralee Jane Strong, November 21, 1853
                    November 23, 1853   By Young T. Taylor, J.P.

William C. Brantley to Sarah Ann Crunk, November 21, 1853
                    November 22, 1853   D. L. Mitchell, M.G.

John M. Smith to Elizabeth A. Gracey, November 24, 1853
                    --   M. Marshall, G.M.

William A. Rhoads to Josephine Smith, November 26, 1853
                    November 30, 1853   William R. Martin, J.P. (Seal)

William Gattis to Mary Burton, November 30, 1853

George N. Tankesly to Caroline Jane Bowles, December 3, 1853

Gideon J. Hamby to Rebecca Warren, December 3, 1853
                    December 4, 1853   Saml. Boon, J.P.

(p 261)
Elijah Floyd to Martha E. D. Phillips, December 8, 1853
                    December 8, 1853   H. C. Cowen, J.P.

A. J. Renegar to Martha J. Thompson, December 12, 1853

Malich B. Land to Emeline Cole, December 15, 1853
                    December 15, 1853   Amos Small, J.P. for L.C.

Newton Hamilton to Lucinda C. Abernathy, December 17, 1853

William B. McMillen to Nancy M. Spence, December 19, 1853

Jackson Smith to Coladonia Cowen, December 20, 1853
                    December 20, 1853   By F. M. Ventress, J.P.

Thomas Timmons to Susan A. Hamilton, December 22, 1853
                    December 22, 1853   John Mathews

Dozier T. Weaver to Alice M. Reddingfield, December 22, 1853
                    December 22, 1853   John W. Braden, J.P. for L.C.
                                        (Seal)

Henry L. Smith to Amanda M. McClure, December 22, 1853

Austin Raslick to Ann Cashin, December 22, 1853
                    December 22, 1853   W. M. Newman, J.P.

(p 262)
N. P. Hedgepeth to Catharin Strong, December 22, 1853
                    December 22, 1853   William R. Hedgepeth, J.P.

James S. Sumners to Martha Wright, December 27, 1853
                    December 29, 1853   By Jacob Nare, J.P.

Newton Dickey to Amanda Abbott, December 29, 1853
                    December 29, 1853   Robert Drennon, J.P.   L.C.

William R. Smith to Martha Jane Shull, December 29, 1853
December 29, 1853 John Mathews, M.G.

Levi W. Hazzellwood to Amanda M. Duke, January 4, 1854

George W. Trim to Caroline Foster, January 7, 1854

R. B. Gibson to Jane Rebecca Walier, January 12, 1854
January 12, 1854 A. G. Gibson, M.G.

James F. Forsyth to Sarah Snow, January 13, 1854

James S. Maupin to America W. Whitaker, January 17, 1854

David Luttrell to Eliza Jane Blackwell, January 17, 1854
January 18, 1854 L. H. Freeman, J.P.

(p 263)
Jesse Marbery to Nancy Catharine Elam, January 19, 1854
January 19, 1854 Robert Drennon, J.P.

James McCoy to Elizabeth Files, January 23, 1854
January 23, 1854 Jacob Gillespie, J.P.

Alfred Williams to Minerva E. Bowols, January 24, 1854
January 26, 1854 Joseph Dean, J.P.

William T. Darnell to Mary Ann Rhoden, January 30, 1854
February 18, 1854 By G. M. Pucket, M.G.

Milton A. Edminston to Susan K. Williams, January 30, 1854
February 2, 1854 Wm. Dyer, J.P.

William E. Hunter to Sarah Ann Ellis, January 31, 1854
February 1, 1854 Orrin P. Hill, J.P.

William W. Eaton to Sarah Ann Little, February 2, 1854
February 5, 1854 Samuel Boon, J.P.

Jesse Claunch to Nancy Womack, February 6, 1854

John P. A. Coble to Martha Ann Smith, February 7, 1854
February 7, 1854 By Jno. Corder, J.P.

George W. Murry to Charity Burrow, February 7, 1854
February 7, 1854 By G. W. R. Moore, J.P.

George Brewer to Louisa Tucker, February 11, 1854
February 11, 1854 H. C. Cowen, J.P.

(p 264)
William H. Taylor to Mary Jane Kenedy, February 13, 1854
February 14, 1854 By Thomas W. Parkerson

James H. Deford to Margaret Jane Allen, February 13, 1854
February 16, 1854 By Thos. W. Parkerson

Jesse J. Price to Mary A. W. Gray, February 14, 1854
February 16, 1854, J.L. Thompson, J.P. for L.C.

Holly R. Williamson to Susan D. Tetty, February 15, 1854
February 16, 1854 William Pryor, J.P.

Hugh T. Terry to Mary B. Morton, February 15, 1854
February 15, 1854 By Thos. W. Parkerson

Cyrus L. Cathy to Eliza Russell, February 16, 1854
February 16, 1854 Matt Marshall, M.G.

William E. McHaffy to Sarah Cason, February 16, 1854
February 16, 1854 Wm. Land

Drewry Wells to Jane Scott, February 16, 1854
February 19, 1854 By H. H. Rivers, J.P.

Wiley G. Milam to Martha E. Bland, February 21, 1854
February 23, 1854 Wm. R. Martin, J.P. for L.C.

N. O. Green to Martha A. Fulton, February 21, 1854
February 22, 1854 By S. M. Cowen, V.D.M.

Thomas Y. Wallace to Mary E. Wiley, March 1, 1854
March 1, 1854 A. H. Bishop, M.G.

(p 265)
David C. Craig to Martha P. Greer, March 1, 1854
March 2, 1853 Matt Marshall, M.G.

George T. Price to Sarah A. Hatchell, March 2, 1854
March 2, 1854 H. C. Holman, J.P.

Joab Neal to Cyntha A. Smith, March 6, 1854
March 26, 1854 Young T. Taylor, J.P.

Jonathan E. Spencer to Nancy Ann Waggoner, March 6, 1854
March 6, 1854 John Copeland, M.G.

Thomas B. Lackey to Sarah Ann Stewart, March 14, 1854

J. C. Irvin to Josephine Davis, March 13, 1854
March 15, 1854 By J. B. Warren, M.G.

Andrew J. Fannon to Malissa Noles, March 15, 1854
March 19, 1854 Young Taylor, J.P.

James T. Beach to Mary E. Sanford, March 18, 1854
March 19, 1854 A. H. Bishop, G.M.

Benjamin J. Noles to Martha E. Noles, March 22, 1854
March 27, 1854 Young Taylor, J.P.

Calvin Smith to Dessa Cannon, March 22, 1854
March 22, 1854 Robt. Drennon, J.P.

Joseph Holt to Mary Jenkins, March 24, 1854
August 23, 1854 By John Bramblet

(p 266)
Isaac R. Pitts to Elvira Reese, March 26, 1845
March 26, 1854 G. H. R. Bray, M.G.

William V. Womack to Catharin S. Bailey, March 28, 1854

John McClure to Susan Hunt, March 29, 1854
March 29, 1854 Wm. C. Jennings, J.P.

Eli Townsend to Susan E. McKee, March 29, 1854
--   30, 1854 Wm. A. Gill, G.M.

Greek T. Rice to M. J. Irwin, March 30, 1854
March 30, 1854 By M. Marshall, M.G.

Edward Smith to Margaret Ann Gray, April 3, 1854

John W. Franklin to Dolpha Ann Fannon, April 5, 1854
April 6, 1854 W. R. Carter, J.P.

Jacob Renegar to Sarah C. Taylor, April 5, 1854
April 6, 1854 By C. R. White, J.P.

Thos. Whitaker to Martha Shofner, April 6, 1854

Lewis Spray to Eliza Billens, April 6, 1854
April 6, 1854 John Caughran, J.P.

(p 267)
David Whitt to Susan J. Browning, April 8, 1854
April 8, 1854 By G. W. Puckett, M.G.

Joel S. Brewer to Nancy B. Tamplin, April 11, 1854
April 11, 1854 H. C. Holeman, J.P.

James W. Tamplin to Nancy Ann Tamplin, April 13, 1854
April 15, 1854 By M. W. Yant, J.P.

John B. Hardy to Pheobe C. Horwood, April 19, 1854
April 20, 1854 A. G. Gibson, M. G.

V. M. Rhyne to Joseph Duckworth, April 20, 1854
April 20, 1854 Jacob Gillespie, J.P.

J. G. Prosser to Martha Jane Barham, April 22, 1854
April 23, 1854 G. W. R. Moore, J.P. for L.C.

B. R. Melear to Elizabeth F. Kimes, April 26, 1854
April 26, 1854 By J. B. Warren, M.G.

Thomas M. Blakemore to Virginia F. Smith, April 26, 1854
June 11, 1854 H. H. Rivers, J.P.

Calvin Harris to Amanda Jane Vinson, April 27, 1854

G. F. Ison to Syntha C. McAfee, April 27, 1854
April 30, 1854 M. W. Yant, Esqr.

George W. Gattis to Mary Jane Mitchel, April 29, 1854
May 2, 1854 By William Gattis, J.P.

(p 268)
Wm. F. Watson to Mary Ann Gillam, May 11, 1854
May 11, 1854 John Roach, J.P.

Wm. G. Sexton to Mary Ann Sanderson, May 15, 1854
May 16, 1854 G. M. Pucket, M.G.

George Edmison to Ann Eliza Kasey, May 16, 1854
May 16, 1854 W. F. Holman, J.P.

Harden Wardon to Mary Keith, May 23, 1854
May 27, 1854 Joseph Smith, M.G.

Jas. N. Bland to Permelia S. Smith, May 24, 1854
May 25, 1854 By William Gayle

W. L. Shelton to Sarah F. Whitworth, May 27, 1854
May 30, 1854 --

Wm. D. Faulkenbury to Jane Dillions, May 29, 1854
May 29, 1854 By John Caughran, J.P.

H. F. Dusenberry to Ann James, June 2, 1854
June 6, 1854 By Lemuel Brandon, M.G.

F. A. Fucher to Tempe Forester, June 3, 1854
June 4, 1854 N. W. Wyat, Esqr.

D. Womack to Lannet Keller, July 3, 1854

(p 269)
N. B. Pierce to Margaret V. George, July 3, 1854
July 4, 1854 John Copland, M.G.

C. J. McKinney to S. E. Reid, July 3, 1854
July 4, 1854 B. M. Allsup, J.P.

Jas. B. Carty to S. E. W. Elliott, -- 1854
July 4, 1854 William Pryor, J.P.

Elisha Womack to Laurett Keller, July 3, 1854
July 16, 1854 L. Maltom, J.P.

J. B. Marshall to Bethena Pitts, July 4, 1854
July 4, 1854 M. W. Yant, J.P.

Wm. W. Stringer to Barbary Parrish, July 6, 1854

Eli Evans to Mary M. Waggoner, July 17, 1854
July 18, 1854 John L. Ashby, J.P.

Alexander Hamilton to Synnica A. Boles, July 17, 1854
July 18, 1854 L. Jacks, M.G.

William Heathcook to Elmina Heathcock, July 17, 1854

Campbell Douthett to Elisabeth Fox, July 24, 1854
--   J. W. Holman, M.G.

Jas. H. Sanders to Louisa J. Hedgepeth, July 24, 1854
July 25, 1854 Henry Turney, J.P.

(p 270)
David J. Kimes to Mary G. M. Daniel, July 25, 1845

Lewis A. Colbert to Martha E. Jones, July 27, 1845

Alexander Edmunson to Catharine Alley, July 27, 1854
July 29, 1854 B. Christian, J.P.

Navis Flynt to Sophronia Easlick, August 3, 1854
August 3, 1854 B. Christian, J.P.

J. E. Humphreys to M. E. Cummins, August 3, 1854
August 3, 1854 A. G. Smith, M.G.

Samuel Smith to Sarah Mitchell, August 5, 1854

S. A. Slaughter to Josephine Edmiston, August 7, 1854
August 9, 1854 By S. M. Cowen, V.D.M.

John M. Buchanan to Eliza J. Williamson, August 12, 1854
August 16, 1854 By S. M. Emmons, M.G.

James L. Moorehead to Mary Spencer, August 14, 1854
August 15, 1854 John Copland, M.G.

Joseph Holt to Mary Jenkins, August 23, 1854

(p 271)
Jas. L. Dickson to Martha Barker, August 24, 1854
August 24, 1854 B. Christian, J.P.

John Letteral to Mandana E. Cox, August 26, 1854
August 29, 1854 B. Christian, J.P.

Wm. B. Roughton to Martha C. Pegram, August 26, 1854
September 10, 1854 By Demsey Sullivan

Wm. A. Findly to Isabelar Murdock, August 29, 1854
September 1, 1854 W. H. McRee, M.G.

Jas. Lane to Martha Cuningham, August 30, 1854
April 30, 1854 Orrin P. Hill, J.P.

William M. Scott to Virginia F. Wells, September 2, 1854
September 4, 1854, Jacob Gillespie, J.P.

J. W. Caney to Lyda Jane Coller, September 4, 1854
          September 4, 1854 Robt. M. Chilman

Rufus K. Smith to Unice C. Casey, September 7, 1854
          September 7, 1854 B. Christian, J.P.

Thos. D. Adverton to Nancy E. Rheah, September 4, 1854
          September 7, 1854 Jaron Ray, M.G.

John Bonner to Mary Jane Clark, September 4, 1854
          --   By William N. Hicks, J.P.

(p 272)
John R. Johnson to Rebeca Ann Buchanan, September 8, 1854
          September 7, 1854 A. G. Smith, M.G.

Nathan Boone to Orpha Johnston, September 9, 1854
          September 10, 1854 By Jo Smith, M.G.

William A. Brown to Milly A. Landess, September 11, 1854
          September 13, 1854 John A. Jones

Thos P. Arnold to Mariah Stanley, September 12, 1854
          September 21, 1854 B. Christian, J.P.

L. L. Leftwich to Elisabeth Reese, September 12, 1854

John R. Hague to Margaret S. McGhee, September 13, 1854
          --   B. McGaugh, M.G.

Henry Green Swinebrand to Martha Ann Wilson, September 14, 1854
          September 14, 1854 By J. B. Warren, M.G.

A. G. H. Brandon to Hester R. Simpson, September 20, 1854
          --   By J. M. Holman, M.G.

Samuel Crabtree to Charlotte Stephenson, September 21, 1854
          September 21, 1854 John Roach, J.P.

George P. Stephens to Nancy Wells, September 21, 1854
          October 2, --   By Rev. Jo Smith

(p 273)
Alerin Bates to Elizabeth Gail, September 22, 1854
          September 23, 1854 R. D. Hardin, J.P.

James Roland to Nancy Miles, September 22, 1854

Daniel B. McCann to Mary Ann Maroney, September 22, 1854
          September 24, 1854 R. D. Hardin, J.P.

Jas. McCartney to Mary E. Lillen, September 25, 1854

Saml. C. McCollum to Elizabeth Armstrong, September 26, 1854
          September 28, 1854 Howell Harris, J.P.

James F. Sanford to Elisabeth Smith, September 27, 1854
                    September 27, 1854   Robt. Brennon, J.P.

Soloman Mason to Mary E. Scoggins, September 27, 1854
                    September 27, 1854   John Caughran, J.P.

Davis Smith to Elinor M. Robeson, September 29, 1854
                    October 1, 1854   B. M. G. Allsup, J.P.

Joseph M. Wakefield to Elizabeth S. Wright, October 2, 1854
                    October 10, 1854   B. F. Ments, L.D.

Martin Smith to Elisabeth H. Majors, October 4, 1854
                    October 5, 1854   D. S. Patterson, J.P. for L.C.

(p 274)
Daniel W. Sanders to Louisa Jane Griffin, October 6, 1854
                    October 7, 1854   W. L. Beene, J.P.

Jasper Dickey to Pheby E. Bradford, October 11, 1854
                    October 11, 1854   A. H. Bishop, G.M.

John Hill to Catharine McGeehee, October 11, 1854
                    October 12, 1854   Nicholas Copeland, J.P.

David F. Brown to Altalitha C. Howell, October 13, 1854
                    October 13, 1854   Smith L. Walker, J.P.

A. J. Hamilton to Narcissa Stone, October 13, 1854

Robt. Searcey to Martha Grigory, October 19, 1854
                    October 19, 1854   By Alex Smith, M.G.

Thomas C. Ray to Elizabeth J. Adkins, October 20, 1854
                    October 24, 1854   Thomas B. White, M.G.

David M. Smith to Martha Jere Cowden, October 24, 1854
                    October 26, 1854   F. W. Brents, M.G.

William Sumerford to Sarah E. Allen, October 24, 1854
                    October 26, 1854   Jacob Gillespie, J.P.

Samuel Hall to Rachell A. Pitts, October 26, 1854
                    October 26, 1854   J. B. Warren, M.G.

(p 275)
John Noah to Nancy J. Roberts, October 28, 1854
                    November 2, 1854   S. M. Emmons, M.G.

Charles G. Taylor to Alley Leonard, October 31, 1854
                    October 31, 1854   B. Christian, J.P.

Joseph M. Rich to Sarah E. Brown, November 1, 1854
                    November 3, 1854   D. Jacks, G.M.

Isaac Majors to Rhody Paysinger, November 1, 1854
                    November 2, 1854   D. S. Patterson, J.P. for L.C.

William Bunn to Mary A. Bryant, November 2, 1854
                    November 2, 1854   C. B. McDaniel, J.P.

Rogin Foster to Letha King, November 4, 1854
                    November 5, 1854   G. W. P. Moore, J.P. for L.C.

Dennis Fowler to Margaret Pauls, November 4, 1854
                    November 5, 1854   D. S. Patterson, J.P.

Reuben Seamore to Norah Heirs, November 10, 1854

David Sanders to Mary Jane Watt, November 14, 1854
                    November 15, 1854   John Roach, J.P.

John D. Laseton to Terresa C. Land, November 21, 1854
                    November 30, 1854   Wm. Pryor, J.P. for L.C.
(p 276)
Chamen Grant to Sarah Commons, November 22, 1854
                    November 22, 1854   Moses Yant, Esq.

W. D. Moore to Susan Danil, November 22, 1854
                    November 23, 1854   Lemuel Brandon

N. C. Ward to Anna Brown, November 23, 1854
                    November 29, 1854   W. A. Hobbs, Esqr.

William Copeland to Mary Ann George, November 24, 1854
                    --   J. W. Holman, M.G.

F. M. Banks to A. J. Sykers, November 25, 1854
                    November 26, 1854   W. A. Hobbs, Esqr.

John Warren to Louisa Abels, November 25, 1845
                    November 25, --   By W. L. Reese, J.P.

John Wood to Mary Russell, November 25, 1854
                    November 26, 1854   By James Kirkland, G.M.

Daniel Tucker to Margaret Heirs, November 28, 1854

George Moyers to Catha Easlick, November 29, 1854
                    November 30, 1854   John L. Ashbey, J.P.

(p 277)
James Brents to Stacy Ellis, December 2, 1854
                    December 3, 1854   L. B. Warren, M.G.

Jacob B. Pitcock to Martha Ann Rick, December 2, 1854
                    December 21, 1854   By D. Jacks, M.G.

John D. Campbell to Sally Ann Been, December 5, 1854
                    December 7, 1854   D. Jacks, M.G.

C. C. Eaton to Martha McLain, December 9, 1854
                    December 10, 1854   By Demps Sullivan, J.P.

James H. Culbreath to Caroline A. Overby, December 13, 1854
December 14, 1854 W. A. Hobbs, Esqr.

John W. Watson to Sarah L. Steelman, December 15, 1854
December 19, 1854 Wm. H. Hicks, Esqr.

Joseph A. Hicks to Ann Land, December 14, 1854
December 19, 1854 Wm. Pryor, J.P.

Alex Scoggins to Eliza Rhodes, December 20, 1854
December 27, 1854 R. S. Hardin, J.P.

Jonathan Sandlin to Elizabeth M. Smith, December 21, 1854

William N. Wright to Mary Buchanan, December 25, 1854
December 25, 1854 By S. M. Cowen, V.D.M.

J. L. Lively to Mary Ann Brown, December 28, 1854
December 28, 1854 James G. Harrison, J.P.

(p 278)
Jesse L. Jones to Martha Hawbwood, January 1, 1855
January 2, 1855 Thos. H. Freeman, J.P. for L.C.

Hopson Lewis to Sarah Ann Murphrey, January 1, 1855
January 2, 1855 By Saml. M. Cowen, V.D.M.

Benj. F. Martin to Martha J. Ewing, January 2, 1855
January 2, 1855 S. E. Douthet, M.G.

F. P. L. Farr to Rebeca E. Sawyers, January 2, 1855
January 2, 1855 James C. Elliott, M.G.

William P. Wright to Elizabeth Swan, January 13, 1855
January 3, 1855 John Wagster, M.G.

John G. McCalla to Lydy L. Roman, January 3, 1855
January 4, 1855 By M. L. Slone

William M. Smith to Amanda Tucker, January 3, 1855
January 4, 1855 By B. Christian, J.P. for L.C.

Temple Scott to Nancy Roane, January 3, 1855
January 3, 1855 A. S. Moor, J.P.

W. W. Haithcock to Sarah L. Franklin, January 3, 1855
January 4, 1855 Wm. H. Hicks, Esqr.

J. E. McWherter to Frence Noe, January 5, 1855
January 7, 1855 A. G. Smith, M.G.

(p 279)
Wm. H. Thompson to Jane Howard, January 6, 1855
January 7, 1855 Wm. Gattis, J.P.

G. M. Swayers to Sarah E. Wackefield, January 6, 1855
January 7, 1855 By James Kirkland, G.M.

Alexander Waggoner to Mary E. McGee, January 6, 1855
January 7, 1855 Moses Yant, Esqr.

J. H. Molden to Nancy J. McKinney, January 8, 1855
January 9, 1855 Henry Turney, J.P.

Henry Carty to Margaret E. Blake, January 9, 1855
--   M. Marshall, Minister

Samuel A. Hopkins to Elizabeth Petty, January 9, 1855
January 11, 1855 Wm. Pryor, J.P.

A. J. Whitaker to S. J. McMillen, January 9, 1855
January 10, 1855 By R. B. McGaugh, M. G.

William Stanley to Martha C. Arnold, January 13, 1855
January 14, 1855 W. P. Holman, J.P.

Joel K. Pamplin to Cynthia E. Yant, January 13, 1855
January 14, 1855 H. C. Holman, J.P.

Jas. M. Smith to Selia J. Dameron, January 16, 1855

(p 280)
Robert Gillaspie to Elizabeth Corepland, January 20, 1855
--   25, --   By Rev. J. Scivally

John Millen to Jane Tucker, January 20, 1855

A. F. D. Goodwin to Mary Jane Hailey, January 24, 1855
January 25, 1855 A. F. Driskell

John W. Armstrong to Nancy Jane Collins, January 25, 1855
January 25, 1855 By R. B. McGaugh, M.G.

A. M. Collins to Sarah J. Allsup, January 29, 1855
January 31, 1855 By J. M. Emmons, M.G.

Larkin A. Smith to Cynthia Landers, January 29, 1855

Jas. A. Franklin to Lovina Heathcock, February 1, 1855
--   1855 By Wm. N. Hicks, Esqr.

George Church to Sarah Dameron, February 3, 1855

George T. Martin to Mary J. Wright, February 5, 1855
--   1855 By Wm. N. Hicks, Esqr.

John H. Coats to Nancy J. Hartgross, February 5, 1855
February 6, 1855 G. M. Pucket, M.G.

Wilkinson Reese to Martha Wagstan, February 6, 1855
February 7, 1855 W. P. Arnold, M.G.

(p 281)
Lewis Fleming to Saline P. Ashbey, February 12, 1855
February 13, 1855 Mat Marshall, Minister

Benj. F. Womack to Susan E. Green, February 12, 1855
        --   By J. W. Holman, M.G.

K. A. McKenzie to Susan E. Higgins, February 14, 1855
          February 14, 1855 By W. E. McKenzie, M.G.

James Marr to Jane Crane, February 15, 1855
          February 19, 1855 By Demps Sullivan, J.P. L.C.

Thos. B. Clelift to Parthena C. Swinebroad, February 20, 1855
        --   By James Kirklan, G. M.

E. H. Stedman to Mary Bland, February 22, 1855
          February 22, 1855 Hugh Parkinson, J.P.

Wm. Patrick to Margaret Ann George, February 22, 1855
          February 22, 1855 A. S. Moore, J.P.

Robt. T. Collins to Lucy C. A. Clark, February 24, 1855
          February 25, 1855 Henry Turney, J.P.

Robert F. Gattis to Harriet Rany, February 26, 1855

Joseph Jones to Elisabeth M. Beard, March 3, 1855
          March 4, 1855 By A. S. Moore, J.P.

(p 282)
Jas. W. Draper to Lucian Karanaugh, March 19, 1855
          March 20, 1855 Y. G. Woods, J.P.

Joseph Jeans to Martha L. Pamphlin, March 22, 1855
          March 22, 1855 By J. W. Cullum, M.G.

Felix Clanch to Bertald Koonce, March 22, 1855
          March 29, 1855 Smith L. Walker, J.P.

James N. Clift to Manerva L. Swinebroad, March 31, 1855
          April 1, 1855 By L. J. Neeley, M.G.

Henry B. McDaniel to Loisa A. Jefferson, Aprile 4, 1855

William Shapard to Elizabeth V. Grills, April 7, 1855
          April 8, 1855 By Jas. E. White, M.G.

George M. Strong to Margarett B. Moore, April 14, 1855
          April 18, 1855 James C. Elliott, M.G.

David Sims to Angeline Greer, April 30, 1855

Nathaniel Mills to Susanah Conaway, May 2, 1855
        --   Rev. William Land, M.G.

Brown Parkison to L. C. C. Bearden, May 3, 1855
          May 3, 1855 A. S. Slone

William D. Walker to Nancy E. Culberson, May 4, 1855
          May 6, 1855 By Rev. William Tillery

(p 283)

Henry M. Powell to Becky Ann Pollock, May 7, 1855
                    May 7, 1855 Wm. F. Zimerman, J.P.

A. P. Clift to Elizabeth Epps. May 7, 1855
                    May 8, 1855 By James G. Harrison, J.P.

Jas. M. Taylor to Elizabeth R. Hawkins, May 8, 1855
                    April 8, 1855 By A. J. Childress, J.P. for L.C.

J. W. Perry to Nancy White, May 15, 1855
                    May 27, 1855 Thos. H. Freeman, J.P. for L.C.

George W. Allison to Anne Ramsey, May 16, 1855
                    May 17, 1855 C. B. McDaniel, J.P.

James R. Routt to Mary J. Wells, May 22, 1855
                    May 22, 1855 Nat Marshall, Minister

G. W. Stephenson to Martha J. Thorp, May 22, 1855
                    May 28, 1855 C. W. McGuern, J.P.

Robt. McMullen to Rebeca E. Holt, May 22, 1855

Augus N. Bryan to Francis A. Martin, May 23, 1855
                    May 23, 1855 Benj. F. Clark, J.P. for L.C.

James Bates to Mary Ann Gale, May 29, 1855

Jacob B. Allison to Nancy R. Thompson, June 6, 1866
                    Juen 7, 1855 Thos. H. Freeman, J.P. for L.C.

(p 284)

N. O. Wallace to M. E. McKinney, June 7, 1855
                    June 7, 1855 By Rev. S. M. Cowen

Wm. L. Allison to Loucenda E. Thompson, June 20, 1855

A. J. Ivy to Malinda Roland, June 23, 1855
                    June 24, 1855 W. A. Hobbs, Esqr.

William H. Shelton to Mary E. Smith, June 25, 1855
                    June 27, 1855 Burrell Christian, J.P.

Virgil A. Dudley to Mary Beavers, June 27, 1855
                    June 28, 1855 By Jeremiah Dean

William Cross to Malinda Shipman, June 28, 1855
                    June 28, 1855 Wiley A. Hobbs, Esqr.

L. L. E. Bearden to Martha Elrells, June 28, 1855
                    June 28, 1855 Nat M. Marshall, D.D.

John T. Phillips to Mary L. Cole, June 28, 1855

Wm. L. Youngblood to Martha J. Hooper, July 2. 1855
                    August 17, 1855 Howell Harris, Jr., J.P.

Wm. Ashworth to Mary R. E. McKee, July 3, 1855
July 10, 1855 By Joseph White, M. G.

(p 285)
John R. Jeater to Elizabeth Ann Wells, July 7, 1855
July 8, 1855 John Rauch, J.P. for L.C.

William A. Watson to Jane Holley, July 10, 1855

William G. Gillam to Agness Y. Tate, July 11, 1855
July 9, 1855 Moses Yant, J.P.

James E. Smith to Margaret L. Majors, July 11, 1855
July 12, 1855 D. S. Patterson, J.P. (Seal)

John C. Arnold to Martha J. Taylor, July 12, 1855
-- 13, -- Burrell Christian, J.P.

F. W. Waggoner to Susan F. Ingle, July 16, 1855
-- J. W. Holman, M.G.

Green B. Casey to Elizabeth L. Hill, July 18, 1855
July 18, 1855 B. Christian, J.P.

James D. Smith to Mary C. Casey, July 18, 1855
July 18, 1855 B. Christian, J.P.

Frances M. Edens to Pheby S. Overby, July 18, 1855
-- J. W. Holman, M.G.

William R. Evens to Frances L. Waggoner, July 21, 1855
July 22, 1855 John L. Ashbey, J.P.

J. H. Look to Indiana Renfro, July 24, 1855
July 24, 1855 By Dempsy Sullivan, J.P.

(p 286)
James G. Land to Nancy T. McDugal, July 24, 1855

Benj. F. Odell to Mary Ann Towry, July 26, 1855

John P. Turney to Tabitha J. Compton, July 30, 1855
July 30, 1855 By Thos. Childs

William Dossey to Piety Weaver, July 31, 1855
July 31, 1855 John L. Gordon, J.P.

Wm. Buffalo to T. J. Majors, August 3, 1855
August 4, 1855 G. W. Pucket, M.G.

William Eddens to Martha Ann Allen, August 6, 1855
August 18, 1855 Wiley A. Hobbs, Esqr.

A. M. Brown to E. C. Russell, August 6, 1855
August 6, 1855 John H. Holman, J.P.

Francis Hudson to Elvira Coulter, August 8, 1855
                    August 8, 1855 John H. Steelman

A. J. Gulley to Lucinda Gulley August 9, 1855
                    August 9, 1855 G. W. R. Moore, J.P.

A. M. Anderson to Isabella Edmonson, August 11, 1855
                    August 13, 1855 By William Gayle, M.G.

John Owens to Elizabeth Brown, August 13, 1855
                    --   By James W. Holman, M.G.

(p 287)
Wm. W. Hindman to Susan A. Wright, August 18, 1855
                    August 19, 1855 By Demps Sullivan, J.P.

William C. Fincher to Fanney B. Reese, August 18, 1855

John S. Wiseman to Juliann Cartright, August 20, 1855

Isom Wills to Eliza Stanley, August 21, 1855
                    --   W. S. Bachman, L.D.M.E.S.

Mathew N. Grinnette to Ruth Hambrick, August 22, 1855
                    August 23, 1855 D. Jacks, M.G.

James W. Hatchell to Elizabeth Webster, August 23, 1855
                    August 23, 1855 J. L. Gordon, J.P. for L.C.

Wm. W. Childs to A. A. Dennis, August 30, 1855
                    August 30, 1855 J. G. Woods, J.P.

James P. Doss to Martha E. McLin, September 1, 1855
                    September 2, 1855 Mat Marshall, Minister

Francis H. Bell to Mary C. Grizard, September 2, 1855
                    September 2, 1855 By T. I. Neeley, Minister

John M. Cook to Nancy Ann Smith, September 3, 1855
                    September 5, 1855 By S. M. Emmons, M.G.

Isaac Grammer to Margarett Ann Bruce, September 4, 1855
                    September 9, 1855 John L. Ashby, J.P.
(p 288)
William J. Jeffries to Lucinda Pamplin, September 5, 1855
                    September 9, 1855 By I. W. Callum, Offi Min

A. M. Brown to E. C. Russell, September 6, 1855

James R. Smith to Nancy Brown, September 7, 1855
                    September 9, 1855 By Wm. Gattis, J.P.

Travis A. Yant to Permilea A. Holman, September 8, 1855
                    September 9, 1855 By I. W. Callum, Min

F. M. Pratt to Elizabeth Edde, August 3, 1855
                    September 2, 1855 F. Motlow, J.P.

John Street to Martha E. Stanly, September 8, 1855
                    September 9, 1855 W. P. Holman, J.P.

James W. Heeter to Mary Ann Scott, September 11, 1855
                    September 11, 1855 Jacob Gillespie, J.P.

John E. Spencer to Alley J. Waggoner, September 12, 1855
                    September 12, 1855 By John Copeland, M.G.

Rufus C. McElroy to Amanda A. Smith, September 18, 1855
                    September 18, 1855 A. G. Smith, M.G.

Isaac Keller to Elizabeth McClure, September 20, 1855
                    September 20, 1855 Smith L. Walker, J.P.

(p 289)
L. H. Fartner to Synthy E. Smith, September 20, 1855
                    September 23, 1855 By Jeremiah Dean, M.G.

Jas. L. Jordon to Aetsey Lutterell, September 20, 1855
                    September 21, 1855 W. F. Holman, J.P.

Jas. H. Forkner to Viny E. Jackson, September 20, 1855
                    September 23, 1855 By Rev. William Tilby

Green W. Nichols to Sarah E. Pirce, September 20, 1855
                    September 20, 1855 W. W. Arnold, M.G.

Samuel Eaton to Jane C. Glasscock, September 22, 1855

Ruffus Harries to Nancy E. Blake, September 25, 1855
                    September 26, 1855 By Saml. M. Cowan, V.D.M.

C. B. Carty to Martha E. Johnson, September 25, 1855
                    September 25, 1855 By Saml. M. Cowan, V.D.M.

Galen P. Wilson to Malinda Jane Hill, September 27, 1855
                    September 28, 1855 J. N. George, J.P.

John B. Cole to Emily Street, September 27, 1855
                    September 27, 1855 Rev. R. D. Hardin

Wm. W. Rogers to Martha Jane Pettes, September 29, 1855
                    October 4, 1855 William A. Gill, G.M.

Dillard Deal to Marthann Hall, October 3, 1855
                    October 3, 1855 Y. W. Cullom, M.G.

(p 290)
William J. Miller to Louisa Southworth, October 4, 1855
                    October 4, 1855 Joseph E. White, M.G.

William Gold to Sarahann Cummins, October 6, 1855
                    October 7, 1855 G. W. R. Moore, J.P. for L.C.

John W. Braden to Sarah A. Taylor, October 8, 1855
                    October 9, 1855 C. W. McGuire, J.P.

James D. Randolph to Louisa Street, October 11, 1855
                    September 11, 1855 Rev. D. Hardin. M.G.

E. W. Ellis to Elizabeth McCoy, October 11, 1855
                    October 10, 1855 G. W. R. Moore, J.P. for L.C.

S. D. Ellis to Mary E. Cummins, October 11, 1855
                    October 18, 1855 G. W. R. Moore, J.P. for L.C.

William M. Henderson to Martha J. Whitworth, October 11, 1855
                    October 11, 1855 John P. McGee, J.P.

George W. Summers to Mary Amanda Frances Pamplin, October 12, 1855
                    October 13, 1855 Thos. H. Freeman. J.P.

Thos. J. Whitworth to Mariah A. Brass, October 19, 1855

R. C. Blackwell to Julian Davidson, October 19, 1855
                    October 20, 1855 By J. B. Waren, M.G.

(p 291)
William J. King to Mary G. Russell, October 25, 1855
                    October 25, 1855 M. M. Marshall, M.G.

Phillip Cooper to Elizabeth Cooper, October 27, 1855
                    October 31, 1855 William J. Grills, J.P.

Thomas Spelce to Catharine Baker, October 27, 1855
                    October 27, 1855 A. J. Steel, M.G.

John Warden to Martha Ann Dunkin, October 27, 1855
                    October 28, 1855 M. W. Yant, J.P.

Andrew Wagoner to Hester Baxter, October 27, 1855
                    October 28, 1855 Dempsy Sullivan, J.P.

Reuben W. Wells to Mary D. Ashbey, October 30, 1855
                    October 31, 1855 M. W. Yant, J.P.

Thos. F. Moore to Elizabeth Blain, November 1, 1855
                    November 1, 1855 T. W. Parkinson

Theodore Smith to M. V. Moores, November 1, 1855
                    November 1, 1855 A. H. Berry

J. A. Martin to Mary Holt, November 3, 1855
                    November 6, 1855 By Jeremiah Dean, M.G.

Robt. Fackender to Mary Ann Oquin, November 3, 1855
                    November 4, 1855 By Dempsey Sullivan, J.P.

M. J. Clunn to L. T. Robertson, November 5, 1855
                    November 7, 1855 D. Jacks, M.G.

(p 292)
Henry B. McCown to Elizabeth McCormack, November 7, 1855

R. M. Carter to Mary J. Davidson, November 7, 1855
                    November 8, 1855   C. B. White, J.P.

Stephen Cole to Sarahann Leatherwood, November 13, 1855
                    November 15, 1855   S. M. Emmons, M.G.

Jas. M. Price to Francis E. Woodard, November 14, 1855
                    November 14, 1855   A. G. Smith, M.G.

James Mims to Julia Ann Wells, November 15, 1855
                    November 15, 1855   By R. B. McGaugh, M.G.

Shepard Hunter to Mary E. Goodrich, November 15, 1855
                    November --, 1855   By Samuel M. Cowan, V.D.M.

Benjamin Bedford to Nancyann Gowan, November 19, 1855
                    November 21, 1855   R. M. Waggoner, M.G.

G. W. Harvey to Nancy E. Gulley, November 21, 1855
                    November 21, 1855   By R. B. McGaugh, M.G.

H. H. Sugg to Sarah Bruce, November 21, 1855

John H. Hutcherson to Margaret E. Meeks, November 26, 1855
                    November 27, 1855   John Caughran, J.P.

Pleasant D. Noah to Mary A. Roberts, November 26, 1855
                    November 29, 1855   By S. M. Emmons, M. G.

(p 293)
Wm. L. Carty to Sarah Jane Moore, November 27, 1855

Siles Lutterell to Parneeda Taylor, November 29, 1855
                    November 29, 1855   W. P. Holman, J.P.

Theordore J. Pickett to Nancy L. Landers, November 29, 1855
                    November 29, 1855   W. T. Holman, J.P.

George Wadkins to Martha Jane Hedrich, December 1, 1855

Benjamin W. Murphy to Elizabeth Jane Ewing, December 3, 1855
                    December 11, 1855   Jas. C. Elliott, M.G.

W. P. Wood to Lucinda E. Chitwood, December 4, 1855
                    December 6, 1855   By S. M. Emmons, M.G.

James Evans to Elizabeth M. King, December 5, 1855
                    --   6. --   D. L. Mitchell, M.G.

Jas. A. George to Jane Cunningham, December 7, 1855

Jas. Philpot to Martha J. Brown, December 8, 1855
                    December 11, 1855   James G. Elliott, M.G.

A. J. Minatree to Mary A. Clark, December 15, 1855

John Price to Mary Mason, December 20, 1855

(p 294)
F. M. Cole to Delila Ellis, December 24, 1855
                    December 25, 1855 By J. B. Marveen. M.G.

William Fonvill to Mary E. Old, December 26, 1855
                    December 27, 1855 John W. Ogden, M.G.

Stephen B. Nelson to Sarah H. Anderson, December 26, 1855

Moses H. Hawkins to Julia A. Surber, December 27, 1855
                    December 27, 1855 A. G. Smith, M.G.

F. H. Lewis to Matilda Dunn, December 28, 1855

James B. Wyatt to Mary E. Wilson, December 31, 1855
                    January 3, 1856 L. W. Parkinson

Lemuel D. Sugg to Margaret F. Holbert, December 31, 1855
                    January 3, 1856 By S. M. Cowan, V.D.M.

Willis M. Holman to Martha D. Higgins, January 1, 1856
                    January 3, 1856 R. B. McGaugh, M.G.

John White to Elizabeth Lackey, January 1, 1855
                    January 6, 1856   --

Jesse Prosser to Mary Jackson, January 4, 1856
                    January 6, 1867 By Dempsy Saulivan

(p 295)
James Massey to Margaret Cunningham, January 5, 1856
                    January 6, 1867 John L. Ashby, J.P.

Demarcus P. Cunningham to Prissilla A. Allsup, January 9, 1856
                    January 9, 1856 By W. M. McKinney, J.P.

William M. Becket to Eugeni C. Hague, January 11, 1856

William G. Pylant to Drusilla Ann Young, January 11, 1856
                    January 13, 1856 G. W. F. Moore, J.P. for L.C.

Joshua Saunders to Lucinda Tucker, January 13, 1856
                    January 13, 1856 James G. Woods, J.P.

Martin F. Hampton to Mary E. Abernathy, January 14, 1855

Albrert Catum to Sarah Hobbs, January 14, 1856
                    January 15, 1856 By William R. Martin, J.P.

Robert Lund to Elizabeth Pigg, January 14, 1856
                    January 15, 1856 By J. Roach, Esq.

A. H. Bell to Martha E. MaGee, January 15, 1856
                    January 15, 1856 William Pryor, J.P.

Wiley Spray to Nancy J. Abbot, January 16, 1856

William Beckett to Eugine C. Hague, January 16, 1856
                    January 15, 1856 Mat M. Marshall, V.D.M.

(p 296)
Thos. Nichols to Elizann Wagster, January 16, 1856

Hicks Bennett to Fanny Ann McChristian, January 17, 1856

John B. Daniel to Emaline Parrish, January 19, 1856
                    January 20, 1856 J. P. McGee, J.P.

Jasper Renegar to Mary J. Buchanan, January 19, 1856
                    January 20, 1856 W. R. Martin, J.P.

Ruben Goldern to Awna Stone, January 19, 1856
                    --   20, 1856 D. Jacks, M.G.

John M. Shaw to Mary E. Evans, January 22, 1856
                    January 22, 1856 William N. Hicks, J.P.

William H. Letteral to Luzena A. Sanders, January 22, 1856
                    January 23, 1856 W. T. Holman, J.P.

James O. Rew to Nancy Jane Freeman, January 24, 1856
                    January 24, 1856 John Wagster, M.G.

Thomas Jean to Martha Emley Rutledge, January 25, 1856
                    January 27, 1856 By R. B. McGaugh, M.G.

A. C. James to Margaret McBride, January 30, 1856
                    February 3, --   S. Leatherwood, J.P.

John Leonard to Sarah E. Templeton, January 30, 1856
                    February 5, 1856 W. C. Jennings, J.P.
(p 297)
A. F. Stone to Susan F. Hoskins, January 30, 1856
                    January 31, 1856 John L. Ashby, J.P.

James Henderson to Nelly F. Harben, February 2, 1856
                    February 7, 1856 William J. Grills, J.P. for L.C.

Wm. M. Franklin to Mary Jane Renerger, February 4, 1856

P. G. Gilbert to Delila J. Edde, February 11, 1856
                    February 18, 1856 J. Smith, M.G.

Charles M. Beard to Clerasa J. Locker, February 11, 1856
                    --   Jas. G. Wood, J.P.

R. F. Evans to Julia E. Creer, February 12, 1856

Joseph C. Wallace to Catharine B. Wiggins, February 13, 1856
                    February 14, 1856 D. S. Patterson, J.P. for L.C.

Esrom C. Loyd to Sarah Catharine Gattis, February 13, 1856
                    February 14, 1856 William Gattis, J.P.

James A. Moore to Sarah L. McDaniel, February 13, 1856
                    February 14, 1856 By T. W. Parkinson

James T. Woodard to E. A. Conway, February 14, 1856
                    February 14, 1856 S. D. Ogburn, M.G.

Edmond C. Jones to Mary L. Demaster, February 16, 1856
                    -- 17, --   John L. Gordon, J.P. for L.C.

(p 238)
Boyers S. Pollock to Martha Renegar, February 18, 1856
                    February 18, 1856 By W. L. Reese, J.P.

John Panter to Elizabeth Story, February 19, 1856
                    February 19, 1856 F. Motlow, J.P.

J. E. Caldwell to Amanda F. Yeats, February 20, 1856
                    February 26, 1856 By R. B. McGough, M.G.

Cornelius B. Adams to Martha E. Jones, February 20, 1856

Josiah J. Land to Mary F. Pickett, February 25, 1856
                    February 28, 1856 Smith L. Walker, J.P.

Hardin J. Gulley to Susanah Bradford, February 25, 1856
                    March 6, 1856 G. W. R. Moore, J.P. L.C.

Joseph Cole to Sarah Jane Armstrong, February 26, 1856
                    February 26, 1856 By Howell Harris, J.P.

C. M. Wilson to Elizabeth Ann Womack, March 4, 1856
                    March 5, 1856 By Lemuel Brandon

Robert A. Shaw to Millie Connelly, March 4, 1856
                    March 4, 1856 By L. M. Cowan, V.D.M.

Bennett W. Childs to Fannie A. Boon, March 5, 1856
                    March 5, -- By B. Chapman, M.G.

(p 299)
Francis M. Moyers to America H. Tucker, March 5, 1856
                    March 5, 1856 John L. Ashby, J.P. for L.C.

H. C. Whitaker to L. L. Whitaker, March 8, 1856
                    March 11, 1856 J. W. Holman, M.G.

Josephus West to Manerva J. West, March 15, 1856
                    March 20, 1856 By T. W. Parkinson, M.G.

J. W. Wilson to A. J. Tate, March 17, 1856

David Laws to Mary Painter, March 19, 1856
                    March 19, 1856 By Lemuel Brandon

John M. Hutchiser to Mary C. Cowan, March 20, 1856
March 24, 1856

Hickman M. Koonce to Helen M. Dennis, March 22, 1856
March 23, 1856 Wm. Pryor, J.P.

Absolum Webster to Rebeca Adcock, March 20, 1856

Johnson Warren to Egletine Freeman, March 27, 1856
March 27, 1856 John Wagster, M.C.

William Tafts to Frances Carpenter , March 27, 1856
March 27, 1856 By William P. Martin, J.P.

James C. Ellis to Nancy D. Pigg, March 27, 1856
March 27, 1856 John Roach, J.P.

(p 300)
J. C. Parr to Elizann Donner, March 29, 1856
April 3, 1856 D. C. Patterson, J.P. for L.C.

James W. Mitchell to Susan E. Gattis, April 3, 1856
April 3, 1853 John Copeland, M.G.

James Richison to Jane Sorrells, April 3, 1856
April 3, 1856 G. W. R. Moore, J.P. for L.C.

John H. Ray to S. A. E. Pamphlin, April 5, 1856
April 6, 1856 By John H. Steelman, J.P. for L.C.

Joseph H. Pollock to Sarah T. Dillingham, April 7, 1856

Richard S. Williamson to Martha Jane Walrup, April 7, 1856
April 8, 1854 M. W. Yant, J.P.

John Halftock to Mary C. Anderson, April 7, 1856
April 10, 1856 Wily A. Hobbs, J.P.

M. M. Caldwell to Julia Ann Alexander, April 7, 1856
April 8, 1856 By S. M. Cowan, V.D.M.

William J. Scoggins to Elizabeth Good, April 16, 1856
April 17, 1856 Robt. Drennon, J.P.

John Sims to Rebeca Pylant, April 17, 1856
April 17, 1856 William Pryor, J.P.

(p 301)
Benj. Fannon to Julia Yarbrough, April 20, 1856
April 22, 1856 W. E. Carter, J.P.

James E. Bray to Mary C. Shappard, April 21, 1856

Samuel H. Phone to Raney Brown, April 24, 1856
April 24, 1856 John P. McCee, J.P. for L.C.

John C. Carter to Sarah P. Stone, April 25, 1856
April 27, 1856 D. Jacks, M.G.

J. S. Hambrick to Emley Pennington, April 21, 1856

William Hise to Cynthie J. Abbott, April 21, 1856
April 23, 1856 W. A. Holes, Esq.

William Gatlen to Martha Ann Vanhooser, April 30, 1856
June 6, 1856 G. M. Pucket, M.G.

Jefferson Flippo to Susan Ann Jane Simmons, May 1, 1856
May 1, 1856 Wiley A. Hobbs, Esqr.

James M. Curtis to Lydia F. Lankston, May 5, 1856
May 6, 1856 Green Nickle, G.M.

Chesbey Hanvey to Margaret E. Warren, May 16, 1856

Ebenezer Hill to Ruth A. Gregory, May 20, 1856
May 20, 1856 A. A. Bell, M.G.

(p 302)
G. M. Steele to Louisa Whitaker, May 21, 1856
May 23, 1856 Mat M. Marshall, M.G.

Jasper Williams to Jane Counts, May 22, 1856
May 22, 1856 By John Corder, J.P.

Jacob C. B. Runnels to Elizabeth Catharine Simmons, May 22, 1856
May 22, 1856 W. A. Hobbs, Esqr.

George W. Posey to Sarah Jane Stewart, May 31, 1856
June 1, 1856 John H. Steelman, Esq.

Pleasant W. Beaver to Priscilla E. Heath, June 3, 1856
June 15, 1856 John L. Ashby, J.P.

T. D. Hill to Julia F. Whitaker, June 25, 1856

Jas. M. Johnson to Sarah H. Jones, June 27, 1856
January 29, 1856 M. W. Yant, Esq.

Thomas Holley to Edde Emeline Wright, July 2, 1856
July 6, 1856 G. W. R. Moore, J.P. for L.C.

John W. McClure to Rebecca D. Mitchel, July 3, 1856
July 3, 1856 L. F. Spencer, J.P.

John M. Alford to Frances Ann Luck, July 3, 1856
July 3, 1856 By S. D. Ogburn

W. C. Bray to Susan Alexander, July 3, 1856
July 13, 1856 By William Gale

Charles L. Waggoner to E. M. Spencer, June 4, 1856
June 4, 1856 By John Copeland, M.G.

(p 303)
Isaac N. Eslick to Martha E. Taylor, July 7, 1856
July 8, 1856 Stephen F. Spencer, J.P.

William H. Hester to Margaret S. White, July 11, 1856
July 13, 1856 D. L. Mitchell, M.G.

James A. Hedrick to Margaret C. Harkins, July 15, 1856
July 17, 1856 G. W. R. Moore, J.P. L.C.

John H. Lane to Elizabeth Johnson, July 16, 1856
July 17, 1856 M. W. Yant, J.P. for L.C.

Thos. J. Stovall to Selia Dameron, July 16, 1856

James H. Campbell to Amanda C. R. Sloan, July 17, 1856
July 18, 1856 Jas. N. George, J.P.

E. J. Phillips to Margaret Ann Neaves, July 17, 1856
July 17, 1856 By John Caughran, J.P.

William Rae to Sarah Ann Campbell, July 17, 1856
July 17, 1856 Henry Henderson, J.P.

James C. Beck to Sytha A. Wilson, July 19, 1856
July 20, 1856 By S. D. Ogburn, M.G.

David G. Smith to A. H. Whittington, July 19, 1856
July 20, 1856 B. M. G. Alsup, J.P.

Cornelius B. Adams to Martha E. Jones, July 20, 1856

(p 304)
Bennett Solomon to Nancy P. Stubbifeeld, July 23, 1856
July 24, 1856 J. H. Eslick, J.P.

Thos. B. Whitworth to Ziephy Killings, July 26, 1856

Bennett B. Merritt to Elizabeth McDaniel, July 28, 1856
July 31, 1856 H. W. Overall, M.G.

Zebulon Parr to Dona E. D. Swinebroad, July 29, 1856
August 4, 1856 S. E. Wilsen, M.G.

John W. Cashion to Charlot J. Arneld, July 29, 1856

Frances M. Williams to Susan Coleman, August 2, 1856
August 7, 1856 William Gayle, M.G.

Davis Call to Mary Jane Wilson, August 4, 1856
--   J. W. Holman, M.G.

John Y. Gill to Mary E. Podgers, August 4, 1856
                    August 5, 1856 By John Caughran, J.P.

James M. Sorrells to Martha Ann Armstrong, August 7, 1856
                    August 7, 1856 G. W. K. Moore, J.P. for L.C.

Peter J. Anderton to Nancy M. Cox, August 8, 1856

(p 305)
J. W. Hodge to Perthena Bledsoe, August 13, 1856
                    August 14, 1856 By G. W. Puoleeled, M.G.

F. M. Colter to Martha A. Nicks, August 13, 1856
                    August 14, 1856 By John H. Steelman, J.P. for L.C.

Joel B. Raney to Huldah Neese, August 16, 1856
                    August 17, 1856 John Wagster, M.G.

Josiah A. Biggs to Frances H. Andrews, August 18, 1856
                    August 18, 1856 By R. Farguharson, J.P.

A. J. Mullins to Martha Ann Vickers, August 25, 1856
                    August 28, 1856 By Wm. N. Hicks, Esqr.

George W. Fields to Nancy M. Bailey, August 25, 1856

David C. Jean to Mary E. Jones, August 25, 1856
                    August 25, 1856 M. W. Yants, Esqr.

Thomas Lock to Margart Ann Marshall, August 25, 1856
                    August 27, 1856 W. N. Hicks, Esqr.

William Marlen to Ann Forsythe, August 27, 1856
                    August 27, 1856 By J. H. Eslick, Esqr.

A. C. Freeman to Mary Ann Perry, September 3, 1856
                    September 3, 1856 Green Nickles, M.G.

(p 306)
Martin V. Pope to Hester Ann Berrien, September 5, 1856
                    September 7, 1856 Henry Henderson, J.P.

John M. Routt to Louisa J. Kelso, September 5, 1856
                    --   5, 1856 W. A. Gill, M.G.

James M. Wells to Isabella McKinny, September 10, 1856
                    September 11, 1856 John P. McGee, J.P.

J. L. Burgess to Lucetta McLaughlin, September 13, 1856
                    September 14, 1856 John Wagster, M.G.

James Gullett to Maurning Ann Shields, September 13, 1856

Robt. Boyd to Cynthia Adcock, September 14, 1856
                    September 14, 1856 R. Forguherson

S. E. H. Dance to M. A. Berry, September 15, 1856
                    September 16, 1856 By T. S. Petway

J. M. Bates to Lucinda J. Jenkins, September 15, 1856
                    September 18, 1856 John S. Ashby, J.P.

M. M. Young to Malinda Jones, September 15, 1856
                    September 15, 1856 Green Nichles, M.G.

John Ralty to Eliza Ann Walker, September 15, 1856
                    September 19, 1856 By John Caughran

(p 307)
Joseph Brooks to Artenia Reese, September 17, 1856
                    September 17, 1856 By Dempsey Sullivan

Wilson R. Call to Martha J. Waggoner, September 17, 1856
                    --   18, --   By J. Scivally

W. H. Davidson to Nancy Warren, September 20, 1856

E. G. Bevill to Lucinda E. Holt, September 22, 1856
                    September 6, 1856 By S. M. Emmons, M.G.

F. L. Ezell to Mary J. McCrackin, September 22, 1856
                    September 23, 1856 M. L. Boho, V.D.M.

Thos. J. Clark to Mary E. Rodgers, September 22, 1856
                    September 22, 1856 Wm. F. Blake, J.P.

David George to Martha C. Hampton, September 24, 1856
                    September 25, 1856 J. N. George, J.P.

William B. McKenzie to Ann E. Sherrill, October 1, 1856

James B. Wilson to Mae A. Whitaker, October 6, 1856
                    October 6, 1856 S. M. Cowan, V.D.M.

Wm. B. McKenzie to Ann E. Sherrill, October 1, 1856
                    October 2, 1856 By W. E. McKenzie, M.G.
(p 308)
Joel Steelman to Belinda Freeman, October 7, 1856
                    October 7, 1856 Green Nicholas, G.M.

Jo. P. Williams to Sarah Ann Foster, October 8, 1856

C. G. Spillman to Molly Ann Gill, October 11, 1856
                    October 12, 1856 W. A. Gill, M.G.

Ambrose Holt to Martha Webster, October 15, 1856
                    October 15, 1856 By John Caughran, J.P. L.C.

James C. Cobb to Emeline Petty, October 15, 1856

David M. Wilson to Melinda J. Mullins, October 17, 1856
                    October 18, 1856 Wm. R. Martin, J.P.

Jesse M. Loveless to Eleanor A. E. Ware, October 18, 1856
                    October 19, 1856 Wm. H. Riggan, M.G.

James L. Clark to Susan R. Smith, October 22, 1856
                    --   Saml. M. Cowan, V.D.M.

Joseph D. McLelland to Mary A. Stonebreaker, October 25, 1856
                    October 26, 1856 B. C. Chapman, M.G.

Wm. Chapman to Nancy Jones, October 25, 1856

(p 309)
Elijah B. Brown to Sarah C. Mitchell, October 29, 1856
                    October 30, 1856 M. W. Yant, Esqr.

Sylvester Pinckney to Mary M. Benningfield, November 3, 1856
                    November 4, 1856 By John Milton, J.P.

F. E. Fleming to N. A. Neeld, November 5, 1856
                    October 5, 1856 By Saml. M. Cowan, V.D.M.

Benjamin A. Beard to Hetty F. Moyers, November 12, 1856
                    November 12, 1856 John P. McGee, J.P.

Jas. A. Panter to Armacinda Miles, November 12, 1856
                    November 13, 1856 C. B. White, J.P.

F. M. Couch to Sarah J. McClure, November 13, 1856
                    November 13, 1856 S. F. Spencer, J.P.

James M. Brown to Susan C. M. L. Carrigen, November 14, 1856
                    November 16, 1867 W. A. Hobbs, J.P.

Daniel G. Story to Nancy L. Stewart, November 18, 1856
                    November 19, 1856 W. F. Zimmerman, J.P.

James B. Pigg to Martha J. Morten, November 20, 1856
                    November 20, 1856 O. P. Hill, J.P. for L.C.

John Braidy to Lucinda Williams, November 24, 1856
                    November 27, 1856 B. M. G. Alsup, J.P.

(p 310)
Robt. Hughy to Sarah Tate, November 24, 1856
                    November 25, 1856 By Alexr. Smith, M.G.

James W. Berry to Laurit M. Motlow, November 26, 1856

Isham J. Towery to Celia Raney, November 26, 1856
                    November 26, 1856 By John Caughran, J.P. L.C.

R. H. Reese to Nancy Phelps, November 26, 1856

I. M. Muse to Martha Nichols, November 26, 1856
                    November 26, 1856 G. Nichols, M.G.

James K. Moores to M. L. Smith, November 29, 1856
November 30, 1856   A. G. Smith, M.G.

John Yeats to Amanda Yarborough, December --, 1856
December 2, 1856   W. D. Carter, J.P.

L. M. Patterson to Lucy A. P. Leatherwood, December 2, 1856
December 4, 1856   S. M. Emmons, M.G.

C. A. Deimer to Rebecca J. Green, December 3, 1856
December 3, 1856   Matt M. Marshall, Minister

James R. Bradford to Elizabeth A. Dickey, December 5, 1856
December 8, 1856   Robert Drenon, J.P.

(p 311)
J. J. Gulley to Almedia D. Y. Pitts, January 3, 1856
(p 312)
R. M. Taylor to Eliza C. West, December 6, 1856

N. M. Jinkins to Elizabeth E. M. S. Nicks, December 8, 1856
December 11, 1856   By John Caughran, J.P.   L.C.

James R. Chilcoat to Susan Flack, December 11, 1856
December 11, 1856   By S. M. Cowan, V.D.M.

Samuel A. Thompson to Melvina L. Tucker, December 11, 1856
December 11, 1856   C. B. White, J.P.

M. H. Roberts to Sarah L. Waterman, December 11, 1856
December 11, 1856   James R. Chilcoat, Judge

John J. Banner to Elizabeth Smith, December 17, 1856
April 6, 1857   William H. Hicks, Esq.

B. F. Whitaker to Manerva A. Buchanan, December 17, 1856
December 18, 1856   A. G. Smith, M.G.

Wm. F. Nave to Martha F. Stuart, December 19, 1856
December 23, 1856   C. B. McDaniel, J.P.

Henry McNeese to Martha Wilkins, December 20, 1856

Saml. Hanie to Anna Morse, December 20, 1856
December 21, 1856   Amos Small, J.P.

(p 313)   Blank

(p 314)
M. C. Story to Mary D. Ship, December 22, 1856

William M. Walker to Martha A. E. Walker, December 23, 1856
December 25, 1856   William Pryor, J.P. for L.C.

William B. Roseboro to Ann F. Harven, December 24, 1856
December 25, 1856   W. T. Grills, J.P.

Thadeus White to Nancy A. Smith, December 27, 1856
                    December 28, 1856 W. E. Carter, J.P.

A. Milliken to Mary Rees, December 30, 1856
                    January 1, 1857 A. G. Smith, M.G.

George F. Gaddis to Susan Hill, December 31, 1856

George W. Budd to Martha Y. Cummins, January 1, 1857
                    January 1, 1857 By Saml. M. Cowan

William J. Rodgers to Francis A. Smith, January 5, 1857

John R. Patterson to Sarah P. Beavers, January 7, 1857
                    January 12, 1857   --

O. P. Owen to Mary Ann Rowell, January 10, 1857
                    January 13, 1857 R. D. Hardin, J.P.

(p 315)
William P. White to Mary Ann Blackwell, January 12, 1857
                    January 15, 1857 C. B. White, J.P.

Albin Roden to Elizabeth Lewis, January 14, 1857
                    January 15, 1857 W. M. McKinney, J.P.

Isaac R. Cole to Nancy A. Buchanan, January 14, 1857
                    January 16, 1857 William F. Zimmerman, J.P.

Alfred Holt to Mary C. Edgeman, January 15, 1857
                    June 11, 1857 Martin Towery, M.G.

Johnathan W. Rowell to Lucinda C. Smith, January 16, 1867
                    January 21, 1857 A. F. Drekill, M.G.

Thos. Bryant to Nancy J. Pickle, January 19, 1857
                    January 22, 1857 John Roach, J.P.

William B. George to Hester M. Stubblefield, January 19, 1857
                    January 22, 1857 Smith L. Walker, J.P.

William S. Moores to Nancy A. Bunn, January 22, 1857
                    January 22, 1857 J. G. Woods, J.P.

Y. C. Ewing to Nancy C. Creacks, January 31, 1857

(p 316)
Samuel B. Roseborough to Nancy C. Snoddy, January 22, 1857
                    January 25, 1857 William E. Carter, J.P.

Wm. P. Lemmonds to N. J. Woodard, January 24, 1857

James H. Hamlin to Emily D. Glen, January 24, 1857
                    --   26, --   By J. W. T. Lee

James L. Currin to Arabella J. Franklin, January 29, 1857
January 29, 1857 Smith L. Walker, J.P.

John L. Tennison to Susan Jane Satterfield, January 31, 1857

Joel R. Neece to Sarah E. Jones, February 2, 1857
February 4, 1857 By Dempsey Sullivan. J.P.

John Jones to Emly Pehnington, February 2, 1857

Henry S. Clift to Sarah J. Pigg, February 5, 1857
February 5, 1857 John Roach, J.P.

Andrew J. Patrick to Eliza Marshall, February 9, 1857
February 10, 1857 Thos. H. Freeman, J.P.

Wiley Lungstin to Martha Bragg, February 9, 1857
February 9, 1857 By John Corder, J.P.

J. C. Ewing to Nancy C. Grubs, January 31, 1857
February 2, 1857 By James C. Elliott, M.G.

(p 317)
John Collins to Mahala Carpenter, February 9, 1857
February 10, 1857 By W. M. McKinney

John A. Silvertooth to Marilda Cox, February 9, 1857
February 17, 1857 Joseph Smith, M.G.

Martin Smith to Rhoda Eislick, February 11, 1857
February 11, 1857 S. F. Spencer, J.P. L.C.

James W. Dyer to Narcissa J. Woodard, February 11, 1857
February 12, 1857 O. P. Hill, J.P.

Benjamin F. Cochran to Louisa J. Pickett, February 16, 1857
March 1, 1857 D. E. Jones, M.G.

Enoch N. Bradley to Helenor Boren, February 18, 1857
--   Isaac H. Eslick, J.P.

John Little to Martha Howard, February 20, 1857
February 22, 1857 C. B. McDaniel, J.P.

H. L. Thornton to Eliza J. Snoddy, February 25, 1857
February 26, 1857 W. E. Carter, J.P.

James B. Lamb to Elizabeth F. Bonner, February 26, 1857
February 26, 1857 C. D. Elliott, M.G.

Daniel B. Downing to Margarett Tempelton, March 2, 1857
March 5, 1857 John Caughran, J.P. L.C.
(p 318)
Wiley Bunn to Rebecca Wells, March 4, 1857
--   4, --   John L. Gerchen, J.P.

J. W. Dryden to Arabella C. Bradshaw, March 5, 1857
     March 5, 1857 W. F. Blake, J.P.

Soloman Roland to Sarah Womack, March 5, 1857
     March 5, 1857 W. A. Hobbs, J.P.

William Lindsey to Margarett Ann Shackelford, March 11, 1857
     March 11, 1857 C. B. White, J.P.

Samuel McCalister to Malinda Walker, March 11, 1857
     March 11, 1857 John Caughran, J.P. L.C.

W. W. McDaniel to Susan Carpenter, March 11, 1857
     March 12, 1857 William F. Martin, J.P.

R. K. Hill to Caroline King, March 23, 1857
     March 23, 1857 Jas. W. Holman, M.G.

Geo. W. Summers to Lyda C. Brotherton, March 26, 1857
     March 27, 1857 By W. M. McKinney

James S. Keith to Mary Ann Sims, April 9, 1857
     April 9, 1857 Amos Small, J.P. for L.C.

Henry Williams to Mary Ann Pigg, April 10, 1857
     April 12, 1857 By Zebulen Parr, M.G.

John S. Hoskins to Nancy M. Collins, April 11, 1857
     April 12, 1857 By Jeremiah Dean, M.G.

(p 319)
William V. Tate to R. K. Alexander, April 15, 1857
     April 15, 1857 By Alexander Smith, M. G.

Reece Williams to Elizabeth Watson, April 22, 1857
     September 1 --, 1857 William N. Nicks, Esqr.

M. G. Waggoner to Frances Hensley, April 23, 1857
     May 8, 1857 By John Copeland

W. A. Wright to Susan C. Hamilton, April 23, 1857
     April 23, 1857 A. G. Smith, M.G.

John W. M. Dance to Sarah B. Price, April 30, 1857
     May 7, 1857 Wily A. Hobbs, Esq.

D. L. Harris to Jedia Conaway, May 5, 1857
     May 5, 1857 Rev. R. D. Hardin

Thomas H. Boles to Eliza Bunn, May 6, 1857
     May 7, 1857 M. W. Yant, J.P.

Willis White to Martha E. Arnold, May 9, 1857
     May 12, 1857 W. E. Carter, J.P. L.C.

George L. Beck to Amanda S. Rowell, May 12, 1857
                    May 13, 1857 W. R. Martin, J.P.

John Reese to Nancy Allen, May 14, 1857
                    May 14, 1857 By Dempsey Sullivan, J.P.

(p 320)
Hillory Mosely to Parthenaia Chilcoat, May 18, 1857
                    May 18, 1857 Mat M. Marshall, V.D.M.

Joseph Jean to Catharine McClure, May 20, 1857
                    --   J. H. Eslick

H. W. Hamblin to Mary A. Bright, June 4, 1857

Bascom Peverly to Eliza P. Sixton, June 6, 1857
                    --   P. --   Willis A. Gill, C.M.

John M. Brown to Nancy P. Kelly, June 6, 1857
                    June 9, 1857 Smith L. Walker, J.P.

Smith L. Walker to Susan J. Stubblefield, -- 1857
                    June 7, 1857 W. Pryor, J.P.

Jesse Peynolds to Enicy L. Hamilton, June 9, 1857
                    June 12, 1857 D. Jacks, M.G.

George Saunders to Alphoo P. Pope, June 11, 1857
                    June 11, 1857 Henry Henderson, J.P.

S. J. Gilliland to Sarah Jane Alsbrooks, June 11, 1857
                    --   11, 1857 J. T. Gander, J.P.

S. M. White to Sarah Owen, June 13, 1857
                    June 16, 1857 Thos. H. Freeman, J.P.

Huston Hill to Martha Jane Adcock, June 18, 1857
                    June 18, 1857 R. Farguharson

(p 321)
Hamilton White to Nancy Brown, June 20, 1857
                    June 26, 1857 C. B. White, J.P.

William P. Lindsey to Martha J. Wiley, June 24, 1857
                    June 24, 1857 A. S. Sloan

George Campbell to Emeline Campbell, July 2, 1857
                    July 3, 1857 John Corder, J.P.

Charles Cunningham to Sarah Willis, July 8, 1857
                    July 9, 1857 By J. N. George, J.P.

Samuel Mason to Mary E. Delaney, July 9, 1857
                    July 9, 1857 L. B. Wiley, Esqr.

William Y. Lackey to Mary Jane Cox, July 14, 1857
                    July 14, 1857 W. E. Carter, J.P.

Elijah Edgemon to Isa Henseley, July 20, 1857
       July 20, 1857 Thomas H. Freeman, J.P.

Alfred Walker to Martha Walker, July 21, 1857
       July 21, 1857 John Caughran, J.P. L.C.

Wm. William to Sarah Jane Shaw, July 22, 1857
       July 23, 1857 Robt. Drennon, J.P.

James L. Thompson to Matilda Ann Strong, July 25, 1857
       July 29, 1857 C. B. McDaniel, J.P.

Samuel W. Browning to Margaret M. Smith, July 27, 1857
       August 28, 1857 Rev. R. D. Hardin

(p 322)
Francis A. Thompson to Frances A. Noles, July 28, 1857
       July 29, 1857 C. B. McDaniel, J.P.

A. B. Scott to Mary Jane Ford, July 30, 1857
       July 30, 1857 Jacob Gillespie, J.P.

Samuel McNabb to Jane Watson, August 1, 1857
       August 1, 1857 Moses W. Yant, Esqr.

J. V. Allsup to Mary Elizabeth Wright, August 1, 1857
       August 2, 1857 By S. M. Emmons, M.G.

M. L. Noles to Caroline Payne, August 7, 1857
       August 11, 1857 C. B. McDaniel, J.P.

M. V. Riddle to Catherine L. Tucker, August 7, 1857
       August 9, 1857 By John Copeland

James A. C. Milliken to Margaret C. Barnes, August 10, 1857
       August 10, 1857 Benjr. F. Clark, J.P. L.C.

James B. Taylor to Nancy Ann McClure, August 12, 1857
       August 13, 1857 W. T. Holman, J.P.

James H. Darnel to Delia Margarett Scott, August 12, 1857
       August 13, 1857 Green Nichols, M.G.

Gray J. Pylant to Ann E. Adkins, August 17, 1857
       August 20, 1857 Rev. A. Tribble

Thos. B. McElroy to Frances E. Smith, August 19, 1857
       April 20, 1857 Rev. R. D. Hardin

(p 323)
James R. Gunter to Martha Pigg, August 22, 1857
       August 23, 1857 Benjr. F. Clark, J.P. L.C.

Wright W. Tooley to Louisa J. Collins, August 24, 1857
       August 25, -- W. M. McKinney

John H. Bryan to Martha Jane Blue, August 25, 1857
                        August 26, 1857 Rev. R. D. Hardin

P. S. Hanks to Mary Riddle, August 26, 1857

Wiley Jean to Mary E. Bunn, August 27, 1857
                        August 27, 1857, C. B. McDaniel, J.P.

John Jean to Lucinda Hazelwood, August 28, 1857
                        August 30, 1857 Wm. Gattis, J.P. L.C.

Milton S. Ray to Mary Emery, August 31, 1857
                        September 3, 1857 By Jeremiah Dean, M.G.

Jesse Ortner to Elizabeth Cates, September 1, 1857
                        --   By W. Reas, J.P. for L.C.

Henry P. Pitts to Harriatt S. Allbright, September 2, 1857
                        September 3, 1857 A. S. Sloan

Eli Brown to Elvira Duke September 4, 1857
                        September 6, 1857 Wm. Gattis, J.P.

Joseph Sebaston to Rebecca Bledsoe, September 7, 1857
                        --   J. W. Holman, M.G.

(p 324)
Thos. B. McGeehee to Mary Jane Rutledge, September 8, 1857
                        September 10, 1857 By John Copeland

George Brewer to Emeline Martin, September 8, 1857
                        September 8, 1857 R. Farguharson, J.P.

L. F. Mitchell to E. M. J. Grant, September 9, 1857
                        September 10, 1857 Jas. C. Stevenson

James W. Braden to Sarah B. Gill, September 9, 1857
                        September 10, 1857 James C. Stevenson

Wm. Anderson to Emeline E. Bagley, September 10, 1857
                        September 11, 1857 John L. Gordon, J.P.

Jackson Richardson to Susan C. Duncan, September 10, 1857
                        September 11, 1857 By Dempsey Sullivan. J.P.

John V. McKinney to Mary E. Thomison, September 15, 1857
                        September 15, 1857 John Harris

Joseph S. H. Gilliam to Rebecca S. Pigg, September 16, 1857
                        September 17, 1857 John Roach, J.P. L.C.

John Rogers to Julia Anh Campter, September 17, 1857
                        September 17, 1857 By Martin Towery, M.G.

Robert F. Fox to Eliza Jane Harrison, September 19, 1857
                        September 20, 1857 Amos Small, J.P.

174

Moses W. Yant to Eliza E. Bunn, September 19, 1857
                    September 20, 1857 John Copeland

(p 325)
John T. Shires to Milley Ann Jackson, September 22, 1857
                    September 24, 1857 Wm. F. Zimnerman, J.P. L.C.

James D. Evens to Martha E. Darnal, September 24, 1857
                    September 25, 1857 John L. Ashby, J.P.

Benj. Jackson to Eliza Bryant, September 24, 1857
                    September 24, 1857 By John Milton

R. H. Berry to Louiza Burned, September 25, 1857
                    September 25, 1857 Hugh Thomison, J.P.

John D. Harris to Eliza C. Woodward, September 26, 1857
                    September 27, 1857 Jas. C. Stevenson

Middlton McGeehee to Louisa Dennis, September 26, 1857
                    September 27, 1857 J. H. Eslick, J.P.

John W. Moore to Martha H. Redd, September 26, 1857
                    September 27, 1857 G. W. R. Moor, J.P. for L.C.

John J. Grayham to Susan M. Barker, September 28, 1857
                    --   29, --   W. P. Holman, J.P.

John Mason to Sarah Boyd, September 21, 1857
                    September 21, 1857 Smith L. Walker, J.P.

Jas. M. Brady to Mary A. Sumners, October 2, 1857
                    October 3,   --   By W. M. McKinney

Joseph Mansfield to Margarett Denml, October 3, 1857
                    October 4, 1857 John H. Stedmon, J.P.

(p 326)
P. H. Reeves to Caroline Pelps, October 5, 1857
                    October 6, 1857 By T. P. Wells, M.G.

Saml. H. Locker to Elizabeth M. Rowe, October 6, 1857
                    October 6, 1857 Henry Henderson, J.P.

Thomas R. Curtis to Frances E. Wright, October 7, 1857
                    October 17, 1857 Green Nichols, G.M.

H. S. Davis to Fannie P. Strong, October 7, 1857
                    October 7, 1857 A. A. Bell, M.G.

J. W. Cullum to Mary B. Isom, October 12, 1857
                    October 13, 1857 Matt M. Marshall, Minister

D. M. Patterson to Bettie Woodruff, October 14, 1857
                    October 15, 1857 Matt M. Marshall, Minister

W. H. Rees to Susan Sullivan, October 15, 1857
                  October 15, 1857 By John H. Steelman, J.P.

William Ables to Jane Brown, October 15, 1857
                  October 15, 1857 S. H. McCord, J.P.

James Foster to Mary Jane Lambert, October 17, 1857

William Hamilton to Elizabeth E. Wyatt, October 21, 1857
                  October 21, 1857 By A. S. Sloan

(p 327)
R. W. Long to Tabitha Bledsoe, October 21, 1857
                  October 22, 1857 J. S. Davis, M.G. (Seal)

Wiley Runnl to Elizabeth Rowlen, October 22, 1857
                  October 23, 1857 By J. T. Gordon, J.P.

Samuel Hall to Sarah Ann Henderson, October 22, 1857
                  October 26, 1857 Isaac R. Nelson, J.P.

E. S. Wilson to Mary S. Kimes, October 24, 1857
                  October 27, 1857 Matt M. Marshall, Minister

C. B. Oliver to Elizabeth Tucker, October 25, 1857
                  --   25, 1857 J. T. Gordon, J.P.

John Jones to Mary Boyd, October 25, 1857
                  October 25, 1857 By J. T. Gordon, J.P.

Martin Bryant to Susan E. Branham, October 28, 1857
                  October 28, 1857 W. C. Jennings, J.P.

John L. Bennett to Milessa M. Couch, October 28, 1857
                  October 28, 1857 W. C. Jennings, J.P.

Nicholas Sandlin to Susanah Womack, October 28, 1857
                  October 28, 1857 John Caughran, J.P.

M. M. Story to Lucinda C. Braden, October 29, 1857
                  October 29, 1857 James C. Stevenson

John V. Moyers to George Ann Wiegart, October 29, 1857
                  October 30, 1857 By J. T. Gordon, J.P.

(p 328)
Reubin Echels to Mary E. Benson, October 31, 1857
                  November 2, 1857 W. E. Carter, J.P.

H. C. Luna to Sarah E. Blakemore, November 2, 1857
                  November 3, 1857 C. R. Darnell, M.G.

W. P. Chiles to Mary W. Glenn, November 3, 1857
                  November 4, 1857 By J. W. T. Lee

A. W. Tripp to Susan E. McClure, November 4, 1857
        November 5, 1857 S. F. Spencer, J.P.

Druiry M. Wims to Martha M. Wisner, November 4, 1857
        November 4, 1857 A. G. Smith, M.G.

George W. Tipps to Lucinda Lembock, November 7, 1857
        November 8, 1857 By John Caughran, J.P. of L.C.

W. H. Riley to Nancy Jane Stovall, November 7, 1857
        --   By R. D. Harden, M.G.

Allen Elston to Manerva Gibson, November 7, 1857
        November 8, 1857 A. G. Smith, M.G.

B. W. L. Rivers to H. E. Flynt, November 7, 1857
        November 10, 1857 L. D. Mitchell, M.G.

J. P. McGuire to Rachel J. Allsup, November 9. 1857
        November 12, 1857 W. F. Zimnerman, J.P.

Stephen Sawyer to Sarah George, November 10, 1857
        November 10, 1857 By Martin Towry, M.G.

(p 329)
Drury M. Mims to Martha M. Wisner, November 11, 1857
        November 11, 1857 A. G. Smith, M.G.

Zera Sawyers to Elizabeth Hencely, November 17, 1857
        November 19, 1857 John Copeland, M.G.

J. W. Hester to Sarah A. Stephenson, November 16, 1857
        November 17, 1857 J. S. Davis, M. G.

J. C. Goodrch to C. H. Massey, -- 1857
        November 17, 1857 Matt M. Marshall, Minister

David Jean to Elizabeth Bryant, November 19, 1857
        November 20, 1857 W. T. Holman, J.P.

Hiram Cole to Clerissa Smith, November 20, 1857
        November 23, 1857 William N. Hicks, J.P.

John R. White to R. S. C. Smith, November 26, 1857
        --   J. Stephenson, M.G.

James E. Brown to Mary A. Brown, --   1857
        November 26, 1857 R. M. Haggard, M.G.

Samuel Cheek to Finnella Rowlin, November 28, 1857
        November 30, 1857 J. T. Gordon, J.P.

Robert Taylor to Sarah Jinkins, November 30, 1857

(p 330)

William Noles to Prudy McWhorter, December 2, 1857
                      December 2, 1857 C. B. McDaniel, J.P.

James H. Phagan to Martha A. Strong, December 3, 1857
                     --   A. S. Sloan

Patrick Ray to Decy Evans, -- 1857
                      December 3, 1857 By William R. Waggoner, J.P.

James Pigg to Elizabeth S. Patterson, December 8, 1857
                      December 8, 1857 By Howell Harris, J.P.

P. T. Murray to C. J. Morgan, -- 1857
                      December 8, 1857 Matt M. Marshall, Minister

Robert Reese to Mary J. Puckett, December 14, 1857
                      December 15, 1857 A. G. Smith, M.G.

Rev. L. D. Jones to Sarah A. Kimbrough, December 14, 1857
                      December 17, 1857 By A. D. Trimble, M.G.

Wm. Michael to Elizabeth Cox, December 14, 1857

William Posey to Martha Warren, December 14, 1857
                  --   15, --   By Thomas H. Freeman, J.P.

C. A. McDaniel to Margaret Buchanan, December 15, 1857
                      December 15, 1857 M. M. Marshall, Minister

(p 331)

Jeremiah Prince to Mary A. Rolin, December 17, 1857
                      December 17, 1857 By W. A. Hobbs, Esqr.

Alexander S. Lee to Francis M. Vickers, --
                      December 17, 1857 Smith Walker, J.P.

William Smith to Susanah Woodard, --
                      December 20, 1857 J. N. George, J.P.

S. Gilbert Stovall to Sarah A. Sanderson, December 18, 1857
                      December 22, 1857 William R. Martin, J.P.

E. W. Stone to Mary Gore, December 23, 1857
                      December 23, 1857 By W. A. Hobbs, Esqr.

D. J. Hill to P. E. Rowel, --
                      December 24, 1857 John Caughran, J.P. L.C.

Isaac Williamson to Rhoda Ann Oldham, December 24, 1857
                      December 24, 1857 J. T. Gordon, J.P.

Henry A. Waggoner to Emeline Tucker, December 28, 1857
                      December 31, 1857 By William R. Waggoner, J.P.

Nathaniel Millard to Manerva S. Nichols, January 2, 1858
                    January 5, 1858 M. Marshall, Minister

H. J. Renager to Louisa Stubblefield, January 4, 1857
                    January 6, 1858 By Wm. Gattis, J.P.
(p 332)
Elifeus G. Shelton to Mary A. Luttrell, January 5, 1858
                    January 6, 1858 W. E. Carter, J.P.

J. R. Nelson to Jane Turney, January 7, 1858
                    January 7, 1858 By J. B. Warren, M.G.

Andrew J. Wright to Sarah J. Lauderdale, January 12. 1858
                    January 12, 1858 A. G. Smith, M.G.

N. A. Bailey to Ann B. Hester, January 16, 1858
                    January 17, 1858 Bradley Kimbrough, M.G.

William A. Metcalf to Mary Ann Pitcook, January 16, 1858
                    January 19, 1858 Smith L. Walker, J.P.

Miles J. Reeves to Tempa A. Milton, January 18, 1858
                    January 20, 1858 By S. M. Emmons, M. G.

James Bailey to Sarah A. Wright, January 19, 1858
                    --   By R. D. Hardin, G.M.

John Clark to Sarah Gully, --
                    January 21, 1858 By J. B. Warren, M.G.

Hyson M. Howell to Sarah Smith, --
                    January 19, 1858 S. L. Walker, J.P.

Charles Smith to Elizabeth Isom, January 19, 1858
                    January 20, 1858 Thos. H. Freeman, J.P.

(p 333)
James Hamilton to Mary Ann Smith, January 20, 1858
                    January 20, 1858 By D. S. Patterson, J.P.

Anderson W. March to L. M. McDaniel, January 21, 1858
                    January 21, 1858 D. R. Marshall, M.G.

Jasper N. Perry to Elizabeth Tennison, January 22, 1858
                    January 22, 1858 J. T. Gordon. J. P.

H. D. A. Thomas to Cynthia Millard, January 23, 1858
                    --   27, 1858 Matt M. Marshall, Minister

R. D. McMillen to Mary Jane Millard, January 23, 1858
                    January 27, 1858 Matt M. Marshall, G.M.

Isaac M. Holman to Susan Nix, January 23, 1858
                    January 25, 1858 By J. H. Eslick, Esqr.

W. S. Sherrell to Permelea T. George, January 24, 1858
                    January 26, 1858 G. W. Puckett, G.M.

G. W. Massey to Mary Ann Sawyers, January 26, 1858
                    January 26, 1858 By William R. Waggoner, J.P.

Charles R. Browning to Sarah F. Grubbs, January 25, 1858
                    January 28, --   Wm. A. Gill, G.M.

William Donald to Polly Frazier, January 26, 1858
                    January 26, 1858 By W. R. Waggoner, J.P.

(p 334)
Nicholas Evans to Martha Chapman, January 27, 1858
                    --   By J. W. Holman, M.G.

George Burrough to Pitty C. Bartlet, January 27, 1858
                    --   W. Rees, J.P. L.C.

William C. Tripp to Martha Ann Shelton, --
                    January 28, 1858 S. F. Spencer, J.P. L.C.

Wm. A. Pitts to Polly Ann Wyles, January 31, 1858
                    January 31, 1858 Robert Drennon, J.P.

Isaac Evans to Elizabeth Massey, February 1, 1858
                    February 5, 1858 J. L. Ashby, J.P.

John Coleman to Sarah Patterson, February 3, 1858
                    February 4, 1858 By A. S. Sloan

Henry S. Commons to Jane Griffis, February 4, 1858
                    February 4, 1858 Benjr. F. Clark, J.P.

J. E. McAdams to Mary L. Patton, --

J. W. Nelson to Sarah E. Watt, February 8, 1858
                    February 9, 1858 By J. B. Warren, M.G.

Jacob Gillespie to Julia Butler, February 9, 1858
                    January 9, 1858 Matt M. Marshall, G.M.

(p 335)
James H. Castleman to Catharine Carly, February 9, 1858
                    February 9, 1858 G. W. Martin, G.M.

James H. Heralson to Martha J. Webb, February 10, 1858
                    February 11, 1858 William N. Hicks, J.P.

T. M. Bell to S. J. Pearson, February 11, 1858
                    February 11, 1858 W. A. Gill, G.M.

Emery M. Posey to Martha Stewart, --
                    February 11, 1858 By John H. Steelman, J.P.

T. J. Russell to Mary F. Cathey, February 13, 1858
                    February 16, 1858 Matt M. Marshall, G.M.

Foah H. McEluy to Jane Edens, February 15, 1858
                    February 18, 1858   W. A. Hobbs, Esqr.

Elisha Hicks to Frances Raines, February 15, 1858
                    February 16, 1858   By W. L. Rees, J.P.

Kelly Norman to Sarah Cobb, February 17, 1858
                    February 18, 1858   By R. B. Magugh, M.G.

John H. Taylor to Martha C. Styles, --   1858
                    February 23, 1858   By J. H. Eslick, Esqr.

Anderson Cole to Lucy C. Cummins, February 18, 1858
                    February 18, 1858   By J. B. Warren, M.G.

(p 336)
W. B. Hamilton to Harriett M. Smith, February 26, 1858
                    February 25, 1858   A. G. Smith, M.C.

Samuel Hill to Martha Porlr, March 2, 1858
                    March 2, 1858   J. T. Gordon, J.P.

Joel E. Yowel to Martha E. Holbert, March 2, 1858
                    --   2, 1858   G. M. Martin, M.G.

W. W. McCloud to Mary A. Shook, March 3, 1858
                    March 3, 1858   By Henry Larken

Wm. B. Taylor to Angeline O. Scott, March 4, 1858
                    March 4, 1858   J. H. Eslick, J.P.

Jackson O. Mitchal to Rutha Swanner, March 9, 1858
                    March 10, 1858   S. M. Emmons, M.G.

Claiborn Harris to Mary Moore, March 10, 1858
                    April 5, 1858   Henry Turney, J.P.

Reubin J. Stone to Elizabeth M. Hoskins, March 11, 1858
                    March 10, 1858   John L. Ashby, J.P.

E. M. Posey to Martha Stuart, March 11, 1858
                    February 11, 1858   By Jno. H. Steelman, J.P.

John Commons to Elizabeth Ellis, March 11, 1858
                    March 11, 1858   G. W. R. Moore, J.P.

John T. Renarger to Lucinda Stubblefield, March 13, 1858
                    March 14, 1858   By I. H. Eslick, J.P.

(p 337)
John Strickland to Martha R. Abbott, March 15, 1858
                    March 15, 1858   S. K. McCord, J.P.

W. A. Eorton to M. A. Waggoner, March 15, 1858
                    March 18, 1858   W. W. Shaw, M.G.

Presley R. Johnson to Martha J. Paysinger, March 20, 1858
                    March 25, 1858 D. S. Patterson, J.P.

Frances M. Gatlin to Martha M. Nelson, March 20, 1858
                    -- 23. 1858 By John A. Milhous

Peterson Grainnor to Mary Ann Evens, March 20, 1858
                    March 21, 1858 By Wm. R. Waggoner. J.P.

Henderson Speck to Racheal Davis, March 22, 1858
                    April 4. 1858 William Gattis, J.P.

John B. Derick to Martha Jane Jening, March 23, 1858
                    March 23, 1858 By R. B. McGough, M.G.

R. Y. Salmon to H. C. Taylor, March 24, 1858
                    March 25, 1858 By James V. Holman, M.G.

John C. Walker to Nancy M. Walker, March 24, 1858
                    March 28, 1858 By John A. Milhous

W. L. Mitcalfe to Elizabeth B. Pitcock, March 29, 1858

(p 338)
Thomas J. Gaddy to Martha J. Maddox, March 29, 1858
                    April 1, 1858 By James C. Stevenson

A. A. Tate to James C. Galoway, March 30, 1858
                    March 30, 1858 J. H. Bryson

Edward B. Durn to Sarah E. Womack, April 15, 1858
                    April 16, 1869 J. T. Gordon, J.P.

L. C. Blear to Julia Ann Luttrell, April 17, 1858
                    April 19, 1858 By William N. Hicks, Esqr.

Milton Ervin to Mary Ann Morris, April 17, 1858
                    April 21, 1858 W. A. Hobbs, Esqr.

Allen Coble to C. A. W. Bradey. April 17, 1858
                    April 17, 1858 Wm. M. McKinney, J.P.

Tilmon Towry to Nancy Burrs, April 17, 1858

C. T. Chesor to Mourming Washburn. April 20, 1858
                    April 20, 1858 By J. B. Warren, M.G.

Jackson Whittock to Nancy C. Davis, April 23, 1858
                    April 25, 1858 By John L. Ashby, J.P.

J. F. Wakefield to Nancy E. Chesser, April 24, 1858
                    April 24, 1858 Benjr. F. Clark, J.P.

(p 339)
John Porter to Lou M. Doss, April 28, 1858
                    April 29, 1858 G. W. Martin, M.G.

J. T. Pinkerton to M. E. Templeton, May 3, 1858
                    May 4, 1858 John Caughran, J.P.

James F. Alexander to Louisa McMullin, May 6, 1858
                    May 6, 1868 J. H. Bryson

Henry Dunn to C. K. Yant, May 8, 1858
                    May 10, 1858 John T. Gordon, J.P.

J. B. Davis to Mary Ann Smith, May 13, 1858
                    May 13, 1858 Wm. M. McKinney, J.P.

J. T. Maxwill to Elizabeth Caddy, May 13, 1858
                    May --, 1858 John T. Gordon, J.P.

George Rolin to Elizabeth Miles, May 15, 1858
                    May 16, --   By W. A. Hobbs, Esqr.

James C. Flynt to Lizzie P. Buchanan, May 27, 1858

Isaac H. Gray to Sarah Miller, June 14, 1858
                    June 15, 1858 Wm. Carter, J.P.

William R. Rison to Mariah L. Jones, June 18, 1858
                    June 18, 1858 R. Farguharson, J.P.

John D. Carter to M. Annie Neald, June 22, 1858
                    June 23, 1858 G. W. Martin, M.G.

(p 340)
John W. Smith to Susan Young Smith, June 23, 1858
                    June 24, 1858 S. F. Spencer, J.P.

M. J. Wills to A. F. Dowing, June 23, 1858
                    June 24, 1858 Wm. A. Gill, M.G.

Moses C. Freeman to Martha Jane Prosser, June 28, 1858
                    June 28, 1858 G. W. Nichols, M.G.

John R. Williams to Elizabeth Beavers, June 28, 1858
                    June 28, 1858 Jeremiah Dean, M.G.

William F. Nesoe to Martha M. White, June 30, 1858
                    June 30, 1858 R. Farguharson, J.P.

John Copeland to Rutha Watson, July 1, 1858
                    July 1, 1858 I. F. Spencer, J.P.

David H. Coble to Juley Ann Coble, July 1, 1858
                    July 1, 1858 Wm. M. McKinney, J.P.

M. M. Hairston to Eliza Bell, July 1, 1858
                    July 1, 1858 By Martin Towry, M.G.

E. L. M. Shelton to Elizabeth Hunt, July 1, 1858
                    July 11, 1858 By W. C. Jennings, J.P.

George S. Wright to C. C. Hill, July 2, 1858
    July 5, 1858 By Joseph Dameron, J.P.

Stephen Touchstone to Mary E. Hayes, July 3, 1858
    July 4, 1858 John Cary, J.P.

Henry Henderson to Sarah E. Crawford, July 4, 1858
    July 4, 1858 S. H. McCord, J.P.

(p 341)
Robert F. Wicker to Phebe E. Rees, July 7, 1858
    July 7, 1858 John Cary, J.P.

A. G. Dowing to Catharine Cray, July 7, 1858
    July 13, 1858 By John Caughran, J.P. L.C.

Wm. J. Wilson to Jane E. Harkins, July 8, 1858
    July 8, 1858 G. W. R. Moore, J.P.

Thos. L. Dougan to Henretta Colman, July 10, 1858
    July 10, 1858 By Joseph Dameron, J.P.

Elijah Hester to Mary Ann Ingle, July 12, 1858
    July 13, 1858 N. A. Bailey, M.G.

James Corder to Sarah Ann Cummins, July 13, 1858
    July 14, 1858 C. B. McDaniel, J.P.

J. E. Spencer to C. J. Wade, July 14, 1858
    July 18, 1858 S. F. Spencer, J.P.

James D. Stedford to Elizabeth C. Luttrell, July 17, 1858
    July 18, 1858 W. E. Carter, J.P.

Luke W. Marbary to Jane Hill, July 17, 1858
    July 19, 1858 Robt. Drennon, J.P.

Wm. Buchanan to Ann Thomison, July 20, 1858
    July 20, 1858 A. G. Smith, M.G.

James M. Bright to Elizabeth E. Stephens, July 22, 1858

(p 342)
Abner S. Woodward to Elizabeth A. Young, July 23, 1858
    July 25, 1858 W. F. Zimmerman, J.P.

Caleb Smith to Palmyrah E. Byers, July 24, 1858
    July 29, 1858 Wm. Land, G.M.

Abraham Summers to Elizabeth Brady, July 26, 1858
    July 26, 1858 W. M. McKinney, J.P.

John George to Catharine Allison, July 27, 1858
    July 27, 1858 By James C. Stevenson

Jesse M. George to Mary J. Ashby, July 27, 1858
    July 29, 1858 John H. Steelman, J.P.

C. L. Smith to Mary Majors, July 29, 1858

George W. Leeley to Nancy E. Evens, July 31, 1858
August 1, 1858 Saml. Stiles. J.P.

Briggs Nicholas to Alsey Foster, July 31, 1858
July 31, 1858 W. W. Arnal, M.G.

C. A. Rees to Sarah Milliken, August 4, 1858
August 5, 1858 John Cary, J.P.

Erastus Taylor to F. L. Randolph, August 10, 1858
August 11, 1858 A. S. Sloan

(p 343)
A. T. Deloney to Bettie L. Pearson, August 11, 1858
August 12, 1858 M. H. Bone, M.G.

William P. Hobbs to Mary Ann Harris, August 12, 1858
August 12, 1858 By James C. Stephenson

Eli Simmons to Sarah C. Riley, August 16, 1858
August 19, 1858 Rev. R. D. Harden

J. D. Harden to Elizabeth Fox, August 18, 1858
August 18, 1858 By R. L. McCree, Minister

James L. Dyer to V. T. Nelson, August 18, 1858
August 20, 1858 J. G. Bledsoe, M.G.

William J. Caldwell to Nancy Simmons, August 19, 1858
August 19, 1858 By Saml. M. Cowan, V.D.M.

Charles W. Smith to Mary Ann Dunn, August 20, 1858

John L. McCoy to Lucinda Rowe, August 21, 1858
August 22, 1858 James C. Stevenson

Benj. F. Fannon to Syntha F. Thompson, August 25, 1858
August 26, 1858 By I. H. Dalick, Esqr.

George W. Dunn to Sarah Ann Smith, August 28, 1858
September --, 1858 Wm N. Hicks, Esqr.

(p 344)
John W. Franklin to Lucy Ann Haithcook, August 30, 1858
September 1, 1858 Wm. H. Hicks, Esqr.

Calvin Gilbert to Tranquila R. Gracy, August 31, 1858
August 31, 1858 By Rev. R. L. McElree

James C. Clarke to Bettie A. Allison, September 4, 1858

Robert Farguharson to Sarah A. Burke, September 6, 1858
September 7, 1858 A. S. Slone, M.G.

John B. Luttrell to Caroline Duke, September 8, 1858

John C. West to Elizabeth J. Taylor, September 9, 1858

J. M. Kibbe to Susan Sulenger, September 9, 1858
                    September 9, 1858 Thomas H. Freeman, J.P.

James P. McCown to J. A. McDill, September 14, 1858

Wilford Abbott to Caroline Dickey, September 16, 1858
                    September 16, 1858 Robt. Brennon, J.P.

John W. Howard to Nancy Ann Pudd, September 17, 1858
                    September 18, 1858 By Dempsey Sullivan, J.P.

(p 345)
John E. Blackwell to Agness Rorax, September 22, 1858
                    September 24, 1858 Wm. Cattis, J.P.

Joseph Simpson to Elizabeth Jane Banks, September 23, 1858
                    September 25, 1858 Samuel Brandon

Wm. C. Burg to Mary S. Wood, September 23, 1858
                    September 23, 1858 A. H. Berry, M.G.

Rufus Harris to Susan Ann Blake, September 27, 1858
                    October 2, 1858 D. L. Mitchell, M.G.

George W. Waggoner to Martha Ann Gattis, September 27, 1858
                    September 30, 1858 G. W. Holman, M.G.

John C. Birdsong to Eliza Cail, September 27, 1858
                    September 27, 1858 Rev. P. D. Hardin

Isaac Rutledge to R. A. Johnson, September 29, 1858
                    --   J. W. Holman, M.G.

John F. M. Hathcock to Eliza Ann Delia Vanhoozer, September 30, 1858
                    September 30, 1858 William N. Hicks, Esqr.

Wilson Ashby to Cynthea B. Pitts, September 30, 1858
                    September 30, 1858 H. A. Bailey, M.G.

Adam Landess to Manerva Williamson, September 30, 1858
                    September 30, 1858 Thos. H. Freeman, J.P.

William Knight to Elizabeth Asa, September 30, 1858
                    September 30, 1858 R. Farguharson, J.P.

(p 346)
W. J. Bryant to Mary Jane Fitch, September 30, 1858
                    October 3, 1858 W. E. Carter, J.P.

John S. Sanders to Surfrona Pope, October 2, 1858
                    October 4, 1858 Hugh Parkinson, J.P.

Franklin A. Hughey to Sarah Margaret Smith, October 2, 1858
                    October 3, 1858 A. C. Dicky, J.P.

James Howard to Huldah Thompson, October 4, 1858
                    October 5, 1858 C. B. McDaniel, J.P.

Siliams Sullivan to Palina A. Rice, October 4, 1858
                    October 4, 1858 John H. Steelman, J.P.

Robert W. Wilson to Mary Elizabeth Hughy, October 6, 1853

William Epps to Francis Richerson, October 6, 1858
                    --   By W. L. Rees, J.P.

John J. Rhea to Catherine E. Ward, October 6, 1868
                    November 7, 1858 N. A. Bailey, M.G.

S. A. Bond to Mary Milton, October 7, 1858
                    October 8, 1858 B. M. G. Allsup, J.P.

Z. R. Dotson to Sarah Ann Radegan, October 11, 1858
                    October 11, 1858 S. H. McCord, J.P.

Benjamin Howard to Mary Jane Gattis, October 12, 1858
                    --   J. W. Holman, M.G.

(p 347)
Eli Abbott to Sarah E. Weaver, October 12, 1858
                    October 12, 1858 Robert Drennon, J.P.

Nathaniel Tucker to Martha Spick, --
                    October 12, 1858 Thos. H. Freeman, J.P.

George, W. Waggoner to Lutisha A. McAfee, October 13, 1858
                    October 19, 1858 John H. Steelman, J.P.

James R. Brewer to Sue E. Rivers October 13, 1858
                    October 14, 1858 N. A. Baily, M.G.

Wm. P. White to Adaline Dickson, October 14, 1858
                    October 14, 1858 Thos. H. Freeman, J.P.

James Massey to Mary Holley, October 14, 1858
                    October 14, 1858 Green Nichols, M.G.

John C. Crabtree to Mary Spencer, October 15, 1858
                    October 21, 1858 Elder John Copeland

Andrew M. Harbin to Vina E. Fowler, October 16, 1858
                    October 23, 1858 Geo. W. Carmechael, M.G.

E. P. Gibbs to Syntha O. Smith, October 18, 1858
                    October 26, 1858 Rev. R. D. Hardin

J. B. Tigert to Margaret A. Crawford, October 19, 1858
                    October 19, 1858 J. B. Warren

Benj. F. Womack to Mildred H. F. Green, October 20, 1858
           --   J. W. Holman, M.G.

G. H. Ray to Sarah Ann Couser, October 21, 1858
         October 21, 1858 By W. A. Hobbs, J.P.

(p 348)
H. C. Roussean to Bethenid Dobbs, October 22, 1858
         October 24, 1858 W. E. Carter, J.P.

J. W. Causby to Mahala Panter, October 23, 1858
         October 26, 1858 G. W. R. Moore, J.P.

H. H. Logan to Sallie K. Caldwell, October 23, 1858
         --   J. W. Holman, M.G.

Joseph H. Baxter to Samantha J. Guthrie, October 26, 1858
         October 26, 1858 By W. A. Hobbs, Esqr.

James F. Byers to Eliza J. Grubbs, October 27, 1858
         October 30, 1858 W. A. Gill, G.M.

Fleming J. Sisco to Mary Elizabeth Hill, October 31, 1858
         October 31, 1858 W. E. Carter, J.P.

Michal Sulivan to Joannah Sulivan, November 1, 1858
         November 4, 1858 H. V. Brown, C. Priest

George W. Steelman to Vitilea Fleming, November 1, 1858
         November 3, 1858 Thos. H. Freeman, J.P.

Thomas M. Harkins to Elizabeth M. Davidson, November 8, 1858
         November 9, 1858 G. W. R. Moore, J.P.

W. D. Yant to Sarah E. Commons, November 10, 1858
         November 10, 1858 R. L. McElree, M.G.

Carrol Commons to Elizabeth W. Harrison, November 11, 1858
(p 349)
John R. McCown to Martha K. Taylor, November 11, 1858
         November 10, 1858 By Henry P. Turner, M.G.

Bolen Merrett to Mary Birdsong, November 12, 1858
         November 12, 1858 John Caughran, J.P.

Moses S. Story to Susan Zimmermon, November 13, 1858
         November 14, 1858 G. E. Eagleton, V.D.M.

Wm. M. Spencer to Martha L. Haisellwood, November 13, 1858
         November 25, 1858 By Wm. R. Waggoner, J.P.

Hestarpas Stewart to Naomi E. J. Stinson, November 16, 1858
         November 16, 1868 Morton Towry, M.G.

John H. Kennday to Isabell C. West, November 16, 1858

Frances D. Epps to Sarah Frances Moore, November 16, 1858
                         November 11, 1858 Thomas Childs, M.G.

John J. Rowels to Elizabeth Griffis, November 18, 1858
                         November 18, 1858 R. D. Hardin, M.G.

Solomon Smith to Louiza Henslee, November 23, 1858
                         November 25, 1858 John Copeland, M.G.

R. M. Brown to M. E. V. Bearden, November 24, 1858
                         November 26, 1858 By A. S. Sloan, M.G.

R. L. McElvee to Mary E. Smith, November 24, 1858
                         November 24, 1858 S. E. Wilson, M.G.

(p 350)
John F. Gregory to Mary Cruse, November 25, 1858
                         November 25, 1858 R. L. McErae, M.G.

Amasa Flynt to Mariah W. Clarke, December 2, 1858
                         December 2, 1858 By Rev. N. T. Tower

William R. Lee to Sarah Stalloup, December 6, 1858
                         December 6, 1858 W. E. Carter, J.P.

James J. McCann to Sarah F. Webb, December 6, 1858
                         December 8, 1858 Wm. N. Hicks, Esqr.

Danl. T. Norman to Sarah Brown, December 6, 1858
                         December 7, 1858 By R. B. McGaugh, M.G.

Saml. Holt to Angaline Stewart, December 7, 1858
                         December 8, 1858 John Caughran, J.P.

J. H. Southworth to Mattie Y. Stonebraker, December 9, 1858
                         December 9, 1858 J. C. Elliott, M.G.

J. C. Brown to A. L. Hamilton, December 11, 1858
                         December 12, 1858 B. M. G. Allsup, J.P.

Willis Blankenship to Martha J. Thomison, December 14, 1858
                         December 14, 1858 E. Strode, M.G.

James A. Byors to Leah A. Jeffiers, December 14, 1858
                         December 14, 1858 John T. Gordon, J.P.

Manson E. Rowell to Nancy M. Smith, December 14, 1858
                         December 14, 1858 William N. Hicks, J.P.

(p 351)
Theophilus Pepper to Jane Carpenter, December 15, 1858
                         December 16, 1858 Wm. R. Martin, J.P.

A. H. Robinson to E. A. Emmons, December 15, 1858
                         December 16, 1868 G. S. Marcon, M.G.

Charles Fowler to Hannah Harbin, December 15, 1858
December 16, 1858   W. E. Carter, J.P.

Joseph S. Powe to Mary E. Farrar, December 15, 1858
December 19, 1858   Jas. N. George, J.P.

W. T. Armstrong to M. A. McKenzie, December 16, 1868
December 16, 1858   M. W. Yant, J.P.

G. W. Jones to Elizabeth M. Whitaker, December 20, 1858
December 21, 1858   Bradley Kimbrough, M.G.

Thos. Hale to Emeline Barnes, December 20, 1858
December 20, 1858   G. W. R. Moore, J.P.

G. A. Robertson to Martha F. Parker, December 20, 1858
December 23, 1858   R. B. McGough, M.G.

Marcus D. Motes to Emely F. Nelson, December 20, 1858

James W. Newsom to Sarah C. H. Overby, December 20, 1858
December 21, 1858   W. L. Rees, J.P.

Joseph G. Caragan to Franse E. Higgins, December 21, 1858
December 22, 1858   N. A. Bailey, M.G.

(p 352)
Wm. A. Lee to Marica Ambrox, December 22, 1858
December 23, 1858   T. S. Corder, J.P.

Andrew Waggoner to Emely Jane Edens, December 22, 1858
December 23, 1858   W. A. Hobbs, J.P.

Thos. J. Coats to Mary A. Stewart, December 22, 1858

J. W. Lemmon to Martha C. Pigg, December 22, 1858
December --, 1858   J. B. Warren, M.G.

Isaac F. McElyea to Milta C. Woodward, December 22, 1858
December 23, 1858   J. N. George, J.P.

George R. Allen to Isabella Strong, December 22, 1858
December 23, 1858   A. S. Sloan, M.G.

William M. Woodard to Eveline P. Grills, December 23, 1858
December 23, 1858   John H. Bryson, M.G.

David M. Tafts to Sarah A. F. Powell, December 24, 1858
December 26, 1858   J. A. Methous

M. C. Ratliff to Sarah C. Rickey, December 24, 1858
December 26, 1858   W. E. Carter, J.P.

A. J. Waggoner to Susan Hensley, December 24, 1858
December 25, 1858   John Copeland, M.G.

J. M. Smith to Mary E. Evans, December 29, 1858
                    February 8, 1859 S. F. Spencer, J.P.

(p 353)
James C. Halbert to Frances D. Gibson, December 29, 1858
                    December 30, 1858 A. G. Smith, M.G.

John Mingea to Margaret V. Grisard, December 30, 1858
                    December 30, 1858 J. T. Gordon, J.P.

D. A. Benson to Ruth J. Harben, January 3, 1859
                    January 4, 1859 T. S. Corder, J.P.

Samuel Stallcup to Julia Ann Hunter, January 4, 1859
                    January 6, 1859 W. L. Rees, J.P.

Harmiston Gowen to Frances Prosser, January 4, 1859

J. W. Forsyth to Isabella C. Lesley, January 6, 1859
                    January 7, 1859 John Copeland, M.G.

Spencer C. Dodson to Permelea Ralekid, January 8, 1859
                    January 10, 1859 John Coland, M.G.

Joseph Lock to Jane Rhodes, January 8, 1859
                    January 12, 1859 Wm. R. Marlin, J.P.

Nathan Moore to Alsa Couser, January 10, 1859
                    January 18, 1859 W. A. Hobbs, J.P.

John F. Redd to Eliza A. Burnes, January 11, 1859
                    January 17, 1859 G. W. R. Moore, J.P.

Cullen Bailey to S. A. Holman, January 12, 1859
                    January 13, 1859 J. W. Holman, M.G.

(p 354)
J. H. Milliken to D. A. Anderson, January 12, 1859

A. M. Walker to A. M. Gibson, January 13, 1859
                    January 13, 1859 A. F. Rankin, M.G.

John Hoots to Hattie N. Hill, January 17, 1859
                    January 18, 1859 J. W. Holman, M.G.

Wyatt Jean to Susanah Bryant, January 21, 1859
                    January 21, 1859 Thos. S. Corder, J.P.

Thomas Daniel to Nancy Billings, January 25, 1859
                    January 27, 1859 John Caughran, J.P.

James M. Rowell to Sarah J. McKinny, January 28, 1859
                    January 29, 1859 Wm. R. Martin, J.P.

Benjamin F. McAfee to Sarah J. Bates, January 29, 1859
                    February 3, 1859 John L. Ashby, J.P.

C. Forrister to Sarah B. Taylor, January 31, 1859
February 1, 1859 Bradley Kimbrough, M.G.

W. F. Stockstill to Nancy Ashby, January 31, 1859
February 1, 1859 F. R. Waggoner, J.P.

William Cobb to Sarah Norman, February 1, 1859
February 3, 1859 P. R. McGough, M.G.

R. F. Holman to A. E. Shoffner, February 5, 1859
February 8, 1859 John Copeland, M.G.

(p 355)
Millford Grammar to Eliza Ann Lock, February 7, 1859
February 8, 1859 J. L. Ashby, J.P.

Champion Smith to Frances E. Smith, February 7, 1859
February 10, 1859 S. F. Spencer, J.P.

Samuel Price to Sarah L. Call, February 12, 1859
February 17, 1859 C. E. McDaniel, J.P.

James Kirkland to Susan Bowers, February 22, 1859
February 22, 1859 John S. Davis, M.G.

James Parkinson to Mary Pinkerton, February 24, 1859
February 24, 1859 A. S. Sloan, M.G.

W. B. Smith to Sarah E. Vaugh, March 9, 1859
March 10, 1859 Wm. B. Martin, J.P.

Wm. R. Bonner to Sarah T. Moodey, March 10, 1859
March 10, 1859 D. S. Patterson, J.P.

William Scott to Carlotta Daniel, March 10, 1859
March 10, 1859 John Caughran, J.P.

M. A. Prosser to L. J. Leftwick, March 12, 1859
March 13, 1859 W. E. Jewell, M.J.

W. W. James to S. V. Freeman, March 16, 1859
March 17, 1859 J. W. Holman, M.G.

E. H. Brewer to R. J. Smith, March 22, 1859
March 22, 1859 Bradly Kimbrough, M.G.

(p 356)
William L. Thomas to Elizabeth B. Clerk, March 28, 1859
March 30, 1859 G. E. Eagleton, V.D.M.

W. W. McNelly to Mary A. Johnson, March 31, 1859
March 31, 1859 W. L. Tarbet, G.M.

Thos. H. Silvester to Mary Merrell, April 4, 1859
April 5, 1859 G. S. Marcon, M.G.

F. E. B. Stevenson to M. L. Franklin, April 7, 1859

R. M. Dunlap to Mary E. Cole, April 7, 1859
                    April 7, 1859   W. F. Zimnerman, J.P.

Leonard Marberry to Mary Dosier, April 11, 1859
                    April 11, 1859   Robert Drennon, J.P.

Saml. E. Gowen to Mary E. Prosser, April 12, 1859
                    April 19, 1859   G. W. R. Moore, J.P.

Alexander Thompson to Mary Jane Bradford, April 12, 1859
                    April 13, 1859   L. L. Clark, J.P.

Bennet Whitaker to Sarah Shipp, April 16, 1859
                    April 17, 1859   William Pryor, J.P.

Rowlen Newsom to B. A. Jackson, April 16, 1859

Jas. B. Armstrong to Mary E. Sharp, April 20, 1859
                    April 21, 1859   G. W. R. Moore, J.P.

(p 357)
William C. Yeats to Sarah J. Fincher, April 28, 1859
                    April 28, 1859   J. A. Edmondson, M.G.

Charles Bettitcalf to Sarah Rivers, May 2, 1859
                    May 2, 1859   William R. Smith, J.P.

Wm. R. Brown to Sophy A. Mitcalfe, May 3, 1859
                    May 3, 1859   W. A. Hobbs, Esqr.

D. O. Hicks to Mary Ann Holder, May 3, 1859
                    May 3, 1859   Amos Small, J.P.

John B. Hamilton to Sarah H. Smith, May 14, 1859
                    May 15, 1859   J. B. Tigert, M.G.

James Shires to Manda Huckabee, May 17, 1859
                    May 17, 1859   B. M. G. Allsup, J.P.

Henry H. Sugg to Elvira Allen, May 19, 1859
                    May 19, 1859   A. H. Berry, M.G.

John Holly to Nelly Sorrels, May 21, 1859
                    May 22, 1859   G. W. R. Moore, J.P.

Archabald Davis to Margaret Massey, May 25, 1859
                    May 26, 1859   John L. Ashby, J.P.
(p 358)
B. F. Holley to Mary Ann Simmons, May 28, 1859
                    May 29, 1859   G. W. R. Moore, J.P.

Maxfield Henslee to Nancy A. Haizlewood, June 1, 1859
                    June 5, 1859   W. R. Waggoner, J.P.

Robert W. Williamson to Louisa Thompson, --
                    June 2, 1859   Thomas H. Freeman, J.P.

Joseph H. Ringo to Martha E. Gillespie, June 8, 1859
June 9, 1859 Matt M. Marshall, M.G.

T. M. Ramsy to Mary Ann Elizabeth Jean, June 11, 1859
June 12, 1859 C. B. White, J.P.

Kennett M. Loyd to Martha Jane Allen, June 15, 1859
July 3, 1859 W. A. Hobbs, Esqr.

M. A. Wisener to E. O. Sawyers, June 30, 1859
June 3, 1859 A. H. Berry, M.G.

Lorenzo Dow to Mary F. Price, July 4, 1859
July 4, 1859 John Caughran, J.P.

Levi Michael to Melissa Tunkenley, July 4, 1859
July 5, 1859 Samuel Stiles, J.P.

John A. Cracy to Frances M. Smith, July 7, 1859
July 7, 1859 R. L. McGeehee, M.G.

Alfred D. Stovall to Jane Maroney, July 9, 1859

(p 359)
Jas. J. Pitts to Martha Jane Albright, July 9, 1859
July 10, 1859 N. A. Bailey, M.G.

Lewis G. James to Sytha Ann Taylor, July 9, 1859

M. A. Edmondson to Charlotta H. Foster, July 12, 1859
July 13, 1859 John Roach, J.P.

Joseph L. Hudson to Easther E. Moon, July 14, 1859
July 14, 1859 M. W. Yant, J.P.

R. L. Weaver to Mary Randolph, July 14, 1859
July 14, 1859 C. B. McDaniel, J.P.

Patrick Snow to Sarah Jean, July 18, 1859
July 18, 1859 Thos. S. Corder, J.P.

James L. Thompson to Jane Worshburn, July 20, 1859
July 20, 1859 Amos Small, J.P.

Gabriel Young to Adaline Sorrells, July 21, 1859
July 21, 1859 Green Nichols, M.G.

J. L. Burrow to Margaret Binhjam, July 23, 1859

David Jolly to Sarah A. Bryant, July 25, 1859
July 25, 1859 Thos. S. Corder, J.P.

(p 360)
J. P. Ensley to Julia Clift, July 25, 1859
July 26, 1859 W. M. McKinny, J.P.

John W. Hobbs to Martha Ann Roe, July 28, 1859

Wm. C. Taylor to Elizabeth Jean, July 29, 1859
                      August 1, 1859 S. F. Spencer, J.P.

Joseph R. Nichols to Pantha R. Overby, August 1, 1859

Wm. H. Brown to Frances J. Martin, August 2, 1859
                      August 7, 1859 W. A. Hobbs, J.P.

John H. Cox to Elizabeth A. King, August 2, 1859
                      August 2, 1859 A. C. Dickey, J.P.

J. E. Remells to Mary F. Rees, August 3, 1859

A. J. Fitch to Nancy J. Webster, August 4, 1859
                      August 4, 1859 T. S. Corder, J.P.

Joseph D. Hester to Frances A. Stephenson, August 5, 1859
                      August 7, 1859 G. W. Pucket, M.G.

Wm. E. Moon to Eliza Stockstill, August 15, 1859
                      August 16, 1869 Hugh Thomison, J.P.

(p 361)
John A. Reavis to Susan C. Byrum, August 20, 1859
                      August 28, 1859 Jeremiah Dean, M.G.

Henry J. Pamplin to Mary D. McLaughlin, August 23, 1859
                      August 23, 1859 R. M. Haggard, M.G.

George P. Landman to Mary Frances Sivley, August 24, 1859
                      August 24, 1859 J. A. Edmondson, M.G.

William Street to Mary Louisa Jones, August 24, 1859
                      August 25, 1859 Henry T. Turner, M.G.

Ethelbert Palmer to Mary Lucinda Hardeman, August 26, 1859
                      September 6, 1859 Wm. J. Bachman, M.G.

Colman Roggers to Lyddia Polly, September 6, 1859

Jas. A. Shoemake to Nancy Cole, September 6, 1859
                      September 6, 1859 J. S. Davis, M.G.

John R. Austin to Elizabeth Partain, September 7, 1859

W. R. Driver to Margaret A. Cox, September 8, 1859
                      September 8, 1859 Jeremiah Dean, M. G.

Thomas Dickey to Elvera A. McGeehee, September 9, 1859
                      September 11, 1859 J. H. Eslick, J.P.

H. H. Hunter to Elvira Powers, September 10, 1859
                      September 11, 1859 Saml. Stiles, J.P.

E. McKee to Sally Campbell, September 10, 1859
            September 11, 1859 D. Jacks, M.G.

(p 362)
Brown Pinkerton to Narcissa Hedgepeth, September 14, 1859
            September 14, 1859 Hugh Parkinson, J.P.

J. B. Bedwell to Sarah A. Fells, September 14, 1859
            September 15, 1859 Robt. M. Haggard, M.G.

William F. M. Oliver to Louisa J. Perry, September 14, 1859
            September 14, 1859 J. T. Gordon, J.P.

D/ M. Holloway to Phebe Elizabeth Clark, September 19, 1859
            September 19, 1859 A. H. Berry, M.G.

Joel T. Pigg to Martha Elizabeth Sullivan, September 19, 1859
            September 21, 1859 John Roach, J.P.

James Tucker to Amy Speck, September 21, 1859
            September 22, 1859 J. H. Eslick, J.P.

James Clark to Sarah Gulley, September 28, 1859
            September 28, 1859 Wm. R. Smith, J.P.

Reubin Webster to Amanda M. Myrick, September 29, 1859
            September 29, 1859 Smith L. Walker, J.P. (Seal)

Pleasant A. Randolph to Lucinda J. Caruthers, October 3, 1859
            October 3, 1859 J. M. Brown, M.G.

James M. Clift to Martha L. Hughey, October 3, 1859
            October 4, 1859 By H. M. McKinney, J.P.

Wm. C. Murdock to Minerva A. Rees, October 3, 1859
            October 6, 1859 R. L. McEhee, M.G.

(p 363)
R. A. McDonald to Martha Cordelia McKinney, October 4, 1859
            October 4, 1859 M. B. Dewitt, M.G.

Henry W. Hamblen to Elizabeth Hall, October 5, 1859

Thos. R. Hicks to Louisa Ann Williams, October 6, 1859
            October 6, 1859 Robt. Drennon, J.P.

Soloman R. Keith to Rebecca E. Ashby, October 6, 1859
            October 6, 1859 R. M. Haggard, M.G.

G. M. Steele to Martha Craig, October 10, 1859
            October 10, 1859 Matt H. Marshall, Minister

John D. Moore to Lucy Ann Caldwell, October 10, 1859
            October 11, 1859 M. B. Dewitt, M.G.

James Sevels to Elizabeth Moss, October 12, 1859
                    October 13, 1859   G. S. Warson, M.G.

Carr D. White to Elizabeth Watson, October 15, 1859
                    October 16, 1859   W. E. Carter, J.P.

H. L. Patton to Mary Bryson, October 17, 1859
                    October 18, 1859   R. E. McMullen, M.G.

S. W. Foster to Martha P. Pinkerton, October 17, 1859
                    October 17, 1859   A. S. Sloan, M.G.

W. S. Curtis to Narcissa Oliver, October 22, 1859
                    October 18, 1859   A. S. Sloan, M.G.

(p 364)
Joseph A. Good to Sarah J. Spencer, October 25, 1859
                    October 26, 1859   A. S. Sloan

A. D. Smith to M. M. Kennedy, October 25, 1859
                    October 28, 1859   S. M. Howell, M.G.

William Norman to L. Dobbs, October 26, 1859
                    October 30, 1859   W. E. Carter, J.P.

A. J. Alford to Margarett A. Russell, October 27, 1859
                    October 27, 1859   M. D. Dewitt, M.G.

John F. Montgomery to Susan H. Askins, October 31, 1859
                    November 1, 1859   --

Newton W. Findly to Harriet Ann Brown, November 5, 1859
                    November 5, 1859   W. H. McKee

N. S. Rees to Nancy Johnson, November 7, 1859
                    November 8, 1859   Wm. F. Anthony

John H. Walker to Nicey J. Crawley, November 9, 1859
                    November 11, 1859   D. Jacks, M.C.

William Grant to Sarah Frances Donaldson, November 10, 1859
                    November 10, 1859   R. J. Scivally

R. L. Whitworth to Malissa Woodall, November 15, 1859

J. F. Webb to Mary Ann McCown, November 16, 1859
                    November 17, 1859   Wm. N. Hicks, J.P.

(p 365)
S. M. Conger to R. C.C. Beall Norton, November 23, 1859
                    November 23, 1859   J. C. Putman, M.G.

G. W. Hopper to E. J. Hedgpeth, November 23, 1859
                    November 24, 1859   S. M. Emmons, M.G.

John H. Scott to Susan Ann George, November 23, 1859
                    November 23, 1859   W. R. Bledsoe, J.P.

John W. Cunningham to Davy Waggoner, November 23, 1859
                     November 24, 1859 John H. Steelman, J.P.

P. G. Cole to Amanda Bosch, November 24, 1859
                     November 24, 1859 William N. Hicks, J.P.

William Williams to Charlotte Watson, November 26, 1859
                     November 26, 1859 John Roach, J.P.

Wm. H. Myers to Amada J. Wright, November 28, 1859
                     November 29, 1859 F. L. Ezell, J.P.

E. F. M. Grace to Susan M. Cluts, November 29, 1859

W. R. Freenwood to Elizabeth Patley, December 3, 1859
                     December 3, 1859 J. L. Gordon, J.P.

Carrell Williams to Catherin Powels, December 6, 1859
                     December 7, 1859 A. J. Steel, M.G.

Shadrack Holly to Mahuld F. Simmons, December 10, 1859
                     December 10, 1859 G. W. R. Moore, J.P.
(p 366)
William Ables to Mary Jane Elizabeth Rebecca Dempsey, December 10, 1859
                     December 10, 1859 M. W. Yants, Esqr.

Wm. T. Gill to May Finer Lloyd, December 12, 1859
                     December 12, 1859 Wm. A. Gill, M.G.

James Pigg to Emeline P. Joter, December 12, 1859
                     December 12, 1859 John Roach, J.P.

James M. Lewter to Caroline York, December 14, 1859
                     December 22, 1859 Jas. L. Coleman

W. Z. Jennings to Margaret A. Stiles, December 15, 1859
                     December 15, 1859 W. E. Carter, J.P.

J. V. Smith to Nancy Stafford, December 15, 1859
                     December 15, 1859 John L. Ashby, J.P.

Wm. R. Smith to Martha E. Koonce, December 17, 1859

L. W. Gale to Caroline Betz, December 20, 1859
                     December 20, 1859 Hugh Parkinson, J.P.

J. F. Ledford to Louisa Lund, December 21, 1859
                     December 22, 1859 John Roach, J.P.

P. E. Gilliland to M. Addie Drake, December 23, 1859
                     December 23, 1859 Matt M. Marshall, M.G.

A. Sutleff to Nancy S. Shaw, December 24, 1859
                     December 25, 1859 J. W. Holman, M.G.

(p 367)

John W. Haizelwood to Mary Ann Jenkins, December 24, 1859
                December 24, 1859 Wm. Cattis, J.P.

F. M. Baldwin to Latisha C. Barham, December 26, 1859
                December 27, 1859 G. W. R. Moore, J.P.

H. C. Shaw to Mary Jane Mullins, December 26, 1859
                December 26, 1859 Robt. Drennon, J.P.

Wm. J. Grills to Sarah Smith, December 27, 1859
                December 27, 1859 Wm. A. Gill, G.M.

Joseph Luttrell to M. Ann Cox, December 31, 1859
                January 1, 1860   --

Wm. Buchanan to Susan Boling, January 2, 1860

Wm. W. S. Luter to Elizabeth C. Bledsoe, January 2, 1860
                January 5, 1860 S. H. Brown, M.G.

J. H. Walker to Nancy E. Maben, January 3, 1860
                January 11, 1860 John Milton

Wm. R. Ellis to Louisa Jane Rowell, January 3, 1860
                January 3, 1860 R. M. Haggard, M.G.

Thos. J. Rich to Clarissa Hill, January 4, 1860
                January 5, 1860 Joseph Dameron, J.P.

James Jolley to Margaret Ward, January 4, 1860
                January 5, 1860 W. L. Reese, J.P.

(p 368)

G. H. Rinfrow to Nancy C. Cates, January 4, 1860
                January 5, 1860 Dempsey Sullivan, J.P.

Wm. A. Sloan to Martha J. Moore, January 5, 1860
                January 5, 1860 A. S. Sloan

Henry Marr to Jane Warren, January 7, 1860
                January 8, 1860 W. L. Reese, J.P.

Jesse Rochel to Margaret Hays, January 11, 1860
                January 12, 1860 A. S. Sloan, M.G.

John P. Stewart to Eliza Lindsey, January 11, 1860
                January 12, 1860 A. S. Sloan, M.G.

Willis Stephens to Cyntha Stephens, January 16, 1860
                January 16, 1860 Thomas S. Corder, J.P.

R. M. Rambo to Elizabeth Jackson, January 16, 1860

Martin V. Clark to Mary A. C. Gully, January 17, 1860
                January 17, 1860 L. L. Clark, J.P.

James A. Clark to Mary E. Gunter, January 17, 1860
                    January 18, 1860 By W. M. McKinney, J.P.

Alexander Riddle to Jane Dean, January 17, 1860
                    January 19, 1860 John E. Holt, M.G.

A. H. Gill to Martha Taylor, January 18, 1860
                    January 18, 1860 W. F. Rees, J.P.

(p 369)
Wm. A. Sullenger to Nancy Ward, January 8, 1860
                    January 19, 1860 J. H. Eslick, J.P.

Jas. S. Conner to M. E. Daniel, January 18, 1860

John W. Hampton to Nancy Jane Farrar, January 20, 1860

J. H. Dobbs to L. H. Hill, January 25, 1860
                    January 26, 1860 J. W. Holman, M.G.

John Vickers to Martha Catharine Swinford, January 26, 1860
                    January 26, 1860 Robt. Drennon, J.P.

Wm. W. Cannon to Nancy E. Claunch, January 28, 1860

J. R. Hinson to N. M. Smith, January 30, 1860
                    January 31, 1860 Rev. R. D. Hardin

Harris Tucker to Adaline Wright, January 30, 1860
                    February 2, 1860 S. M. Emmons, M.G.

W. K. Taylor to L. M. Wiseman, January 31, 1860

J. A. Stiles to Maria Payne, February 1, 1860
                    February 2, 1860 J. H. Eslick, J.P.

R. M. James to Eliza Jane Taylor, February 4, 1860

(p 370)
Daniel Warren to Priscilla Jackson, February 6, 1860
                    February 12, 1860 W. L. Reese

John Dobbs to Priscilla Jane Stanley, February 6, 1860
                    February 12, 1860 W. E. Carter, J.P.

H. P. McElyea to Frances A. Pitcock, February 6, 1860
                    February 12, 1860 D. L. Mitchell, M.G.

R. E. Buchanan to M. A. Horton, February 20, 1860
                    February 20, 1860 J. T. Gordon, J.P.

F. M. Snoddy to Martha G. Howard, February 22, 1860
                    March 1, 1860 W. E. Carter, J.P.

Enoch Cunningham to Nancy K. Noah, February 25, 1860
                    February 28, 1860 A. C. Dickey, J.P.

Wm. N. Young to Nancy M. Woodall, February 27, 1860

A. M. Whitworth to Alpha N. Chiles, February 27, 1860
February 28, 1860 Smith L. Walker, J.P.

Wm. Pigg to Sarah M. Dyer, March 1, 1860
March 1, 1860 John Roach, J.P.

John N. Helton to May Ramsy Read, March 7, 1860
March 8, 1860 G. W. Nichols, G.M.

Wm. Stubblefield to Martha Carter, March 19, 1860
March 26, 1860 J. H. Eslick, J.P.

(p 371)
Jas. A. Albright to Susanna M. E. Baxter, March 28, 1860
March 29, 1860 Smith L. Walker, J.P.

Wm. C. Word to Sarah R. Moyers, March 29, 1860
March 29, 1860 J. H. Eslick, J.P.

John L. Clark to Julea M. C. Neal, March 30, 1860
March 30, 1860 M. B. Dewitt, M.G.

Thos. A. Maddox to Sarah J. Pamplin, March 31, 1860
April 1, 1860 Benj. F. Clark, J.P.

William Williams to Casey Ann Pylant, April 2, 1860

James E. Green to Mary F. Bonner, April 11, 1860
April 12, 1860 G. W. Puckett, M.G.

Lillie Wilson Beck to Angeline Chick, April 14, 1860
April 15, 1860 John T. Gordon, J.P.

Jesse L. Jean to Cyntha Caroline Bogel, April 16, 1860
April 16, 1860 S. H. McCord, J.P.

William A. Walker to Nancy C. Koonce, April 19, 1860

Elisha M. McClure to Susan Catharine Brown, April 19, 1860
April 19, 1860 J. H. Eslick, J.P.

(p 372)
Wm. T. Cartright to Fannie Catharine Hill, April 21, 1860
April 21, 1860 J. H. Eslick, J.P.

G. W. Higgins to Sue Carrigan, May 9, 1860
May 9, 1860 J. B. Warren, M.G.

Wm. T. Baldwin to Adaline Daniel, May 12, 1860
May 24, 1860 Wm. R. Waggoner, J.P.

R. U. McEntire to A. A. Franklin, May 16, 1860
May 17, 1860 Z. T. Ezell, J.P.

Anderson Daves to Manerva Bartlett, May 23, 1860
                     May 23, 1860   J. A. Prosser, J.P.

Wm. Cannon to Nancy Claunch, May 24, 1860
                     May 24, 1860   Martin Towry, G.M.

M. P. Russell to Margaret M. Gibson, May 28, 1860
                     May 31, 1860   J. G. Bledsoe, M.G.

H. M. Bledsoe to Sarah Bond, June 12, 1860
                     June 14, 1860   R. D. Hardin, M.G.

Thos. Connelly to Mary Nealy, June 26, 1860
                     June 27, 1860   M. B. Dewitt, M.G.

John L. Steelman to Mary Steelman, June 27, 1860
                     June 28, 1860   James B. Hudson, J.P.

Thos. J. Tucker to Jane Caroline Armstrong, June 28, 1860

(p 373)
Nathan Gaivey to Patsey Smith, July 1, 1860
                     July 1, 1860   W. W. Wilson, J.P.

George W. Whitworth to Dicey Priscilla Nancy Adeline Dempsey, July 2, 1860
                     July 3, 1860   James B. Hudson, J.P.

Thos. Hart to Sarah E. Hunter, July 3, 1860
                     July 3, 1860   Joseph Damons, J.P.

J. P. Kent to Ruth K. Thompson, July 10, 1860
                     July 10, 1860   Benjamin Fox, J.P.

Berry Gattis to Nancy Howard, July 16, 1860
                     July 24, 1860   J. H. Eslick, J.P.

M. J. Peddingfield to Elizabeth R. Mitchell, July 17, 1860
                     July 17, 1860   Z. T. Ezell, J.P.

S. R. Reynolds to Julea A. Street, July 19, 1860
                     July 19, 1860   W. C. Soloman, J.P.

R. D. C. McMillin to Faney Howard, July 23, 1860
                     July 24, 1860   J. H. Eslick, J.P.

Thos. B. Strong to Willie E. Eltoll, July 26, 1860
                     July 26, 1860   R. Farguharson, J.P.

John Moore to Nancy E. Kiser, July 28, 1860
                     August 2, 1860   J. L. Bryant, J.P.

(p 374)
Josephus Miles to Polly Pearce, July 28, 1860
                     July 29, 1860 Wm R. Waggoner, J.P.

John Honey to Lydia C. Whitworth, July 30, 1860

Joseph H. Pigg to Delinda L. Tamplin, August 1, 1860
                    August 2, 1860 John Roach, J.P.

D. R. Holloway to Elizabeth Spence, August 2, 1860
                    August 2, 1860 A. S. Slone, M.G.

Thos. B. Lee to Priscilla L. Peoples, August 4, 1860
                    August 5, 1860 F. L. Ezell, J.P.

John Hill to Mary Ann Yarborough, August 7, 1860

John Wilson to Mary M. Kiser, August 11, 1860
                    August 17, 1860 Robt. M. Whitman, J.P.

James Brown to Susan E. E. Enochs, August 11, 1860
                    August 12, 1860 Samuel Bobo, J.P.

Wm. M. Smith to Mary E. Hardin, August 14, 1860
                    August 14, 1860 Wm. A. Rhoads, J.P.

George H. Waggoner to Ann Parks, August 14, 1860
                    August 16, 1860 John L. Ashby, J.P.

Martin V. Howell to M. H. Womack, August 15, 1860
                    August 16, 1860 A. G. Smith, J.P.

John P. Keith to E. S. Yant, August 16, 1860
                    August 16, 1860 James B. Hudson, J.P.

(p 375)
William Moyers to Mary Wise, August 18, 1860
                    August 23, 1860 Samuel Bobo, J.P.

Dudley Tipps to Jane R. Tripp, August 20, 1860
                    August 23, 1860 Wm. R. Waggoner, J.P.

James W. Wise to Mary Ann Bailey, August 21, 1860
                    August 21, 1860 Samuel Bobo, J.P.

John B. Gray to Mary Wormack, August 21, 1860
                    August 26, 1860 Samuel Bobo, J.P.

M. A. Clifford to Elizabeth Solomon, August 24, 1860

Wm. Mullins to Selome Sanders, August 27, 1860
                    August 28, 1860 Martin Towry, G.M.

W. B. Hedgepeth to Harriet Luna, September 3, 1860
                    September 4, 1860 John Roach, J.P. for L.C.

George H. Britten to Mary Elizabeth Rice, September 4, 1860

Eli Barns to Ellen Ramsey, September 6, 1860
                    September 6, 1860 Benjamine F. Clark, J.P. L.C.

Jackson Smith to Elzada Hall, September 6, 1860

Charles Moore to Mary F. Gully, September 8, 1860
                September 14, 1860 Martin Towry, G.M.

(p 376)
William M. Phagan to Nancy V. Moore, September 13, 1860
                September 13, 1860 A. S. Slone

Aaron Parks to Angeline McNeese, September 14, 1860
                September 25, 1860 W. H. Thompson, J.P.

James T. Coop to Virginia A. Webb, September 18, 1860
                September 19, 1860 W. E. Carter, J.P.

Pallis Griffin to Elizabeth Pitcock, September 19, 1860
                September 19, 1860 D. L. Mitchell, M.G.

James M. Coats to Orlena B. Shipp, September 19, 1860
                September 20, 1860 William Tillery, M.G.

Benjamin F. Clark to Sarah Jane Sanders, September 20, 1860
                September 20, 1860 David G. Smith, J.P.

Morgan Carter to Elizabeth Davidson, September 24, 1860
                September 25, 1860 Wm. D. Moorhead, J.P.

Jerome B. Williams to Rutha E. Barley, September 25, 1860

William Ray to Manerva E. Dennis, September 27, 1860

Hiram Howard to Elizabeth Rudd, October 1, 1860
                October 4, 1860 J. L. Bryant, J.P.

John C. Mills to Margaret Rutledge, October 3, 1860
                October 4, 1860 James B. Hudson, J.P.
(p 377)
Jacob Mitchel to Letha Ann Elizabeth Trip, October 6, 1860
                October 7, 1860 J. D. Smith, J.P.

C. W. Lucas to J. L. Motlow, October 10, 1860
                October 11, 1860 J. W. Holman, M.G.

C. H. Cunningham to S. N. Story, October 11, 1860
                October 11, 1860 W. W. Wilson, J.P.

Daniel Thompson to Artinesa Clifford, October 12, 1860
                October 12, 1860 J. A. Prosser, J.P.

William Dawson to Pheba T. Sawyers, Oxtober 12, 1860
                October 12, 1860 A. G. Smith, M.G.

James C. Stuard to Marsset R. Patrick, October 13, 1860
                October 14, 1860 Needham Koonce, J.P.

James Roden to Susan Y. Adbit, October 13, 1860
                October 14, 1860 David G. Smith, J.P.

N. J. Smith to Sopha S. Robertson, October 13, 1860
October 14, 1860 W. T. Wilson, J.P.

Wm. J. Harris to Jane Mosely, October 22, 1860

Lewis Sandlin to Elizabeth Howel, October 22, 1860
October 22, 1860 John Caughran, J.P.

(p 378)
Amos Small to Elizabeth M. G. Clark, October 23, 1860
October 23, 1860 James B. Hudson, J.P.

Thomas Croce to Mary M. Creson, October 25, 1860
October 25, 1860 William Ashby, J.P.

W. M. Tucker to Amanda Jane Tanbelerster, October 26, 1860
October 28, 1860 J. H. Eslick, J.P.

James H. Majores to Martha Miles, October 27, 1860

William Harrison to Martha E. Cunningham, October 27, 1860
October 27, 1860 S. M. Hampton, J.P.

T. A. Patillo to Fanny Jane Hale, October 29, 1860
October 29, 1860 D. L. Mitchell, M.G.

Micajah L. McElroy to Martha Whitaker, October 30, 1860
October 30, 1860 A. G. Smith, J.P.

John Mills to Margret Jane Sanders, November 1, 1860
November 1, 1860 L. L. Cole, J.P.

William Carter to Lucretia Jane McCowen, November 4, 1860
November 6, 1860 Rev. John Milton

Isaac J. Smith to L. Z. Hall, November 12, 1860
November 12, 1860 A. T. Nicks, J.P.

(p 379)
John H. Dyer to Dillia E. Chitwood, November 13, 1860
November 14, 1860 Wm. K. Smith, J.P.

Moses Fist to Mary S. Jones, November 14, 1860

Oliver Street to Hester D. Holey, November 14, 1860
November 14, 1860 A. F. Driskill J.P.

John W. Tillery to Nancy Elizabeth McKinney, November 17, 1860
November 17, 1860 J. Vanhoozer, J.P.

Wm. Roland to Terlitha Elizabeth Locker, November 22, 1860

D. J. Noblett to S. Boon, November 22, 1860
November 22, 1860 J. L. Bryant, J.P.

James H. Hanes to Martha P. Riddle, November 23, 1860
November 25, 1860 John H. Holt, M.G.

James P. Carthy to Sarah A. Hughey, November 24, 1860
                     November 25, 1860 G. Eagleton, V.D.M.

Wm. H. Ingle to Mary Catharine Bell, November 27, 1860
                     November 27, 1860 E. L. Bester, M.G.

George A. Andrews to Nancey G. Jones, November 28, 1860

(p 380)
Thomas P. Sumners to Sarah E. Brothertin, December 1, 1860
                     December 2, 1860 David G. Smith, J.P.

B. F. Tiller to Louisa Thompson, December 1, 1860
                     December 4, 1860 Wm. Ashby, J.P.

G. W. Stephenson to Judia L. Gay, December 3, 1860
                     December 6, 1860 A. G. Smith, M.G.

James S. Merroll to Loisa Josephine Feed, December 3, 1860
                     December 11, 1860 J. Vanhoozer, J.P.

Thomas M. Rowell to Isabella D. McCawley, December 4, 1860
                     December 4, 1860 Rev. R. D. Hardin, J.P.

Henry Rutledge to Rachel Thompson, December 5, 1860
                     December 5, 1860 Wm. Ashby, J.P.

W. J. Davidson to Elizabeth A. Smith, December 6, 1860
                     December 6, 1860 M. B. Dewitt, M.G.

D. M. Armstrong to Martha F. King, December 11, 1860
                     December 6, 1860   --

John H. Brewer to Margret D. Donham, December 11, 1860

(p 381)
John W. Kelley to T. C. Moores, December 11, 1860
                     December 11, 1860 W. H. Brown

John F. Fly to Sarah Glen McLaughlin, December 12, 1860
                     December 12, 1860 A. T. Rankin, M.G.

Samuel K. Murdock to Sarah Patterson, December 13, 1860
                     December 13, 1860 A. G. Smith, M. G.

Joseph C. Stephens to Mary Jane Taney, December 13, 1860
                     December 13, 1860 A. J. Childress, J.P.

T. D. Moore to Mary Frances Buchanan, December 18, 1860
                     December 24, 1860 A. T. Rankin, M.G.

James N. Epps to Hepsey Prosser, December 19, 1860
                     December 20, 1860, James B. Hudson, J.P.

J. W. Randolph to Hanah J. Thurman, December 20, 1860
                     December 20, 1860, E. L. Hester, M.G.

E. A. Bray to Joanah McCray, December 20, 1860
                       December 20, 1860 P. P. McGough, M.G.

Robert W. Locker to Rachel T. Rowe, December 20, 1860

James C. Epps to Julia Ann Taylor, December 22, 1860
                       December 24, 1860 P. P. Clarke, J.P.

(p 382)
J. H. Brown to Amanda Shull, December 22, 1860
                       December 24, 1860 A. T. Pankin, M.G.

John Smith to Mary M. Caton, December 24, 1860
                       December 24, 1860 Rev. R. D. Hardin

Smith Ceton to Mary Frances Smith, December 27, 1860
                       December 28, 1860 F. L. Ezell, J.P.

Wm. Thomas Clanton to Nancy Honnez, December 29, 1860
                       December 30, 1860 W. E. Carter, J.P.

J. E. Baily to Nancey Catharine Nash, December 31, 1860

John Stubblefield to Tilitha A. Claunch, December 31, 1860

www.ingramcontent.com/pod-product-compliance
Lightning Source LLC
Chambersburg PA
CBHW082352270326
41935CB00013B/1593